The
Continual
Pilgrimage

The Continual Pilgrimage

American Writers in Paris, 1944–1960

CHRISTOPHER
SAWYER-LAUÇANNO

GROVE PRESS
New York

Published by Grove Press
A division of Grove Press, Inc.
841 Broadway
New York, NY 10003–4793

Published in Canada by General Publishing Company, Ltd.

Due to limitations of space, permissions
and photo credits appear on page 329.

Library of Congress Cataloging-in-Publication Data

Sawyer-Lauçanno, Christopher, 1951–
The continual pilgrimage : American writers in Paris, 1944–1960 /
Christopher Sawyer-Lauçanno. — 1st ed.
        p.   cm.
Includes bibliographical references and index.
ISBN 0-8021-1371-0 (alk. paper)
1. American literature—France—Paris—History and criticism.
2. American literature—20th century—History and criticism.
3. Paris (France)—Intellectual life—20th century.   4. Americans—
France—Paris—History—20th century.   5. Authors, American—20th
century—Biography.   6. American literature—French influences.
I. Title.
PS159.F5S28   1992
810.9'944361—dc20   91-41295
                                                                        CIP

Manufactured in the United States of America

Printed on acid-free paper

Designed by Irving Perkins Associates

First Edition 1992

1   3   5   7   9   10   8   6   4   2

For Patricia L. Pruitt

Acknowledgments

A great many individuals who were present in Paris between 1945 and 1960 helped a great deal with this book. I am particularly indebted to the following: John Ashbery, William S. Burroughs, Evan Connell, Jr., Michel Fabre, Lawrence Ferlinghetti, Edward Field, Herbert Gentry, Allen Ginsberg, James Lord, Harry Mathews, George Plimpton, Ned Rorem, Edouard Roditi, William Targ, the late Virgil Thomson, and George Whitman.

I would also like to express my appreciation for the interest and support of my family: Patricia Pruitt, Jessica Chelsea Pruitt, and Sarah Diane Pruitt. I owe a special debt to Jessica, who carefully prepared the notes. The Garcias, as usual, bolstered my efforts with their enthusiasm for me and my project.

I am grateful as well to the Office of the Undergraduate Research Opportunities Program at the Massachusetts Institute of Technology for a grant enabling me to employ Lesley Schwartz as a part-time research assistant. Lesley's diligent unearthing of countless articles and books from dusty archives contributed substantially to this undertaking.

The indefatigable Roslyn Targ, agent extraordinaire, not only gave me the sort of support any author would envy but also provided valuable insight into the character of Chester Himes. Anna Jardine, the most meticulous and dedicated copy editor I've ever encountered, made sure that my sentences made sense and that my echoes didn't resonate too loudly. Susan Tillack, at Grove, handled myriad details with good humor and aplomb. Finally, I would like to thank my two editors at Grove Press,

Mark Polizzotti and Jim Moser. Mark's continual belief in this
project, in tandem with his remarkable knowledge of contemporary French and American literature, aided me inestimably in
this work. Jim's care and concern with the final editing turned a
manuscript into a book.

Contents

CONTENTS

And what about what was there before?

This is shaped in the new merging, like ancestral smiles, common memories, remembering just how the light stood on the water that time. But it is also something new. Outside, can't you hear it, the traffic, the trees, everything getting nearer. To end up with, inside each other, moving upward like penance. For the continual pilgrimage has not stopped. It is only that you are both moving at the same rate of speed and cannot apprehend the motion.

John Ashbery, "The New Spirit," *Three Poems*

The
Continual
Pilgrimage

"What It Doesn't Take Away"

THEY WERE not a lost generation, but they had not exactly found their way either, except, that is, to Paris. They congregated at cafés—Lipp, Flore, Deux Magots, Monaco, Tournon—read the existentialists, discovered the surrealists, frequented galleries, and listened to jazz, made mostly by their compatriots, until dawn. Many of them lived in fifteen-dollar-a-week rooms, ate fifty-cent meals (wine and service included) in the little restaurants scattered all over the Left Bank. Some were there as students, the GI Bill of Rights and Fulbright Act having recently been passed by Congress. Others were there in less official capacities, living, for the most part meagerly, off savings or allowances. A few actually survived on money earned from their writing. Most had come over for the first time after World War II, drawn to a city they had never seen but already knew through the writings of the generations that preceded them.

Their reasons for being in Paris, then, were varied—and not the least of them was the romance of it all. The same magic had attracted the first great wave of expatriate writers and artists, in the twenties and thirties: the belief that everything was happening in this city. But the attraction lay also in being in the place where Hemingway, Joyce, Pound, Wolfe, Fitzgerald, Djuna Barnes, Cummings, Stein, Miller, and others had flourished. Like their famous predecessors, they too subscribed in advance to Gertrude Stein's dictum: "It's not so much what Paris gives you, as what it doesn't take away."

But once in Paris the younger generation began to realize what Stein's pronouncement actually meant. James Baldwin, who arrived in 1948, perceptively noted that "the American writer, in Europe, is released, first of all, from the necessity of apologizing for himself. . . . It is not necessary for him, there, to pretend to be something he is not, for the artist does not encounter in Europe the same suspicion he encounters here." This was a reason not only for Baldwin but for many others as well. "The artist has got some sort of honor here," explained James Jones. "There is a feeling in Paris that promulgates art in any of its forms. . . . In New York, even a successful writer, if he's serious about writing, always has the feeling of being a little bit on the outside of everything."

This precious sense of artistic enfranchisement was for most of these transplanted Americans an entirely new concept. In France, commented William Styron, "a writer is esteemed, respected as such, and feels himself necessary to the intellectual life of his country at all times. But in America a writer is much less well accepted."

This acceptance as individuals was perhaps most keenly felt by black writers, such as Baldwin, Richard Wright, and Chester Himes. Although initially their major motivation in going to Paris was more to escape the omnipresent American racial nightmare than to satisfy a decided predilection for France, once on French soil the dream of equality was transformed into a vision of the way a society could and should operate. But it took some getting used to: "There is such an absence of race hate that it seems a little unreal," Wright observed shortly after his arrival.

Gay artists and writers too felt considerably more at ease in Paris than they had back in the States. French society was far more tolerant than many others, and—as was not the case in most countries then—homosexuality was not a crime, the Napoleonic Code having more than a century before decriminalized homosexual relations between consenting adults.

Sexual license was also the province (and backbone) of Maurice Girodias's English-language Olympia Press. But along with erotica, supplied primarily by Americans living in Paris, the press published such distinguished literary works as *Lolita*, *Watt*, *Naked Lunch*, and *The Ginger Man*. Neither *transition* nor *The Transatlantic Review* was still in existence, but other little magazines, responding to the influx of young anglophone writers, flourished. Among them were *Points*, *Zero*, *Merlin*, and *New-Story*. But the most enduring publishing venture of the era was *The Paris Review*. Founded in 1953 by George Plimpton, Peter Matthiessen, William Pène du Bois, John Train, Thomas Guinzburg, Harold Humes, and William Styron, it was a worthy successor to the great literary journals of the 1920s and 1930s. Much of its early writing and illustration came from Americans residing in France, including its founders, as well as Evan Connell, Jr., Alfred Chester, James Lord, and Eugene Walter.

With magazines publishing new and important work, with readings at the English-language bookstores the Librairie Mistral and The English Bookshop, with cheap accommodations and food, Paris quickly reestablished itself as the center of American expatriate literary and artistic activity. "To be young and in Paris," noted Styron, "is often a heady experience. . . . We feel peculiarly at ease for a change, we know where we are, and we wish to stick around."

But the American press trying to chronicle the scene was baffled by it. Attempting to attach a convenient label to this group of itinerants and émigrés, they tried out a few names—"new expatriates," "Ameuropeans"—when they profiled the new wave of Parisian settlers in *Holiday*, *Esquire*, and *Life*. But the diversity of these postwar pilgrims defied easy categorization, and soon the glossies switched to glorifying the sights and sounds of Paris, relegating the "bohemians," as usual, to fringe attractions. Hollywood too worked to perpetuate the city's romantic image in films shot on location, among them *An American in Paris*, *Love in the Afternoon*, and *Moulin Rouge*.

Despite overt disapproval of Americans' meddling in their internal and external affairs, exemplified by walls scrawled with such slogans as "*Les Américains en Amérique*" and "U.S. Go Home," the French privately welcomed the young writers who arrived in increasing numbers from the end of the war through the 1950s. The chief reason for the warm individual reception had to do with the attitudes that the members of this literary generation brought with them to Paris. And while the new wave of Americans abroad at first tended to gravitate toward fellow expatriates, there was in general a great deal more interest on their part in France and in the French than among the members of the "Lost Generation."

Many, in fact, came to study French literature. Lawrence Ferlinghetti, who had first seen France as an adult from his command post on a submarine chaser off Normandy Beach in 1944, returned in 1948 as a doctoral student at the Sorbonne. Aside from completing his doctorate, Ferlinghetti began his career as a poet, writing many of the poems that would eventually be included in *Pictures of the Gone World*. He also finished a novel, *Her* (not published until 1960), which like Djuna Barnes's *Nightwood* evokes a Paris of the psyche.

Others came seeking France rather than simply other Americans. The young poet John Ashbery made the Atlantic crossing in the mid-fifties. After two years in France on a Fulbright grant, he was forced by lack of funds to return for a one-year stay in New York, where he taught French at New York University. But he returned to write a dissertation on Raymond Roussel, who would remain a lifelong hero. Though Ashbery never completed his thesis, he did write *The Tennis Court Oath*, a work tangentially indebted to Roussel, who allowed him to see (and hear) "what you can do with language." He stayed on for almost another decade, supporting himself by writing art criticism for *ArtNews* and the [*International*] *Herald Tribune*.

Poet, novelist, and translator Harry Mathews, fresh out of

6

Harvard with an A.B. degree in music, went to Paris in 1952 with his wife, Niki de Saint Phalle, and their young daughter, to continue his studies in conducting. He still lives there, having swapped a career in music for one in writing. In 1960, with the poets James Schuyler and Kenneth Koch in New York, Ashbery and Mathews in Paris founded *Locus Solus,* a short-lived but extremely imaginative experimental review.

Irwin Shaw, a Signal Corps private and scriptwriter, was among the first Americans to enter Paris on Liberation Day, August 25, 1944. Seven years later he returned, and stayed on and off there for the next twenty-five years. Novelist James Jones set up housekeeping in the heart of the city in 1958, creating a central meeting place for Americans abroad that lasted for more than a decade.

In the late fifties the Beats—Allen Ginsberg, Gregory Corso, Peter Orlovsky, and finally William Burroughs—descended on Paris and set up headquarters at 9 Rue Gît-le-Cœur, which became known as the Beat Hotel. Brion Gysin also moved in, helped to edit *Naked Lunch,* and expounded on the theory of cut-ups, the legacy of which would find its way into several Burroughs novels. The Beats also met Henri Michaux, Marcel Duchamp, Man Ray, and Louis-Ferdinand Céline, were featured in *Life,* espoused Beat philosophy at cafés, and read their work at the Librairie Mistral to groups of curious expatriates and Europeans alike.

The diversity within this group of writers was broad; the styles, themes, and forms in which they wrote, unpredictable and not classifiable into any neat categories. If they had been gathered together in the same room, it is unlikely they would all have been able to communicate with one another, despite their having been in Paris during more or less the same period. And yet there were unlikely alliances, formed to some extent by virtue of the simple bond of being Americans in Paris. Writers as different from one another as James Jones and James Baldwin were close friends; Evan Connell, Jr., Peter Matthiessen, William Styron, George Plimpton, and Irwin Shaw all had each other and *The Paris Review* in common. Brion Gysin and Richard Wright were both in the

Stein circle; after Stein's death in 1946 they continued to be recipients of Alice Toklas's hospitality. And though each of these writers had his or her own Paris, and appreciated different aspects of what the city offered, there was also a sense of group identity gained from being American writers in a foreign capital. George Whitman, owner of the Librairie Mistral, a major congregating spot for the anglophone community, stated it succinctly: "Americans who would never have talked to each other in Boston or New York suddenly became fast friends in Paris, uniting precisely because they were Americans living away from America."

THIS BOOK is a chronicle of a generation of American writers who came to Paris after World War II. Intended as a kind of moving picture of an age, it is an exploration of interconnected communities and affinities, of what these Americans discovered in Paris and of what they took away. Many of the writers profiled here made their first major forays into literature while in Paris. Empowered as artists, they went on, often back in the United States, to become leading members of the literary establishment.

By no means is every writer who lived in Paris during the postwar period examined here. Rather, I have concentrated on those who, in my estimation, gained artistically from being in the city. Writers such as Truman Capote, Gore Vidal, Saul Bellow, Carson McCullers, and Eudora Welty, although resident briefly there, are not discussed, as they seem to have benefited little (literarily) from their time in France and they were not key members of the expatriate community. The dominant attention given male writers in these pages also needs to be clarified. The omission of women is not by design; rather, with the notable exceptions of Gertrude Stein and Janet Flanner (who are treated here), the major American writers in Paris in the postwar era were men.

The imprint of place on a writer can be less than obvious. For some in this group—Baldwin, Himes, Ferlinghetti, and Shaw, for example—who wrote directly about their Parisian experiences, the influence is readily discernible. But the use of a backdrop is not the only criterion by which to measure the impact of place. In the works of Ashbery, Mathews, Wright, and even Burroughs and Ginsberg, there are often appropriations of sensibility and style, echoes of French writers from Mallarmé to Robbe-Grillet, from Roussel and the surrealists to Sartre and Céline.

The book begins on Liberation Day. The choice is not arbitrary. First, a number of American writers or would-be writers (some of whom would later return to take up residence in France) entered Paris that day. Second, and more important, the war and the Occupation had a profound impact on life and letters in France, and directly or indirectly influenced the Americans who settled in the capital in the decade following. The book ends, with a few exceptions, in 1960. By this time the migration of Americans to France had greatly diminished. Those—and there were thousands—who wanted to make use of the GI Bill to study in France had generally done so. In addition, the dollar had declined in value, no longer making France so economically attractive as it had been. Politically, the Algerian war discouraged many from moving to Paris. Which is not to say that Paris was still not a haven for individual American artists and writers, but the large American community that had thrived there during the decade and a half immediately after the war had for the most part disintegrated.

But for as long as the postwar pilgrimage lasted, the City of Light was as electric as ever; and while Paris can hardly be given sole credit for enriching contemporary American literature, it nurtured this generation immeasurably by providing an environment that encouraged the arts and artists. Translated into personal experience, this meant belief in the value and viability of writing, and beyond that, belief in oneself as a creative person.

In following a dream, these writers found a vision.

9

Chapter One

The Liberation of Sylvia Beach, and Other Tales of August 1944

HE WAS not there as a fighting man. Indeed, as a war correspondent, he was forbidden by the Geneva Conventions to bear arms. But regulations were one thing, reality another, and Ernest Hemingway, itching to play a part in the Allied invasion, soon managed to find a place for himself as a soldier. He first saw action in Normandy, and later around the village of Rambouillet, where he "commanded" a group of *maquis* chasing down retreating Germans. He relished the opportunity, however slight, to battle the Boches, then typically embroidered his exploits. But now, in his assigned role, that of a reporter for *Collier's* magazine, he felt no need for hyperbole in describing the sight of Paris looming in the distance: "I had a funny choke in my throat and I had to clean my glasses because there now, below us, gray and always beautiful, was the city I love best in all the world."

The date was August 24, 1944, the day before the entrance of the Allies into Paris. A few days earlier Hemingway had learned that the honor of liberating Paris had been given to the troops of General Jacques Leclerc, commander of the French army's Second Armored Division. Hemingway maneuvered his way into their ranks, and was among the first Americans to march triumphantly into the capital.

Although Hemingway later described the entrance into Paris as "chickenshit as to fighting," the official accounts paint a picture of sporadic sniper fire and occasional barrages from German artillery. In fact, in a large square near the Bois de Boulogne, on the city's outskirts, Hemingway and company came close to what could have been a fatal encounter, when rifle bullets peppered the air and an artillery shell brought down a massive chestnut tree directly in front of the advancing contingent. Hemingway and his small group, including Colonel David Bruce of the OSS and Lieutenant Colonel S. L. A. Marshall, the U.S. Army's official war historian, took cover in the doorway of a nearby building to make way for several half-tracks and five tanks to enter the square, machine-gun turrets blazing.

Suddenly Bruce noticed that Hemingway had disappeared. But as the roar of the German fusillade died down, Bruce spied his compatriot crouched on the third-floor balcony of a distant apartment house, carbine in hand, shouting in French that the Germans were in the house behind them and that Bruce, Marshall, and others should get out before the French artillery began pounding the building. While Hemingway covered them with bursts of gunfire, they scurried to another doorway just in time to see a hail of mortar shells come crashing into the façade of the German-held complex.

Despite the continued danger, the most profound sense was that of joy. With each mile gained toward the capital, the conquering army found the streets lined with jubilant, ecstatic crowds. Men and women of all ages, boys and girls rushed forth to kiss and throw their arms around the troops. They showered the liberators with flowers and proffered bottles of champagne, cognac, and wine that had been sequestered for years in cellars in anticipation of this victorious moment. The French flag flew from balconies and rooftops, and shouts of *"Vive la France!"* and the strains of "La Marseillaise" reverberated through the streets. It was a day like no other. After four years of often brutal occupation, a corner of France was again French; the war, many thought, must surely be near an end.

In the early afternoon of August 25, as they moved slowly through the throngs of Parisians along the Avenue Foch, Hemingway and his contingent finally saw the Arc de Triomphe come into view. Hemingway, Bruce, and a few others cautiously got out of their jeeps and strode over to the Tomb of the Unknown Soldier while sniper bullets exploded around them and vehicles burned in the distance. At the monument they found six French World War I veterans and a mutilated ex-soldier in a wheelchair guarding the eternal flame. A French captain approached and asked whether they would like to ascend the arch. "The view was breathtaking," wrote Bruce in his diary. "One saw the golden dome of the Invalides, the green roof of the Madeleine, Sacré-Cœur and other familiar landmarks. Tanks were firing in various streets. Part of the Arc was under fire from snipers. A shell from a German 88 nicked one of its sides."

A couple of bottles of champagne were drunk; Paris was toasted. But the liberators didn't dally long, for Hemingway had seized on a new objective: the "liberation" of the Travellers Club, one of his old haunts. The task was not difficult. No Germans lurked on the premises; only the club president and a few of the old regulars occupied the establishment. To celebrate the Allied arrival, a magnum of champagne was ceremonially uncorked and glasses were raised all around to *l'amitié franco-américaine.*

The next stop was again vintage Hemingway but also served a practical purpose: finding a place to sleep. In this case, Hemingway had his eye on the Ritz. But as he, Bruce, and assorted others were leaving the Travellers Club, small-arms fire broke out, causing them to make a forced stop at the Café de la Paix. Once the shooting died down, they deemed the streets passable again and proceeded without incident directly to the Hôtel Ritz on the Place Vendôme. In front of the hotel they were greeted by the "imperturbable Ausiello," longtime Ritz manager and an old friend of Hemingway's. To his delight, the hotel was both deserted and completely unscathed from the nearby street fighting. After taking possession of their rooms, they ordered fifty martinis from the bar. The bartender was not to be found, but the management, true to style, did not balk at the order. The drinks were promptly delivered, and although judged by Hemingway as "mediocre," they were greedily consumed by the hotel's new guests.

THE AMERICAN army's Twelfth Regiment, Fourth Division, entered Paris just behind General Leclerc's troops on August 25. Assigned to this detachment was a Signal Corps camera unit consisting of two cameramen, a driver, and one writer, whose job was to record in detail the subject of the silent footage. The thirty-one-year-old scripter, PFC Irwin Shaw from Brooklyn, New York, had long dreamed of being a writer in Paris. An extra degree of exultation, therefore, accompanied his entry into the capital. Although he and his jeepmates did not encounter the German opposition experienced by Hemingway and his companions, Shaw did note the same joyful hysteria on the part of the local populace: "Our jeep was banked with flowers, a gift from people in the little towns on our route to Paris, and we had a small store of tomatoes and apples and bottles of wine that had been tossed to us as we slowly made our way through the crowds that tore down barricades in our path."

After witnessing (and filming) a few skirmishes between snipers and Allied troops around the Chambre des Députés and in the Place de la Concorde, Shaw and his cadre registered at the Hôtel Scribe, the official headquarters of the foreign press corps. After a cold-water bath—hot water being virtually nonexistent because of fuel shortages—Shaw headed for the hotel bar to check in with fellow journalists, most of whom he'd known in London before the invasion. Among those present that evening were two of Shaw's comrades, Lieutenant Colonel George Stevens, former Hollywood director, now Shaw's boss and head of the

Special Coverage Unit, and Robert Capa, the distinguished war photographer, on assignment for *Life*.

Capa, Charles Wertenbaker, Time Inc.'s London bureau chief, and their driver laid claim to being the first American contingent to enter Paris, having done so at 9:40 that morning. (Hemingway arrived shortly after noon; Shaw, a couple of hours later.) Capa was quick to inform the "late" arrivals, crowding into the bar, of Time-Life's coup, but the atmosphere that night was not devoted to one-upmanship. Rather, as Shaw noted, "it was possible to feel that a new age of courage, decency, and gratitude was beginning in Europe."

MARY WELSH, also a member of Wertenbaker's crew, finally managed to reach Paris that night, but she found to her dismay that, so many journalists having preceded her, the Scribe was full. Before departing for the room offered her, in a shoddy old hotel across the street, she checked the register to see who was there. The roster brimmed with familiar names from London: Shaw, Capa, Wertenbaker, Stevens. The two names that most interested her, however, were missing: Hemingway's and that of her husband, Noel Monks, an Australian journalist now in British employ. She observed that Martha Gellhorn, Hemingway's wife, was not registered either.

The next morning she checked in with Wertenbaker, who promptly assigned her to get a story on Paris fashion. She decided first to go to the Ritz to see if by chance Hemingway was ensconced there. "Papa, there's a dame here," yelled Hemingway's driver, Private Archie Pelkey, as Welsh stood in the hall outside room 31. A grinning Hemingway soon emerged from the room, threw his arms around Welsh, and whirled her around several times before redepositing her on the carpet. Over champagne, they exchanged news of what had transpired during their month of separation. Around them, Pelkey and several ragtag French partisans, Hemingway's companions since Rambouillet, sat cleaning rifles and sipping from what seemed an inexhaustible supply of champagne. There was clearly too much activity for intimate talk, so Welsh and Hemingway set up a dinner date for that evening and Welsh arranged to move into the Ritz that afternoon.

There was much to discuss. Both were married to other people; neither was sure of what this wartime romance was all about. They had met only three months before, in London. At that time Welsh was engaged in an on-again, off-again affair with the equally married Shaw. At lunch one day in May, Hemingway, who was dining at the same restaurant, ambled over to their table. "Introduce me to your friend, Shaw," said Hemingway. After a couple of minutes of polite conversation, the big, bearded author invited Welsh to lunch the next day. She accepted without hesitation. After Hemingway had departed, Shaw looked across the table at Welsh and dryly intoned: "Well, it's been nice knowing you." "You off somewhere?" asked Welsh. "A monopoly has just been born, you dummy. The Soho answer to De Beers diamonds."

Shaw was right. What he didn't realize was that Hemingway, whom he extravagantly admired, would immediately begin to regard him as a rival, even after Shaw made it evident to all concerned that he had relinquished his claim on Welsh. Later, in his first novel, *The Young Lions*, Shaw would create characters transparently based on Hemingway and Welsh, portraying them and their affair in a somewhat less than flattering manner. But at this point he was not terribly unhappy about the course of events, though he was disturbed by Hemingway's overt jealousy. As they shared friends, particularly Capa, and were involved in chronicling the same momentous events, they worked out a truce, but never really reconciled. After *The Young Lions* was published, Hemingway was so angered by the transparent portraits that he threatened to punch Shaw in the nose. He also initially forbade Welsh, by then Mrs. Hemingway, to see Shaw, and for some time after, when speaking of him, he never failed to interject a barrage of curses and denunciations into the conversation.

*   *   *

WHILE WELSH went on her way to discover what the war had done to Paris fashion, Hemingway had another mission that morning. Along with a few members of his motley crew, he set a course for the Left Bank, specifically for 12 Rue de l'Odéon, longtime home of Sylvia Beach's Shakespeare and Company. Since its opening in 1919, the bookshop and lending library had been the major gathering place for literary expatriates of every stripe and nationality, as well as for French literati. Hemingway, whom Beach had dubbed "her best customer," first borrowed a book from her in 1921. It was at this legendary bookstore that the Lost Generation had congregated: Pound, Stein, Toklas, Joyce, MacLeish, Eliot, Dos Passos, Sherwood Anderson, Hilda Doolittle (H.D.), Bryher, Virgil Thomson, Man Ray, Robert McAlmon, Janet Flanner. It was here that Beach and her partner, Adrienne Monnier, introduced these literary exiles to the likes of Gide, Cocteau, Aragon, Marcel Duhamel, Perse, Romains, and Valéry.

During the Occupation, Beach had been forced to close, but sensing the inevitable, she had managed to hide her treasures just before the Germans came and confiscated her priceless stock. But she did not hide herself. A few months later, despite her American citizenship, the Gestapo arrested her and sent her off to an internment camp. Had an old French friend not intervened on her behalf with the Vichy government, she would likely have spent far more than the six months of confinement she had to endure before being released.

Beach, who had just moved back to her apartment above the vacated bookshop, awoke on the morning of August 26 to the usual sound of gunfire. Despite the "liberation" of the city the day before, snipers, it seemed, were still operating on the Rue de l'Odéon. That afternoon, between shell bursts, she heard a deep voice crying her name. As she did not answer at once, everyone on the street began taking up the cry of "Sylvia! Sylvia!" It was Monnier who first recognized the one deep voice. "It's Hemingway! It's Hemingway!" she exclaimed. "I flew downstairs," wrote Beach. "We met with a crash; he picked me up and swung me around and kissed me while people on the street and in the windows cheered."

In the apartment they talked for a while, catching up on the main events of the last few years. Beach asked if there was anything she could do for him. Hemingway requested a piece of soap, which Monnier cheerfully surrendered even though it was her last cake. He then asked what he could do for Beach. She took down from a bookshelf a copy of *Winner Take Nothing*, which he had inscribed for her in 1937. He seized a pen and wrote a new inscription: *"Lu et approuvé."* She also mentioned the problem of the snipers. "He got his company out of the jeeps and took them up to the roof," recalled Beach. "We heard firing for the last time in the rue de l'Odéon."

For Hemingway, the return to the French capital was filled with special meaning. In a letter to Welsh, he wrote, "Have been to all the old places I ever lived in Paris and everything is fine. But it is all so improbable that you feel like you have died and it is all a dream." Welsh, who had reported from Paris before the war, was also caught up in the exhilaration of being there once again. On her stroll through the city the morning after her arrival, she was struck by how superficially unaltered Paris was despite the years of occupation: "I walked through that lane of enchantment, the Ritz's passage from its Place Vendôme side to the rue Cambon, and after years of seeing drab London shop windows was more intoxicated by the gaiety and imagination of the stylish showcases along the walls than I had been by the champagne." After stopping in at a few boutiques to check up on how the couturiers had survived the war (intact), Welsh hurried over to the Place de la Concorde to get the real story of the day, General Charles de Gaulle's official entrance into Paris. She found the Champs-Élysées mobbed with thousands and thousands of Parisians who nearly drowned out his speech with their continual cries of *"Vive la France!"* and *"Vivent les américains!"*

WHILE HEMINGWAY was exploring his old haunts and Welsh was covering the official Liberation ceremonies, Shaw was gaining a roommate at the hotel: William Saroyan. The two had first met in 1939, when Harold Clurman commissioned Shaw to write a one-act "curtain raiser" to accompany Saroyan's *My Heart's in the Highlands*. The two hit if off immediately, as both were enthusiasts of poker, women, and drink. They admired each other's writing and had a shared understanding of ambition and the quest for fame. Drafted into the service, they both ended up in the Signal Corps and were flatmates in London. Like Shaw, Saroyan was a private in the unit; also like Shaw, he behaved as if he were a colonel, demanding and receiving special privileges, hobnobbing with the officers. But unlike his fellow privates, Saroyan found it virtually impossible to adapt to the army. "He was very antiwar—completely—and anti-Army," recalled Shaw. "He was too much of an anarchist . . . to be able to work for any organization."

Having no interest in the D Day invasion or even in the liberation of Paris, Saroyan had managed to hole up safely in London's Savoy Hotel until being forced to go to Paris the day after Liberation. Once at the Scribe, however, Saroyan fell right into step, drinking, gambling, carousing with his fellow correspondents, revisiting places where he'd "done time" in the mid-thirties.

While Shaw maintained relations with Hemingway, Saroyan did not. The two had become adversaries in 1935, when Hemingway, angered by what he regarded as snide references to his writing in Saroyan's first collection of short stories, fulminated against Saroyan in print. In London they had managed to keep their distances; in Paris it was not possible. A day or two after Saroyan's arrival, one of Hemingway's drinking companions noticed Saroyan lingering outside the bar of the Scribe and called to him to come over. "Here's Bill Saroyan," said Hemingway's drinking buddy. Waiting until Saroyan was in earshot, Hemingway replied, "Where's Bill Saroyan?" Saroyan approached the table and said, "In London you had a beard, but even without it I haven't forgotten you. Did shaving it off make you forget me?" Hemingway ignored the riposte and resumed conversation with his cohorts. Saroyan, fuming, walked away.

This incident, however, turned out to be simply a prelude to further hostilities. A few nights later Hemingway and Saroyan were both dining in the restaurant at the Hôtel George V. Upon noticing Saroyan, a drunken Hemingway began a loud, excoriating tirade: "Well, for God's sake, what's that lousy Armenian son of a bitch doing here?" A few more lines of this sort were uttered before Saroyan and his dining companions were out of their chairs. When oaths and denunciations proved insufficient for either party, a full-scale brawl broke out which required the combined forces of the management and local *gendarmes* to stop. Both factions were ousted. For Hemingway it all seemed like great good fun; for Saroyan, confirmation of Hemingway's barbarousness.

HEMINGWAY DID not spend all of his time brawling (though he did devote considerable attention to getting drunk). While preoccupied with his budding romance with Welsh, he also held court in his room at the Ritz. Among the visitors was a young soldier, a special agent in the Counter Intelligence Corps, Sergeant Jerome D. Salinger. Salinger had already published a number of stories in *Story*, *Collier's*, *Esquire*, and *The Saturday Evening Post* and was gratified that Hemingway knew who he was. Indeed, the meeting was apparently quite amicable; at its conclusion Hemingway asked to see some work. Salinger gave him an early story to read, "The Last Day of the Last Furlough," and Hemingway bestowed his approval on it. In a letter to Hemingway two years later, Salinger wrote that his talks with him had been the only rewarding minutes of the entire war.

Others came too. Marcel Duhamel, Hemingway's French translator, appeared at the Ritz almost immediately upon hearing of the author's arrival and installed himself as Hemingway's personal and social secretary. The first role was really that of publicist: planting stories (rarely a hundred percent accurate) in the French press about Monsieur Hemingway's exploits. As social secretary, Duhamel made sure that Hemingway saw the right people in Paris.

It was Duhamel who invited André Malraux, by now a hero of the Resistance, to visit one afternoon. Accounts vary as to what actually transpired at the meeting. Leicester Hemingway, the writer's brother, who was present, recorded that the visit consisted of a friendly, nonstop exchange of war stories; Hemingway himself, however, circulated a very different version, in which he claimed to have bested Malraux.

According to Hemingway, the meeting went like this:

> [Malraux] had 5 galons [gold braids]—polished cavalry boots—decorations etc. I had one of two shirts I owned.
> I said "Bonjour André," he said
> "Bonjour Ernest. How many have you commanded?"
> I said, "Dix aux douze. Au plus deux cent."
> He said, "Moi: deux mille."
> I said, "What a shame my colonel that we did not have the assistance of your force when we took this small town (a patelin) . . ."
> Then we went on working and let him preen, and jerk, and twitch until he left.
> One of my characters asked me into the bathroom and said, "Papa on peut fusiller ce con?"
> . . . I said, "No. Offer him a drink and he will go by himself."

Hemingway may indeed have felt he got the better of the French author, but Malraux was by far the greater war hero. Not only had Colonel Malraux been a highly decorated Free French leader in the Dordogne, commanding fifteen hundred partisans in daring and successful military operations against the Germans, but he was, on the occasion of his meeting with Hemingway, in charge of the Alsace-Lorraine brigade under General Leclerc. After this brief interlude in Paris, in fact, he would take part in the fighting on the eastern front until VE Day. Compared with these true exploits, Hemingway's were insignificant.

This may account for Hemingway's bravado and later attempts to portray the meeting in a different fashion. There was another reason as well. Although Hemingway had initially expressed admiration for Malraux's novel *Man's Fate*, calling it in 1935 "the best book I have read in ten years," by 1938 he had drastically altered his favorable opinion of the man himself. He felt Malraux had retreated early from the Spanish Civil War simply in order to write a book about it. Hemingway, who had decided that a novel about the war was *his* turf, excoriated Malraux in a 1938 letter to Maxwell Perkins: "Really will have quite a lot to write when this [the war] is over . . . When finished am going to settle down and write and the pricks and fakers like Malraux who pulled out in Feb 37 to write gigantic masterpisses before it really started will have a good lesson when write ordinary sized book with the old stuff unfaked in it." That there might be room for both *For Whom the Bell Tolls* and *Man's Hope* evidently didn't occur to Hemingway.

While he may have sparred with Malraux, Hemingway greeted Picasso, on a visit to his studio a few days after Liberation, with an enthusiastic *abrazo*. The painter was apparently equally excited to see Hemingway, showing him and Welsh around the large studio, pointing out what seemed to Welsh "half a thousand canvases" painted during the war. Over the course of the evening Picasso and Hemingway reminisced about old times, filled each other in on more recent events. Hemingway was particularly interested in the effect of the Occupation on the painter's work. "Les Boches left me alone," Picasso told Hemingway. "They didn't like my work, but they did not punish me for it."

As they were leaving the studio, Picasso summoned Hemingway and Welsh to an open window with a view of roofs and chimney pots, now violet in the last light of the setting sun. "That is the best picture in my studio," he told them. Welsh, who did not particularly appreciate the artist's latest work, "abstractions, two- and three-profiled portraits," felt Picasso was right. When she confided this to her companion after leaving the studio, Hemingway chided her. "He's pioneering. . . . Don't condemn [the paintings] just because you don't understand them. You may grow up to them. . . . If you understand easily, the thing may be spurious."

The writer James Lord, then an Army intelligence officer, visited the artist shortly after Hemingway and recorded a somewhat different version of the meeting. According to Lord, Picasso informed him that Hemingway was a "charlatan." "He came to see me at Liberation," said Picasso, "and gave me a piece of S.S. tunic with the S.S. embroidered on the front, and told me he had killed the man himself. It was a lie. Maybe he had killed a lot of wild animals, but he never killed a man. If he had killed one, he would not have felt the need to circulate souvenirs."

Hemingway also decided to look up Gertrude Stein, with whom he'd had a falling-out years earlier. She wasn't at home, having endured the Occupation first at her country house in Bilignin and then, when that was taken from her, at Culoz. Hemingway left a note. A few months later, they finally did have a reunion at her house on the Rue Christine. Recalling the meeting, Hemingway wrote that "there wasn't a hell of a lot of time then and so I just told her I had always loved her and she said she loved me too which was, I think, the truth from both of us."

WHILE OTHER correspondents were writing stories in a frenzy, Hemingway was far less preoccupied with his occupation as a reporter. In fact, he filed only two stories from Paris during the several months he was in residence, while Welsh and others were cabling two or three dispatches a week. He was instead busy drinking, socializing, pursuing his romance with Welsh, and by early September soldiering.

The new round of battle activity began with a taunt in a message from Colonel Charles (Buck) Lanham, commander of the Twenty-second Infantry Regiment, Fourth Division, with whom Hemingway had become friends during the fighting in Normandy. The cable, which arrived at the Ritz on the first of September, contained the following message: "Go hang yourself, brave Hemingstein. We have fought at Landrecies and you were not there." The language was a parody of Voltaire's rendition of Henry IV's communiqué to Louis de Crillon, but unlike the duke,

Hemingway felt goaded into action, perhaps because the message came on the heels of his similar retort to Malraux about his having been absent at the liberation of Paris. By the next morning, Hemingway was en route to the Belgian front, where Lanham was engaged in mop-up operations.

The trip was totally foolhardy—"jackassery" was Lanham's later characterization. German troops still held many of the roads and villages along the way, and it was necessary for Hemingway and his driver to dodge heavy fire throughout the journey. Despite the perils of the trip, by the time Hemingway arrived and presented himself to an astonished Lanham, there was not much for "brave Hemingstein" to report; the fighting in the region was virtually over. He had, however, proved his valor, at least to his way of thinking.

After a few days of R&R back in Paris, Hemingway joined Lanham again and remained with the outfit for more than three weeks as it crossed the Siegfried Line into Germany with the first of the American troops. The fighting this round was fierce, real; the weather, cold and damp. Hemingway was in his element: "Have a battle jacket with the zipper broken held together by safety pins, wear same two shirts worn last two months, both at once, have head cold, chest cold, trouble on both flanks, shelling the Bejesus behind, shelling the ditto ahead, counter attack on our right, what-all on our left and never felt happier." He later wrote a fictionalized version of the campaign into Germany, "Black Ass at the Cross Roads" (never published in his lifetime), which despite its macho heroics conveys the terrible reality of the situation in a terse, taut narrative.

Hemingway would undoubtedly have stayed longer with Lanham and company, glorying in the hardship, but he was summoned to the headquarters of the inspector general of the Third Army to answer charges of having borne arms as a correspondent during the liberation of Rambouillet, a clear violation of the Geneva Conventions. At the inquest on October 6, bolstered by character testimonials from Colonels Bruce and Lanham, he solemnly denied his past "heroics" and was instantly acquitted.

Upon returning to the Ritz, Hemingway discovered, to his delight, that the hotel had a new resident, Marlene Dietrich, who had been sent over on a USO tour. He had first met Dietrich ten years before, on an Atlantic crossing, and they had instantly formed a mutual admiration pact. At the Ritz it was still in evidence. Welsh remembers Dietrich continually fawning over Hemingway with lines like, "Papa, you are the most wonderful. . . . Papa, you are the greatest man and the greatest artist." This before, during, or after Hemingway had proclaimed her glories to one and all. She quickly became his attendant, frequently wandering into the bathroom to perch on the edge of the bathtub and sing to him while he shaved. She also delighted in getting him to participate in duets with her, during which she continually maintained an amused expression at his notoriously off-key renditions.

While lavishing flirtatious attention on Dietrich, Hemingway nonetheless avidly pursued his courtship of Welsh, to whom he'd been writing jocular love letters and sophomoric poems during the campaign on the German front. She, meanwhile, was ambivalent about the affair, but as he wanted the matter settled, he shocked her by formally proposing to her. Welsh at first demurred, reminding him that they were both still married. This fact he quickly dismissed, saying that since both marriages were clearly over, divorce was merely a formality that could be easily overcome. She agreed in principle but felt that she needed to talk to her husband, Noel Monks. As for Hemingway's marriage to Martha Gellhorn, there was no question that it had already disintegrated. After years of putting up with his abusive behavior, she had informed him in April that she wanted out. But because of the war neither party had initiated divorce proceedings.

In October, Gellhorn arrived in Paris and Hemingway invited her to dinner. She agreed, out of a desire to discuss divorce. To her surprise Hemingway came accompanied by an entourage of young soldiers. With his crew as an audience, he spent the evening insulting and mocking her, until finally she stormed out. On November 3, she wrote to him from the Netherlands: "We are honest people, Bug and this is a no-good silly arrangement. . . . I think it would be best for you to get this finished with me." Although she had been the one to ask for a divorce, Hemingway would later claim that it was he who had done the divorcing. In a way, he had. For the previous six months his treatment of her, including reading aloud to his friends a deprecating poem he had written called "To Martha Gellhorn's Vagina," had been so despicable that she really had little option.

Mary Welsh, meanwhile, found that she did not have to ask Monks for a divorce either. Before she was even convinced herself that marrying Hemingway was what she wanted to do, she received a note from Monks that read: "I'm sorry I had not the necessary qualifications to stay the distance with you."

Even though she was now unofficially detached, Welsh was "feeling shaky and sad and needing to check [her] navigation." An incident a few days after she had extricated herself from her marriage made her seriously question her bearings. Hemingway had organized a dinner at the Ritz to honor some of the officers he'd fought with at the German front. During the course of the evening one of the inebriated officers had been extremely rude and condescending to visiting congresswoman Clare Boothe Luce, who happened to be married to Welsh's top boss, Henry Luce. Disgusted with the whole scene, and fearing for her job, Welsh informed Hemingway she was going to bed. Now it was Hemingway's turn to be abusive: "You insulted my friends. All evening and without cess. . . . You could not have behaved more horribly." Welsh held in her anger for a moment, then let fly: "Your friends are drunks and slobs. They threw up all over my bathroom. They probably lost me my job. They drove Marlene away. They may be heroes in Germany, but they stink, stink, stink here." Hemingway's response was to slap her in the face. Falling on the bed, her jaw aflame, Welsh softly cursed him: "You poor coward. You poor, fat, feather-headed coward. You woman hitter . . . Knock my head off, you coward. . . . Take it to the twenty-second. On a platter. Show 'em you won't let me insult 'em, you bully." Hemingway, after waiting out the tirade, simply replied, "You're pretty when you're mad." At that, she threw him out of the room.

The next day a steady stream of Hemingway's cronies knocked on Welsh's door, bearing his apologies. Finally Dietrich came. "He loves you, as you know," she said. Welsh was unmoved. After a few more remarks of this sort, she cut Dietrich off. "Any man worth his salt would come up here himself instead of sending apologists." A few minutes later, Hemingway appeared. "You were absolutely wonderful last night. . . . You small fighting cock, dancing around giving me hell with your courage." Welsh was disarmed. They talked for a while, she laying out her objections to his behavior, his drinking, he repeatedly countering. The matter gradually began to resolve itself, ending with Welsh's insistence that for the sake of her nose she give him a bath.

Hemingway's most compelling romance that fall, however, was not with Welsh but with the battlefield. Learning that the Fourth Division was about to launch a new offensive, he bade farewell to Welsh, the Ritz, and the bars of Paris, and on November 16 set off for the front accompanied by fellow correspondent William Walton. For the next two and a half weeks the two reporters were firsthand observers of some of the most intense fighting of the war. By early December, Lanham's regiment, among the hardest hit, had sustained more than 2,500 casualties, but in the process it had scored significant victories in what came to be known as the battle for the Hürtgen Forest. With the fighting at a lull, Hemingway and Walton returned to Paris, where Hemingway immediately took to his bed, having come down with pneumonia.

Although quite ill, with a constant fever, he still entertained a stream of visitors to his room. One day his brother Leicester arranged through a common friend for a visit from Jean-Paul Sartre and Simone de Beauvoir. Writing of the encounter years later, Beauvoir noted her surprise at the ugliness of the decor and at the sight of the great American writer prepared to receive them, stretched out on the bed, in pajamas, his eyes shielded by a green eyeshade. Upon their entrance to the room, Hemingway raised himself up, grabbed hold of Sartre, and firmly embraced him. "You're a general," he said. "Me, I'm only a captain." As Sartre was not a general, and Hemingway not an officer at all, the comment seemed rather off the mark, but the French writers chalked it up to ebullience or drunkenness. (Beauvoir noticed several half-empty bottles of scotch on the table next to the bed.)

Over the evening the alcohol flowed—champagne in Leicester's version; scotch in Beauvoir's—as did the conversation. At some point Sartre asked Hemingway's opinion of Faulkner, then Sartre's idol. Hemingway frankly admitted that Faulkner was a better writer than he was, as he in fact stated frequently. By the third bottle, Beauvoir was becoming curious about how sick Hemingway really was. He kicked off the bedclothes, flexed his leg, and announced with a wide grin, "Healthy as hell, see?" Around the sixth bottle, Sartre left; Beauvoir stayed until dawn. Hemingway later boasted that she had wanted to have the "literary experience" of sleeping with him, but although he was willing, because of his illness and general battle fatigue he was not able.

Other encounters were not so gallant. One evening at the Ritz, Hemingway, entertaining Lanham and another colonel on their first leave since D Day, was parading around his room with a pair of loaded German machine pistols, a gift from Lanham, when he came across a portrait of Welsh and her husband. He took the picture into the bathroom, placed it in the toilet, then fired several shots at it. He shattered the toilet, flooding the room and sending the management upstairs. Hemingway professed amazement at what had occurred, apologized profusely, and the next day wrote a flowery letter in French to the hotel administrator explaining that the toilet had broken when Lanham sat down on it. No doubt the Ritz management knew the true cause, but as he was a revered customer they simply replaced the toilet and Hemingway continued on as a cherished VIP resident. Welsh, who at the time accused Hemingway of being a "bloody fool," in the end was as forgiving as the hotel staff.

Hemingway had finally seen enough of war and believed that the conflict was almost over; he began to make plans to go back to his home in Cuba. He was intent now on creating a new life with Welsh and starting a new book. The germ of it had been in his head for some time. To his editor, Maxwell Perkins, he wrote in mid-October, "Have stuff for wonderful book. Have been with every action of the Div. . . . and if I have good luck a little longer want to lay off and get to work on the book. Want to write novel—not war book. It should have the sea and the air and the ground in it." To Welsh he characterized it as a "very fine, good, grownup novel." Although he would not begin the writing of what would become *Across the River and into the Trees* until 1948, he was already collecting incidents, taking mental notes. Some of this material—the liberation of Paris and subsequent experiences on the eastern front—eventually ended up in fictional form in the novel.

HEMINGWAY'S DEPARTURE from Paris in March 1945 coincided with the general exodus of correspondents and troops from the city. Shaw had been sent home in November; Saroyan was in Luxembourg on the verge of being discharged; Welsh was packing up; Capa and many others of the old Scribe crowd were in and out of the city, but more often in Germany now that the war had shifted there. Paris was becoming Parisian again, and despite inflation, acute food and fuel shortages, and a national preoccupation with rounding up suspected *collabos*, the situation in the capital was returning to normal.

For Hemingway, the interlude in Paris was hardly a sentimental return to the city he had done so much to mythologize in the twenties. Aside from reunions with a few old friends, most notably Beach, Stein, and Picasso, there is little evidence that after his first couple of days in the capital he was particularly nostalgic about his past there. This was largely a result of the abnormality of wartime; the Paris of 1944–45 hardly resembled the Paris of the Lost Generation. In addition, there was a great deal to occupy

29

his immediate attention. The glamour and excitement (for him) of war and of a new affair took precedence over sifting through his past. This is not to say that Paris was not pregnant with associations, with meaning. It was simply that there was little time, and less opportunity, to relive the grand era of the moveable feast.

Chapter Two

"Living Largely on Vegetables and Mostly Without Heat"

"EXISTENCE IN Paris is still abnormal with belief, with relief," noted longtime Paris observer Janet Flanner in her first post-Occupation "Letter from Paris," published in *The New Yorker* on December 15, 1944. An ebullient Simone de Beauvoir proclaimed: "It's all over, it's all over. It's all over: everything's beginning." And it was. No more than a day after Liberation, newspapers, censored under the Germans, flourished. Among these publications, the Communist and Communist-front press alone accounted for enough new periodicals to fill an entire news rack. Other papers that had existed before the war, including those which were not so left-leaning but which had been equally suppressed, were now revived. Regardless of political stripe, the dailies were sold out by mid-morning.

It did not take long to read the news. The paper shortage that continued throughout the fall and into winter allowed only for one-sheet tabloids. Reports of the battles on the front, or of rumblings in the Consultative Assembly, therefore, still circulated much the way they had during the Occupation: by word of mouth. The difference was that the whispered anti-German facts or rumors gave way now to unmuzzled, animated conversation. Talk, opinion, and arguments flowed freely at crowded café tables. Laughter was even heard again, and in the streets the children sang: "*Nous ne les reverrons plus / C'est fini, ils sont foutus*" (We will not see them again / It's over, they are screwed).

Even the cultural life of the capital began to come out of hiding. Concerts at the Opéra, closed during the last year of the Occupation, recommenced, with Yehudi Menuhin kicking off the new season. Galleries reopened, as did the first Salon d'Automne since 1940. Major artwork executed clandestinely during the war years was displayed along with prewar paintings that had been hidden from the Germans. The surrealists Ernst, Masson, Dominguez, and Miró were prominently displayed along with Dufy, Matisse, Braque, and Jacques Villon. The ever prolific Picasso was assigned an entire section of the exhibition. As usual, the Salon had its admirers and detractors: some of Picasso's more recent abstract paintings were torn from the walls, while the perpetrators screamed "Explain. Explain." Public readings, often of work banned under the Germans, drew large, enthusiastic crowds.

But the euphoria of liberation was soon subsumed by the grim reality of hardship, of suffering; the only substance in abundance during the fall and winter of 1944–1945 was bitter cold. As the writer James Lord noted, "The nearly hysterical enthusiasm that was felt at liberation was over long before the war itself." The end of occupation, in fact, had not brought with it a respite from the paramount need to survive in a city whose population could not adequately employ, clothe, heat, or feed itself. There was no single cause for the problems; rather, there was a complex chain of causes and effects.

A primary reason for the difficulties was the lack of coal to power factories, railroads, and electrical generating facilities. But even after the coalfields in northern France were liberated, the problems did not end, for the Germans had absconded with two-thirds of the trucks and railroad equipment used to haul the precious fuel. The fact that many roads, rail lines, and bridges had been bombed during the German retreat exacerbated the problem; not only coal shipments were delayed, but also the delivery of food from the newly liberated farms and pastures. Barge transport, the likely alternative to trucks and trains, was also nearly nonexistent after two months of heavy autumn rain that caused rivers and canals to swell to such a point that navigation was precarious if not impossible.

Because of the coal shortage, there was a gas shortage. Cooking gas, as a result, was turned on only between noon and one-thirty and between seven and eight in the evening. Ingenious heating devices, ranging from firetrap sawdust-burning stoves to electrically heated stone-lined stoves were available—for a high price—but finding sawdust or having a constant enough supply of electricity to heat the stones was another matter. To make matters worse, the black market, which had virtually kept Parisians alive under the Vichy government, rapidly deteriorated under the Allies. It was not imposed morality that put an end to the vigorous bartering; instead, inflation made farmers think twice about selling a cow or a pig or a few hundred bushels of wheat, for the price received one day would not compensate for the outlay necessary for other provisions the next.

Idle and angry, many Parisians devoted their time to exacting revenge against those who had collaborated or were suspected of collaborating; aside from the desire to bring traitors to justice, those persecuted by the lack of daily necessities relished the opportunity to round up their compatriots who had prospered under the Germans. Justifiably a noble activity, it was also a way of gaining a modicum of distraction from food lines and ration cards and frequent power outages. Poet Paul Éluard reflected the general sentiments of a population eager for vengeance. In "Les Vendeurs d'Indulgence" ("The Indulgence Sellers"), published in the journal Les Lettres Françaises in March 1945, he wrote:

> Those who have forgotten evil in the name of good
> Those who have no heart preach to us of pardon

. . . .

There is no stone more precious
Than the desire to avenge the innocent

There is no sky more brilliant
Than the morning when the traitors perish

Everyone who had survived the Occupation had a story to tell. Some tales had to do with outwitting the Nazis; others, far less droll and far more frequent, concerned brothers or husbands or sons taken away in the middle of the night to face firing squads or deportation to work or extermination camps in Germany. Eight hundred thousand Frenchmen, in fact, had been sent to work as slave laborers in Germany to fuel the dying Nazi war machine. They were still in captivity. Janet Flanner summed up the situation succinctly in a letter to a friend: "french also sad from head to foot. poor or rich, big or little. i can be wrong surely, but not without authority; i didnt make this up; they told me, they showed me."

Jean Bruller, better known by his pen name, Vercors, who had formed an underground publishing house in 1942, Les Éditions de Minuit, captured the prevalent feeling of post-Liberation Paris in a striking metaphor:

There is at present on the walls of Paris a very beautiful poster. It has been there ever since Liberation Day, or almost, and still I cannot look at it without feeling my heart swell. This poster symbolizes my country through the features of a young girl. It is France as light dawns. As she shields her eyes against the bright sun her hand still bears the mark of the nail which held her crucified. She shields her eyes because after the long night even the gentle light of dawn hurts her. She is not joyful. She is proud. But she is also timid and uncertain. She is like those souls whom illness has tied to their beds through long months, who are not yet cured but who are allowed to get up for the first time and who are full of anxiety at the thought of trusting their legs, which have been immobile for so long.

34

How well the liberating army comprehended France's predicament is hard to judge. The typical press reports depicted the American view, at least initially, as a mixture of equal parts joy and awe at having finally set foot in the legendary City of Light. Awe, however, was a difficult emotion to sustain; elation lasted longer, particularly as Paris was quickly discovered to be a city "with dames to spare." *Life*, spearheading the view of "gay Paree," rarely failed to mention how eager the "girls" of Paris had embraced (literally) the young soldiers. Photographic evidence was usually supplied as well.

Even when alluding to the food shortages, news stories tended to minimize the real problems: "Paris' greatest revelation was that, in privation, it had produced one of the prettiest crops of girls in the memory of living men. For four years they had not eaten too much or loafed. And above all, they had to travel by bicycle. Bicycling Paris in fact was the greatest leg show in the world." To his credit, Time-Life's Charles Wertenbaker, in a commentary that otherwise attempted to portray Paris as getting back to normal, nonetheless managed to report the truth: "Paris is poor in everything: poor in money, poor in food, soap, tobacco and hard liquor, poor in men to make things, and in transport to bring things from elsewhere. Pretty women dive for cigaret butts on the street and a half-eaten tin of Army rations will be grabbed out of the gutter."

Composer Virgil Thomson, who had returned to Paris in 1945, noted that even essential commodities were far beyond the reach of most Parisians:

If new shoes from America pinched the feet, there was no remedy, since others could not be bought. Or only on the black market and for $200—for $100 if you had black-market francs. This also turned out to be the price of a hat. . . . It was also the price of a fair meal for two, with wine, in any of the speak-easy-like black-market restaurants. Unitemized, the total would be jotted on a paper scrap, as if it were a telephone number, should police enquire. At the white-market restaurants, which included all reputable establishments, prices were regulated; and one gave ration points as well.

As a result of such prices, only the GIs and assorted Americans seemed to be able to enjoy the pleasures of Paris. For the Parisians, the presence of the American army in their streets was a mixed blessing. The GIs quickly assumed the role of victors. Paris was their city, as the ecstatic welcome had confirmed. Honored guests, liberators, saviors, they basked in the knowledge that they had been responsible for giving France back its capital. This feeling didn't persist too long, however. "The only thing most of the GIs wanted after glimpsing Paris," noted James Lord, "was to get home, sleep soundly, eat apple pie. The liberation for them was just another indicator that the war was ending, that they'd soon be home. For the French, naturally, it was different."

It was indeed different for the Parisians. In the days after liberation, they generally gave the GIs the key to the city. "For me, these carefree young Americans were freedom incarnate," wrote Simone de Beauvoir. Lord agreed with her observation: "There was a definite advantage then in being an American. And while I couldn't wait to get out of uniform, when I walked through the streets I was constantly overwhelmed by the gratitude. It was a distinctly odd feeling, since I hadn't really done anything personally to warrant such a response. Part of this feeling that Americans were quite wonderful had to do with our having helped throw off the Nazi yoke. In addition, the French had really not seen all that many Americans before. They had a very romantic idea of who we were. They knew the British but they didn't know us. Naturally we benefited from this added aura that we gained from simply being Americans."

Nonetheless, the Americans were still a foreign army. A young woman could not walk down the street without the catcalls and whistles of GIs following her. Well fed, albeit on C rations, the soldiers also had money in their pockets and were eager to spend it, particularly on a "dame." Writer John Phillips (John P. Marquand, Jr.) recalled that just after liberation, Paris was a "sea of cocksmen" who eagerly descended on the Place Pigalle: "We soldier chauvinists called it Pig Alley and GIs in filthy fatigues and muddy boots were hauled in from the front by six-by-six trucks and dumped loose on a forty-eight hour pass. The whores gathered at the truck stops to select the evening's clients, removing a man's helmet liner, running fingers through his scalp to check for lice."

Not just the women who staffed the brothels worked actively at liberating a few francs or commodities from a happy GI. Beauvoir recounts how a young female friend took up the pastime of *"chercher les américains."* It was not difficult. She had only to take a seat at any café on any boulevard and wait for a GI to strike up a conversation. "If she found one who seemed both discreet and entertaining," wrote Beauvoir, "she would accept a drink, a jeep ride, a dinner; in exchange for the promise of a rendezvous, which she generally failed to keep, she would bring back . . . Camels, instant coffee and tins of Spam."

Exploitation of the conquerors was not only a survival technique but a mark of the growing resentment of privilege as well. The Americans stayed in heated hotels, had hot water at least once a week, dined on eggs and fish and meat, and white bread with butter. The French government offices were unheated; every head of household had a ration card that limited a family of three to a half-pound of fresh meat, three-fifths of a pound of butter, and nine twenty-fifths of a pound of sausage per week. Milk was available only to infants. As Janet Flanner noted, the Parisians were "living largely on vegetables and mostly without heat." While the Americans rode through the streets in jeeps, the Free French walked.

Despite the advantages, the "half-million or more" GIs in the capital were already tiring of it. "One used to see them loafing on the streets, stuffed to the throat with all that GI food, bored with no place to go, and feeling sorry for themselves because the French population did not invite them home," noted the visiting

37

Virgil Thomson. "The unowned GIs, lonesome and unhappy, would wish that they were back in Germany, where everything, being run by the conquerors, was simpler, the black market easier to manipulate, and love available for merely cigarettes." Gertrude Stein, though an ardent fan of the soldiers, also took them to task for preferring the "obedience" of the Germans over the independence of the French:

> I got very angry with them, they admitted they liked the Germans better than the other Europeans. Of course you do, I said, they flatter you and they obey you, when the other countries don't like you and say so, and personally you have not been awfully ready to meet them halfway, well naturally if they don't like you they show it, the Germans don't like you but they flatter you, dog gone it, I said I bet you Fourth of July they will all be putting up our flag, and all you big babies will just be flattered to death, literally to death, I said bitterly because you will have to fight again.

WHILE THE Americans compared the French with the Germans, the Parisians began to mumble about the contrast between life under the Germans and life under the Americans. In the Consultative Assembly, de Gaulle's provisional government came under fire for the lack of supplies. Some deputies publicly asked why, during Christmas 1943, under the Nazis, there were turkeys available for those who could pay; this year, one couldn't even get a chicken. De Gaulle's answer was to talk about the war on the eastern front, about the sorry condition of the roads and rails, about the coming glory of a free France. It was not that anyone wanted the Germans back; it was just that the high expectations on Liberation Day had not been met by the reality that followed. Tempers flared even further when stories began to circulate that the German prisoners of war were being fed better than the French. In a Montmartre nightclub, a biting satirical song on the theme, entitled "The Stars and Stripes," was sung nightly to roars of approval from the patrons.

Janet Flanner, perhaps the most astute and honest American observer on the scene, wrote of the deteriorating relations:

> Friction between the Americans and the French has been steadily mounting. The worst of it is that there is always a great deal of truth in every unpleasant claim made by either side. And it is no lie that the occupiers of a country are never popular, either those who want to stay forever or those who are dying to get back home. Good Americans here criticize those French who think their country can remain great no matter how picayunely they find it convenient to act. Good Frenchmen criticize those American Army officers who knowingly frequent the same fashionable salons the Germans frequented. One of the reasons for supposing that the war will soon be over is that all three of us old Allies [the United States, France, the United Kingdom] have been getting along together as badly as we usually do in peace.

The fundamental lesson that the average American in France failed to comprehend was the extent of the suffering that the French had undergone during the Occupation and were still undergoing. To notice shortages (and most did) was one thing; to understand the psychological trauma was another. Not only had France surrendered to a superior German army; it had also, under the Vichy government, surrendered to itself. There was grief at defeat, anger at humiliation, but above all a sense of "the intolerable helplessness of a France covered in crimes and shame." The crimes were those of the government against its own people; the shame, that such a government had been allowed to exist and that so many had gone right along with it.

Addressing Americans, Vercors attempted to explain: "Can the American soldier, when he sets foot on its soil, see . . . France? I do not believe so. What does he see? People who smile, who look rather healthy; not as badly dressed as he expected. . . . What do you think was the suffering of this isolated nation? . . . . To kill either a nation or a man, it is necessary first to tear out its soul. That is what the Nazis tried to do."

During the war France had been a country divided against itself, but the split was easily delineated: the Resistance and the Free French against the common enemy—the Nazis, the Vichy regime, and its collaborators. Now that the war was ending, new ruptures began to develop among those who had previously formed a unified front. Old animosities reared up; prewar feuds were rekindled.

Although for a few brief moments after the Liberation, the Communists and Socialists were united under the banner *"Châtier les Traîtres"* (Punish the Traitors), they quickly began to disagree on who the traitors were. For the Socialists, the major targets were the right, composed mainly of the old aristocracy and bourgeoisie, who did not oppose, at least actively, Marshal Henri Pétain and his Vichy government. The Communists, however, also began to denounce scores of leading leftist intellectuals, including those who had played active roles in the Resistance. Gide, Camus, Sartre, Beauvoir, and Duras were eventually among those on the left vilified by the Communists.

Suddenly the Socialists, who had been on the offensive against the Communists after the Stalin–Hitler pact of 1939, found that they had to defend themselves against an adversary far more powerful than before the war. And while they attempted to revive memories of how the Communists had originally resisted involvement in the "imperialist war" and how their leader, Maurice Thorez, had actually deserted from the French army in 1939, the Socialists could not deny the validity of the Communists' wartime exploits. Under Thorez, they had played a major role in creating and continuing the Resistance. They were, as everyone knew, genuine heroes. They had even been rewarded with cabinet positions in de Gaulle's provisional government. Despite halfhearted attempts on both sides at occasional rapprochement, the split in the left grew deeper and more rancorous month by month. Almost any matter found them on opposite sides. This became the case particularly after VE Day, when the Communists, aligning themselves squarely with Moscow, cranked up their doctrinaire denunciations of leading members of the non-Communist left.

There were also divisions among those who had resisted the Vichy government from within France and those, headed by de Gaulle, who had fought from abroad. Among the conservatives, distinctions were made between those who had actively worked against Pétain, and those who, while not collaborating, had nonetheless not forcefully opposed the puppet regime. From the vantage point of the left, anyone who had not resisted was a traitor, but even within the ranks of the right, many shared this opinion.

Almost any event was cause for partisanship. Early in 1945, the first French literary prize to be granted since the occupation, the Prix Fémina–Vie Heureuse, or Fémina–Happy Life Prize, was awarded to the clandestine writers of Les Éditions de Minuit. Rather than accept the prize as a token of repayment for services rendered the Republic, the majority refused it. In a written statement the writers accused the jurors of never having taken a stand "to combat the invader or his accomplices." The signatories, among them Elsa Triolet, François Mauriac, Éluard, Aragon, Jean Cassou, and Vercors, proclaimed the award "derisory."

Despite the rampant political divisions, de Gaulle at first enjoyed broad-based support. Regarded nearly unanimously as the savior of France, he also proved himself a master politician. A member of no political party save his own, the Gaullist, he used his position to advantage, deftly courting the left while attempting to maintain prewar ties to the moderate right, especially those in the financial community. His first action after entering Paris on Liberation Day, for instance, was to confer with Resistance leaders of all political persuasions. He then almost immediately announced a new program for France based on those talks. The agenda included speedy justice for collaborators, nationalization of French heavy industries, the vote for women, and national unification. His much touted slogan, "*Rénovation*," meant more than simply renewal; it meant creating a France in control of its own destiny.

This concept, sacred to the French, was given a backhanded boost by the British and American governments, which did not recognize de Gaulle's sovereignty immediately upon his formation of the provisional government. Instead, they waited until late October to bestow official recognition on the Provisional Government of the Republic of France. Within France, the lack of recognition by the Allies was denounced from all sides. De Gaulle, however, used the situation to demonstrate that he was not a puppet of the United States and Britain, garnering considerable credibility in the process. Similarly, when the U.S. government expressed concern about his "Socialist" leanings, he used the criticism to rally French support around himself and his programs for an independent France. At the same time he conferred daily with the American and British governments and continued to supply Allied forces with every type of matériel— from trucks to food—that he could reasonably allocate to the war effort.

Even the newspapers, which in France were nearly all aligned with or controlled by political parties, did not initially take swipes at their leader. Instead, they directed their criticism against his provisional government, as if the general had nothing to do with it. Finally, however, after five or six months of worsening conditions, the tide turned against the sacrosanct de Gaulle. Tired of the rhetoric—regardless of its eloquence, its quotations from Shakespeare, its exhortations to the people to rally 'round the Third Republic—the citizenry, and hence the press, opened fire. Deeds not words, was the prevailing tone. The leading Resistance paper, *Combat*, edited by Albert Camus, wrote simply that "when [de Gaulle] ends words and starts acts, he will obtain the gratitude of the entire country." The Communist *L'Humanité* demanded immediate confiscation of "traitors'" fortunes and demanded to know why the two hundred families of the Banque de France, that is, the wealthiest French, were above the law. The Socialist *Populaire* pressed for real nationalization and more vigorous prosecution of collaborators.

The people though were less concerned with nationalization than with butter: "Parisians can now recite by heart the number of bombed bridges still unrepaired and the number of trains and trucks being used to feed the armies at the battlefront. The statistics they would like some news on are the twenty-five thousand pounds of black-market butter and the ten million francs of black-market profit that changed hands in the past six months," commented Janet Flanner.

The problems of butter and fuel were suddenly effaced when, as a result of the Allied liberation of the concentration camps, French prisoners of war and deportees began to return to France. The POWs arrived first: pale, dirty, skeletal. Some were barely able to stand or walk; others, without strength, were carried on litters. Next came the political deportees. A mix of ages, many of them women, some pregnant, all of them exhausted, ragged, skinny, dazed, moved through the reception center at the Gare d'Orsay, repeating their names, the names of their villages to one official after another before finally being released into the cheering crowds outside the center.

But these first two waves of returnees did little to prepare France for the influx of those from the camps. Although news of the atrocities had begun to trickle in, the reality, which confronted the Parisians as they stared into the gaunt faces of former inmates, was more than anyone could have imagined or cared to imagine. Where the crowds had cheered at the return of the POWs and forced laborers, the survivors of the concentration camps were met by sobs, by speechless anger, by profound shock and horror. Flanner wrote movingly of the arrival of the first group, three hundred survivors of the women's prison camp at Ravensbrück:

The first contingent of women prisoners arrived by train, bringing with them as very nearly their only baggage the proofs, on their faces and their bodies and in their weakly spoken reports, of the atrocities that had been their lot and that of hundreds of thousands of others in the numerous concentra-

tion camps our armies are liberating, almost too late. . . .
[They] were met by a nearly speechless crowd ready with welcoming bouquets of lilacs and other spring flowers, and by
General de Gaulle, who wept. . . . There was almost no joy; the
emotion penetrated beyond that, to something nearer pain.
Too much suffering lay behind this homecoming, and it was the
suffering that showed in the women's faces and bodies. . . . In a
way, all the women looked alike: their faces were gray-green,
with reddish-brown circles around their eyes, which seemed to
see but not to take in. They were dressed like scarecrows, in
what had been given them at camp, clothes taken from the
dead of all nationalities. As the lilacs fell from inert hands, the
flowers made a purple carpet on the platform and the perfume
of the trampled flowers mixed with the stench of illness and
dirt.

Marguerite Duras, in her memoir *The War*, describes the condition of her husband after he returned from Dachau:

He must have weighed between eighty-two and eighty-four
pounds: bone, skin, liver, intestines, brain, lungs, everything—
eighty-four pounds for a body five feet ten inches tall. . . . The
head was connected to the body by the neck, as heads usually
are, but the neck was so withered and shrunken—you could
circle it with one hand—that you wondered how life could pass
through it; a spoonful of gruel almost blocked it. At first the
neck was at right angles to the shoulders. Higher up, the neck
was right inside the skeleton, joined on at the top of the jaws
and winding around the ligaments like ivy. You could see the
vertebrae through it, the carotid arteries, the nerves, the phar-
ynx, and the blood passing through: the skin had become like
cigarette paper.

Duras's husband eventually recovered, but thousands of others
of those repatriated eventually succumbed. Many never survived
the return journey, dying en route; hundreds of thousands were
exterminated or perished from disease or starvation before the

camps were liberated. Although Germany's defeat was imminent, the ravages of the war continued in the form of physically and psychically shattered victims. The terrible legacy would hang over France for years; the wounds would never totally heal.

Chapter Three

"Courage to Be Courageous": The Last Works and Days of Gertrude Stein

"WHAT A day is today that is what a day it was day before yesterday, what a day! I can tell everybody that none of you know what this native land business is until you have been cut off from that same native land completely for years. This native land business gets you all right. . . . I am so happy to be talking to America today so happy." Thus spoke Gertrude Stein on September 4, 1944. The occasion was a transatlantic radio broadcast to the American people three days after the liberation of Culoz by the Allies.

Stein was indeed happy. The war years, during which she and Toklas had remained in southeast France, had been fraught with uncertainty, deprivation, anxiety. As Jews, as enemy aliens, they had lived constantly with the possibility of arrest and deportation to the camps. Now, nearly delirious with the arrival of the Americans, she could finally express how truly isolated she had felt. This is not to imply that she and Toklas had bemoaned their wartime fate. Having chosen to stay in France—a decision made with considerable hesitation and anguish—they accepted the situation with equanimity. Stein later recorded how she and Toklas had decided to remain:

> And then Italy came into the war and then I was scared, completely scared, and my stomach felt very weak, because—well, here we were right in everybody's path; any enemy that wanted to go anywhere might easily come here. I was frightened; I woke up completely upset. And I said to Alice Toklas, "Let's go away." . . . And we telephoned to the American consul in Lyon and he said, "I'll fix up your passports. Do not hesitate—leave."
> . . . We went; it was a lovely day, the drive from Bourg to Lyon was heavenly. They all said, "Leave," and I said to Alice Toklas, "Well, I don't know—it would be awfully uncomfortable and I am fussy about my food. Let's not leave." So we came back, and the village [of Bilignin] was happy and we were happy and that was all right.

A few days later, however, they decided again to leave and made the trip to Lyon to renew their passports. But once more, they could not bear the thought of deserting France, where they had resided for more than thirty years. Their friends and neighbors affirmed their decision. One acquaintance in Belley was apparently most responsible for their choice. As Stein recorded it, he told her: "Everybody knows you here; everybody likes you; we all would help you in every way. Why risk yourself among strangers?" This settled the matter: "So back we came and we unpacked our spare gasoline and our bags and we said to Madame Roux, 'Here we are and here we stay.'"

STEIN WAS not idle during the war years. Although at first the time passed quite slowly, with the arrival of the Germans, Stein found herself observing closely small details of daily life: the sound of the cannon on the hillside, the refusal of a local garage keeper to furnish gasoline to the Germans, the anxiety of the young men who feared being rounded up and sent to Germany. Incidents such as these formed the backdrop of three major works that she wrote during the Occupation: a novel, *Mrs. Reynolds*; a chronicle of her life during the war, *Wars I Have Seen*; and a play, *Yes Is for a Very Young Man*. Taken together, they reveal a great deal about Stein's reactions and experiences under the stress of those years. But where *Wars I Have Seen* is a public record of public events, *Mrs. Reynolds* and to a lesser extent the play are accounts of the effect of war and occupation on the psyche. Of the three, *Mrs. Reynolds*, though far less straightforward than the other works, is the most powerful and compelling statement of life under the Germans.

The book tells the story of an American couple, Mr. and Mrs. Reynolds, very reminiscent of Stein and Toklas, who are resident in occupied foreign territory during a war. The novel revolves around Mrs. Reynolds's daily activities—walking, gardening, talking with friends, ruminating on history and books of prophecy, sleeping, sighing, weeping—during what seems an interminable period of war. An additional central but unseen character is Angel Harper, a version of Hitler. He was a local boy, and his odd youth and rise to power are major topics of conversation among the villagers in the first half of the novel; in the second half, through frequent and obsessive mentions of his age, he functions on the periphery as an indicator of passing time. Stalin is also present in a minor role, in the rather undeveloped figure of Joseph Lane.

Written between 1940 and 1943, *Mrs. Reynolds* is really a novel about endurance amid total uncertainty. In a brief epilogue to the book Stein defined it as "an effort to show the way anybody could feel these years. . . . There is nothing historical about this book except the state of mind." The description is apt, for while Mrs. Reynolds has several conflicting emotions, she has one state of mind, one mission: to survive intact. "It takes courage to be courageous," she announces in the book's opening line. The rest of the novel is an articulation of what this means in terms of "a perfectly ordinary couple living an ordinary life." As such, the book is constructed around small, occasionally ominous but more often mundane incidents, all of which contribute to creating a psychologically resonant portrait of despair. Mrs. Reynolds seeks refuge in a variety of ways—through memory, gossip, and belief in medieval prophecy, through her relationship with Mr. Reynolds, through frequent sighs and outbreaks of tears, through sleep—but none really satisfactorily effaces the daily anxiety. Her heroism, her courage, consists in not ultimately succumbing; it is a small-scale triumph, but a victory nonetheless.

Wars I Have Seen presents much of the same terrain, but through a somewhat different lens. Begun while Stein was still writing *Mrs. Reynolds*, it is written from the viewpoint of the intelligence, not of the psyche. Again, observed details of quotidian existence, often paralleling events in *Mrs. Reynolds*, are set next to broader meditations on war, humanity, politics, society, and history. The overall impression, though, is of Stein as a rational, tough-minded, fully engaged human being. It is really only at the end of the book, when the American army finally arrives, that emotion is allowed to enter the narrative. Even when she is evicted in 1943 from her house in Bilignin, where she and Toklas had resided since 1929, and forced to move to the nearby town of Culoz, or when she is made to house German and Italian soldiers in her new residence, she stoically accepts these intrusions into her personal life.

Stein's politics were always conservative. She was an ardent defender of the Falangists in Spain, and in *Wars I Have Seen* she extends her support of conservative values to Marshal Pétain; he was "right to make the armistice," she says, and sees in it not capitulation but "an important element in the ultimate defeat of the Germans." Although she does not mention it in the book, she so believed Pétain had been right that she even translated a volume of his speeches in the early years of the war. Her hope was that she might be able to help Americans understand better what was widely perceived in the United States as his surrender of France to the enemy. But after getting negative reaction from friends in the States, she quietly abandoned the project.

To comprehend Stein's embrace of the Vichy doctrine it is necessary to view it within the greater perspective of her outlook on the war. She believed, at least initially, that by signing the armistice with the Nazis, Pétain had managed to save thousands of French lives: a perception not all that uncommon at the time. On a more personal level, Stein believed that Pétain's action, which nominally left the Vichy government in control of a large portion of France, prevented its occupation by German troops. "We who lived in the unoccupied we knew there was a difference all right. One might not be very free in the unoccupied but we were pretty free and in the occupied they were not free, the difference between being pretty free and not free at all is considerable." It was the case, as a severe critic of her position, her longtime friend W. G. Rogers wrote, that "if I had believed that Pétain helped to save my neck, I too might seek to exculpate him from the more flagrant charges of collaboration."

Despite her early admiration of Pétain, as the war continued she began to give less credence to the Maréchal: "So many points of view about him, so very many, I had lots of them, I was almost French in having so many." By 1943, in fact, her attitude had undergone a considerable transformation when it became clear that the Germans were indeed beginning to occupy the "unoccupied" zone. As a result, she began to write glowingly of the *maquis*. The abrupt switch in allegiance was fairly typical of many in the Vichy sector; to some extent Stein's sentiments were those of her adopted countrymen, determined more by personal circumstances than by ideology.

In *Yes Is for a Very Young Man*, Stein addresses the variety and complexity of individual responses felt by the French during the Occupation. Or as she wrote to the English painter Francis Rose: "Living in an occupied country is very complicated and that is what I have tried to make people understand in my play Yes is for a very young man." No better synopsis of the play exists. Although flawed as drama, as a statement on France during the Occupation, *Yes* is enormously insightful. The central concern is the moral dilemma—to whom do one's loyalties belong?—that an occupied people face; in a more personal sense, it was Stein's way of attempting to sort out her own conflicting emotions as the war dragged on.

The play opens in 1940, just after the armistice has been signed, and ends with the liberation of Paris. It is a drama of ideas, its tensions created through the juxtaposition of small but key events that bring the characters to reveal their feelings about the war and especially the Occupation, then express those feelings through actions. The central characters are Denise, a reactionary Frenchwoman; her bewildered husband, Henry, who eventually participates in actions of the *maquis* after his father is killed by the Germans; Henry's brother, Ferdinand, the "young man" of the title, who is sent as a forced laborer to work in factories in Germany; and Constance, an American woman who, after choosing to stay in France, joins the Resistance. All of these personages, though, are aspects of the one major character in the play: France itself, "a country that can be beaten but not conquered, that can be a phoenix and rise from the ashes."

As in *Mrs. Reynolds*, many of the actual incidents are drawn from life, and a good portion of the dialogue is taken directly from *Wars I Have Seen*. Ferdinand, for instance, is based on an acquaintance, Francis Malherbe, whose description in Stein's nonfictional account of the conditions in Germany is quoted nearly verbatim in *Yes Is for a Very Young Man*. Constance is persuaded to stay in the village by a neighbor, as was Stein. Troops are billeted in her house and her servants have the same names as Stein's servants. What makes the play remarkable is Stein's ability to create a vivid sense of life under the Germans without ever resorting to praise of one action or condemnation of another. Perceptive of detail, she manages to present, as she had hoped, "the divided families, the bitterness, the quarrels and sometimes the denunciations, and yet the natural necessity of their all continuing to live their daily life together, because after all that was all the life they had, besides they were after all the same family or neighbors, and in the country neighbors are neighbors."

Perhaps because it is a play about the "neighbors" of whom

Stein had such an acute awareness and admiration, there is no real hero in the drama, but no true villain either. Everyone's position, as Stein sees it, is worthy of sympathy and requires understanding. This includes even the ultrarightist Denise, with her pro-German pronouncements. The underlying situation for Stein is that, as Ferdinand says near the beginning of the play, "every Frenchman in France is in prison, but you can't take sides in prison."

GIVEN STEIN'S obvious ability to perceive the intricate human questions regarding the war, it is surprising that she seems never to have comprehended fully the Holocaust. Indeed, on her own Jewishness and on anti-Semitism in general, Stein's perspective was not so different from that held by a number of Jews in the early days of the war, who, having identified themselves as Frenchmen first, Jews second, were tragically duped into thinking that their own attitudes would somehow prevail over the rabid tide of anti-Semitic persecution sweeping France. Stein notes at one point in *Wars I Have Seen* that although her lawyer advised her and Toklas to flee immediately, lest they be shipped off to the camps, her reaction was not fear but disbelief, almost as if she did not regard herself and Toklas as Jews: "I felt very funny, quite completely funny."

After she and Toklas discussed the matter, they decided to remain. "What was so curious in the whole affair," commented Stein, "was its unreality." Although she never denied being Jewish, she seems to have felt that as a nonpracticing Jew she was exempt from the concerted campaign to deport all Jews.

To some extent this was simply naiveté, but there is also reason to believe that Stein felt protected from deportation by her friend and French translator, Bernard Faÿ, who as an official in the Vichy government interceded on her behalf with Pétain. Faÿ at least later claimed this to be the case, and it is quite likely that Stein wanted to think it was so. More immediately responsible for her well-being, however, was the mayor of Culoz; well aware of Stein's status as a Jew and a foreigner, he nonetheless refused to denounce her, "forgetting" to mention Stein and Toklas when the Nazis were rounding up enemy aliens. "You are obviously too old for life in a concentration camp," he simply told her. "You would not survive it, so why should I tell them?"

Stein's refusal to categorize herself as a Jew is perhaps responsible for what can be described only as a tendency toward anti-Semitism. When elsewhere in *Wars I Have Seen* she discusses the issue, she proffers a thesis that verges on blaming the Jews for the problem:

> Before industrialism Jews were international bankers and before that international money lenders, but since industrialism, all the Jewish money in the world is only a drop in the bucket. . . . But the European particularly the countries who like to delude their people do not want to know it, they must know it of course, anybody must know it, and the Jews do not want anybody to know it, although they know it perfectly well they must know it because it would make themselves to themselves feel less important and as they always as the chosen people have felt themselves to themselves to be important they do not want anybody to know it.

Even after learning of the horror of the camps, she did not alter her opinion. In a letter to Robert Graves written in 1946, she was even more direct in her assessment that Jews were responsible, at least to some degree, for anti-Semitism. Commenting on a former acquaintance, she wrote:

> She was the materialistic jew camouflaging her materialism by intellectualism, a very common thing in the race, I cannot say camouflaging, really the intellectualism is the reactionary violence of their materialism, in the Jewish race there are really more jews like that than any other kind, I guess it is Semitic that, and it is they that make all the noise and really keep alive Anti-semitism.

Stein's position vis-à-vis her fellow Jews had much less to do with her philosophy of religion, which stemmed from her embrace as an undergraduate at Radcliffe of the work of William James, than with her concept of character, developed in large part from her reading of Otto Weininger's *Sex and Character*. Her enthusiasm for the book, published in English translation in 1906 and read by Stein in 1908, was curious, to say the least, for *Sex and Character* is both virulently anti-Semitic and misogynistic. Stein, however, had the ability to take only what she wanted from people, philosophy, and literature, and ignore what didn't correspond to her own similar (and often preconceived) set of ideas. What appealed to her most was Weininger's "characterology," which attempted to reduce matters such as genius and talent, homosexuality, and relationships between the sexes to a schema involving the intrinsic nature of human beings. She was able to overlook his statements that women, because of their nature, could never be geniuses, and concentrate instead on his pronouncements that the lesbian, because she is "half male," is more predisposed toward achievement.

She apparently adopted a similar point of view on Weininger's anti-Semitic remarks, of which his book is replete. In particular, she appropriated his concept of "genuine" Jews, who like women are incapable of genius, as opposed to Jews in name only. It was always the "genuine" Jew, to use Weininger's classification, who was the target of her blasts. According to her friend Virgil Thomson, Stein's "anti-Semitism" was largely an abstraction, more a result of her penchant for grand likes and dislikes than any sort of codified position. As Thomson noted, her many individual relationships with Jews were marked by a high degree of familial intimacy:

Just as Gertrude kept up friendships among the Amazons, though she did not share their lives, she held certain Jews in attachment for their family-like warmth, though she felt no solidarity with Jewry. Tristan Tzara . . . she said was "like a cousin." Miss Etta and Dr. Claribel Cone, picture buyers and friends from Baltimore days, she handled almost as if they were her sisters. The sculptors Jo Davidson and Jacques Lipschitz, the painter Man Ray she accepted as though they had a second cousin's right to be part of her life. About men or goyim, even about her oldest man friend, Picasso, she could feel unsure; but a woman or a Jew she could size up quickly. She accepted without cavil, indeed, all the conditionings of her Jewish background. And if, as she would boast, she was a "bad Jew," she at least did not think of herself as a Christian.

Ultimately, it is this ability to identify herself as a "bad Jew" or a Jew "in name only" that most significantly affected her position during the Occupation; this explains in part her being able to live under the thumb of the German army without undo concern about her and Toklas's personal safety. Not believing herself or Toklas to be Jews like "most Jews," she did not regard the threat of deportation with much seriousness. Thanks to the concern of others, however, her strategy, if it can be called that, paid off. Many, such as her old friend the poet Max Jacob, were not so lucky. Despite his conversion to Catholicism years before the war, he was arrested and deported from Paris, and died in a concentration camp.

IN IDENTIFYING herself as an American, however, Stein never wavered, although she had lived more of her life in France than in the United States. Indeed, her jubilation at the arrival of American troops and her subsequent embrace of the GIs bordered on the chauvinistic. In the last pages of *Wars I Have Seen* she recorded how ecstatic she was upon coming across the first Americans while on a shopping trip to Belley with Toklas: "We held each other's hands and we patted each other and we sat down together. . . . In the last war we had come across our first American soldiers and it had been nice but nothing like this, after almost two years of not a word with America."

From this encounter until her death nearly two years later, Stein would be surrounded by American GIs. and correspondents. Courting them, and being courted by them, she enthusiastically welcomed practically all Americans into her home, delighting in their speech, regional accents, tales of childhood, of life on farms, in towns, in cities. In a curious way, she achieved fame upon the Liberation that she had never enjoyed before. *Life* magazine sent a cameraman to photograph "America's most famous literary expatriate." She broadcast to America on the radio, traveled to Germany on assignment for *Life* to write a story on servicemen there, wrote a companion piece for the *New York Times Magazine*, was interviewed by French, American, and British newspapers. Cries of "Hiya, Gertie" burst from the mouths of young American soldiers as she walked through the streets. Others swarmed around her asking for autographs. *Wars I Have Seen*, welcomed with rave reviews, became an overnight bestseller and sensation upon its publication in 1945; it was by far the most popular success she'd ever had in the United States. In short, Stein became a literary celebrity, a heroine of the war, a champion of America and Americans.

IN SEPTEMBER 1939, soon after Hitler invaded Poland, Stein and Toklas removed their personal belongings from their Paris apartment at 5 Rue Christine. Of their fabulous collection of paintings they took only two: Cézanne's *Portrait of Hortense* and a Picasso portrait of Stein. They did not return to Paris during the entire Occupation and were unaware of how their belongings had fared under the Germans. Now, at liberation, they were eager to return to the capital. The urgency became even greater when, in November 1944, they received a letter from an American friend, Katherine Dudley, who had remained in the city during the war. The letter contained reassuring but at the same time alarming news. "It's a miracle," wrote Dudley, "that your collection is still there for about 2 weeks before the Boches left 4 men of the Gestapo came, demanded the key of your concierge who protested in vain that you were American." Dudley went on to inform them that their downstairs neighbor, hearing footsteps overhead, rushed upstairs to witness the Gestapo "lashing themselves into a fury over the Picassos saying that they would cut them to pieces and burn them. 'De la saloperie juive, bon à brûler.'" Finally forced out of the apartment, the neighbor called the police, who eventually evicted the Germans on the grounds that they did not have an order of perquisition to enter and confiscate personal possessions.

When Stein and Toklas finally did return to their apartment in mid-December 1944, they took inventory at once. A few items were missing—a footstool covered with a petit point that Toklas had worked from a Picasso drawing, and other small objects— but the collection was intact. Had it not been for the quick intervention on the part of their neighbor, major work would undoubtedly have been lost. A bundle of paintings, already tied up, leaned ominously against a wall.

Stein and Toklas had been back only a few hours when their first visitor arrived: Picasso. They embraced one another, rejoicing that "the treasures of [their] youth, the pictures, the drawings, were safe." From Culoz, Stein and Toklas had brought a Henry IV table; when Picasso expressed his admiration for the design and workmanship, they gave it to him, assuring him it wouldn't fit in their apartment.

Over the next few days others arrived, among them fellow expatriates Sylvia Beach and Katherine Dudley, both of whom had weathered the Occupation in France. Hemingway came too, and although he and Stein had quarreled long before, this reunion was wholly amicable, with the two avowing that they loved one another.

But the majority of those who rang the doorbell were in uniform. Officers and enlisted men, young and not so young, they flocked to the Rue Christine eager for an audience. Without exception, Stein welcomed them. "Paris is so lovely the American army is delightful I like them so much, and it is all every day just that way," she wrote to a friend in the States. The GIs, overwhelmed by her warmth and her interest in them, quickly fell into the pattern of so many of their predecessors. They showed her poems written on the battlefield, expressed to her their dreams, their anxieties, their homesickness. A few, including writers Donald Sutherland and Joseph Barry, and Donald Gallup, eventually curator of the American Literature Collection at Yale's Beinecke Library, would contribute substantially to forwarding Stein's reputation; but at the time they were simply young, anonymous servicemen, awed at having made contact with a great American writer.

Stein also became involved again in promoting the arts. In a gallery announcement for a young Spanish painter resident in Paris, Riba-Rovira, she prefaced her remarks by describing her search for new talent and noting that after having spent so many years in the countryside she was in need of discovering a young painter. "Paris was wonderful, but where was the young painter? I looked everywhere, in gallery after gallery, but the young painter did not exist." Finally she discovered Riba-Rovira, and now consequently felt her return to Paris was complete. She also took up the cudgel for "a very interesting young painter," Jean Atlan. Equally enthralled with the fashions being created by a then unknown designer, Pierre Balmain, she did much to advance his early career by writing a glowing article on him for *Vogue*.

But it was not just new painters and designers who interested her. As before the war, she renewed her championing of the work of Francis Rose, even acting as something of an agent for him. In a number of letters written to Rose, still resident in London, she gave a detailed accounting of how many pictures of his she had sold, and told him she awaited his orders about what to do with the money. By April 1946, she had earned the artist 158,555 francs, about $800.

Another old friend, Bernard Faÿ, also received her support. Arrested as a collaborator, he was eventually sentenced to life imprisonment at hard labor. Stein was appalled. "About Bernard Faÿ, no indeed he never worked against the free French, he was waiting with the greatest excitement the arrival of the Americans and the British, he helped many of the Resistance as well as the Jews, there is no doubt about that." She wrote to him regularly, sent him candy and vitamin pills, even shipped him strictly rationed cigarettes when she learned that he could use them as currency within the prison.

Despite her delight at being back in Paris—"we had so much concentrated country for four years that we do like the life of the city"—daily life in the capital was more complicated than before the war, for Stein and Toklas were not spared the problem of basic commodities shortages. Stein, though, put a good face on it: "It is a happy time in a kind of a way when we can be pleased to have anything, when I think of the old days when we were fussy about the brand of coffee, or the choice of butter, or the cut of meat, it is now as it used to be for the children, you take what you get and be thankful." She also appealed to friends abroad for small items impossible to obtain in Paris: "Could you send us some TEK toothbrushes and toothpaste we need them."

Stein was, as well, ingenious about obtaining precious commodities. A young GI, Leon Gordon Miller, recounted how he had one day accompanied her to a butcher shop, where the customary long queue had formed. But instead of standing in line, she walked directly to the counter, heedless of the loud protests issuing from others waiting patiently. Suddenly the butcher, in an attempt to calm the crowd, shouted, *"Elle est écrivain,"* then took her order. Emerging from the shop, Stein admonished Miller, who had beaten a retreat. In France, she told him, creative people were granted special privileges, as they had "less time to spare on routine."

She could not, however, use her status as a writer to influence the electric company. She and Toklas suffered as much as other Parisians during the extremely frigid winter of 1944–1945, shutting off all but two rooms in their apartment to conserve heat. Yet the excitement at being back in Paris took precedence over the lack of conveniences. "Alice having been raised in a temperate climate California finds it cold well it is cold, but when the electricity goes it is not so cold, but it does not always go, no it doesn't but we are so happy to be here, I walk and walk around and see it all."

Walking in Paris, however, was not the same experience as it had been before the war. Virgil Thomson recalled that Stein used these outings to meet the GIs who swarmed through the streets of

Paris: "Every day, as she walked her dog, she picked up dozens, asked them questions, took them home, fed them cake and whiskey, observed their language." Listening to the young soldiers became a major activity. So enthralled was she with their speech and their preoccupations that she set about to record the GI legend for posterity. The result was a short novel, *Brewsie and Willie*.

The book consists essentially of dialogues among GIs. Brewsie is the philosopher in the group; Willie, loudmouthed, dominant, and sarcastic, is representative of what Stein at least took to be the common man. Other figures, nurses and fellow GIs, move in and out of the conversations, put forth their views as the need arises. Donald Sutherland, who wrote the first substantial book on Stein, noted perceptively that the book is really a series of twentieth-century Platonic dialogues in which ideas hold center stage; the characters exist only as vehicles for debating the central concerns of the time. He also makes a strong case for the accuracy of Stein's ear:

> While the GI legend was really on, in Paris, it was as *Brewsie and Willie* describes it. . . . The legend was not a discipline or code or a dream of heroism, it was not at all rigid and it certainly allowed for the creation of individual legends or "characters" or variations within the range of the key signature, but that key was not determined by any individual personality, it was set by the group which was American and of the time. The book is a kind of quartet or sextet composed exactly in that key. At least it sounds exact to me, and I was in and out of Paris and Germany at the time, being as GI as possible.

Despite the charm of the book, its message was really quite subversive. Through her primary spokesman, Brewsie, Stein launched a spirited attack on what she perceived as the true enemy of America: industrialism. In harangue after harangue, Brewsie denounces the loss of the "pioneering" spirit, which has been replaced by the corrosive trend toward industrial enslavement: "Industrialism . . . produces more than anybody can buy and makes employees out of free men makes 'em stop thinking, stop feeling, makes 'em feel all alike." In the afterword, "To Americans," in an ardent tone reminiscent of Ezra Pound's Rome broadcasts (for which he was charged with treason), Stein addressed her readers directly:

> I am sure that this particular moment in our history is more important than anything since the Civil War. We are there where we have to have to fight a spiritual pioneer fight or we will go poor as England and other industrial countries have gone poor, and don't think that communism or socialism will save you . . . you have to find out how you can go ahead without running away with yourselves, you have to learn to produce without exhausting your country's wealth, you have to learn to be individual and not just mass job workers, you have to get courage enough to know what you feel and not just all be yes or no men, but you have to really learn to express complication, go easy and if you cant go easy go as easy as you can.

While redundantly clear as to the problem, Stein was less able (or willing) to offer a salutary prescriptive. Her vague concept of the "pioneering spirit" is open, apparently by design, to interpretation. Individualism, populism, staying tied to the land are all part of the equation. Curiously enough, although she saw these qualities as quintessentially American, the experience of France during the Occupation seems to have inspired her fervency. With the manufacturing process in collapse, the masses, particularly in the cities, suffered; those in the countryside, with small plots on which to grow basic essentials and raise a few chickens or goats, managed to endure the privation with far greater success.

By turning these immediate memories into object lessons, Stein hoped to convince Americans that a greater danger than international war awaited them back home. Her concern, as expressed through the mouths of GIs in *Brewsie and Willie*, was that the false prosperity that accompanied the war buildup would quickly disintegrate, that economic depression would return, that "life on the installment plan" would cripple the individual's ability to think for himself, to act positively on his own behalf. "It's about that employee mentality we're all getting to have, we're just a lot of employees, obeying a boss, with no mind of our own and if it goes on where is America," says one of the characters in her book. For Stein, it was imperative that the people use their constitutional power to shape the future, to prevent what she saw as the imminent demise of a nation of "pioneers." In an eloquent discourse that mixed GI folksiness with a quotation from the Gettysburg Address, she attempted to rouse her readers to "look facts in the face, not just what they all say, the leaders, but every darn one of you so that a government by the people for the people shall not perish from the face of the earth."

Distrust of authority was always part of Stein's message, and her appeal. America's leaders in particular came in for a fair amount of abuse in *Brewsie and Willie*. Franklin Roosevelt is excoriated by name; non–office holders, governing through their corporations' influence over the political process, are collectively derided as well: "We are being ruled by tired middle-aged people, tired business men, the kind who need pin-ups," says one of her GIs.

It is this realization that is at the root of Stein's last great work, *The Mother of Us All*, written as a free-form libretto at the request of Virgil Thomson, who had received an opera commission from Columbia University. Stein chose Susan B. Anthony and her struggle for the right of women to vote as a vehicle to espouse her latest views on America.

According to Thomson, the subject was entirely of Stein's choosing. His original suggestion was simply that she provide him with a libretto "about nineteenth-century America, with perhaps the language of the senatorial orators quoted." She obliged, in her fashion; Daniel Webster is given a major role as Anthony's chief antagonist. His oratory, however, is inflated, pompous, chauvinistic, while hers is elegant, vibrant, eloquent, and human. Thomson was not displeased: "When [Stein] chose

Susan B. as her protagonist, I could not deny her the feminist approach. When she showed her in a scene of domesticity that might as well have been herself and Alice Toklas conversing about Gertrude's career, I knew that she had got inside the theme and that the work would now be moving rapidly."

The libretto did indeed progress quickly. Within months of Thomson's initial offer, Stein had completed two key scenes and had developed the basic scenario, this despite the rather extensive amount of self-imposed research that she felt was necessary to do justice to the theme. She became so immersed in nineteenth-century American history that she exhausted not only her own collection on the subject but also that of the American Library in Paris. In the end, the library was forced to send to New York for additional volumes to satisfy her required reading list. From this reading she freely borrowed quotations, characters, and situations; at the same time, *The Mother of Us All* is hardly a historical drama in the classic sense. Friends and acquaintances, including Virgil Thomson, Jean Atlan, and GIs Donald Gallup and Joseph Barry are characters in the opera, as are figures such as John Adams who were no longer even alive at the time of Anthony's struggle.

For Stein, Anthony embodied the true revolutionary spirit of America and her crusade must be set against other revolutionary historical events. Chief of these was the Civil War, which, while it resulted in the emancipation of the slaves and the enfranchisement of black men, did not give women the right to vote. Thus Anthony, in Stein's view, is a fervent activist set on completing the revolution that should have taken place at the end of the Civil War, namely, the establishment of universal human rights. The struggle for the vote is symbolic; the real aim is that of creating equality between women and men, of toppling the masculine stranglehold on societal institutions in which "there is no humanity there are only laws."

Powerful men, quite naturally, are the targets of Susan B.'s (and Stein's) wrath. Her first denunciations have the quality of name-calling: "Men said Susan B. are so conservative, so selfish, so boresome and said Susan B. they are so ugly, and said Susan B. they are gullible." Later, however, frustrated in her struggle to get the men "to vote my laws," she proffers a more profound and psychological analysis:

> They fear women, they fear each other, they fear their neighbor, they fear other countries and then they hearten themselves in their fear by crowding together and following each other, and when they crowd together and follow each other they are brutes, like animals who stampede, and so they have written in the name male into the United States constitution, because they are afraid of black men because they are afraid of women, because they are afraid afraid. Men are afraid.

Marriage too is looked at with more than a shred of disdain. Susan B. proclaims: "I am not married and the reason why is that I have had to do what I have had to do, I have had to be what I have had to be, I could never be one of two I could never be two in one as married couples do and can, I am but one all one, one and all one, and so I have never been married to any one." Despite Susan B.'s remarks on marriage, she has an extremely close and nurturing relationship with Anne, very much like Stein's with Toklas. Anne, however, is clearly the follower, often literally echoing Susan B.'s statements. She is also Susan B.'s most ardent admirer, bolstering her, defending her, championing the cause. In short, she plays the supporting role; she is the woman behind the woman.

How Stein rationalized such a contradiction is not apparent, but it is evident that she did not see Susan B.'s union with Anne as a marriage in the conventional, and destructive, sense. Instead, she saw the two women as individuals united in a cause; Anne, in spite of her allegiance to Susan B., is not subservient, nor does she lack courage. She is every bit the fighter that Susan B. is. At times she even fuels Susan B.'s flagging energy, reaffirms the importance of the struggle. As such, her identity is not fused with that of Susan B.; she is her own person, a true comrade-in-arms.

The Mother of Us All was completed a few months before Stein's death from stomach cancer. Whether or not she knew she was dying (Thomson thinks not), the closing scene is clearly a meditation on mortality. Susan B. is dead, and speaks from behind her marble-and-gold statue as her followers file past. It is a polemical ending, for on the surface she seems a disappointed heroine, uncertain of the victory gained since her death: "But do I want what we have got, has it not gone, what made it live, has it not gone because now it is had, in my long life in my long life." A closer reading, however, reveals that this statement is actually a call to continue the struggle in which gaining the right to vote was simply the first step. For Stein, as for Susan B., the real cause, not yet fully achieved, was that of self-determination, of overthrowing the established patriarchal order. As "Mother's" true child, Stein was bent on continuing that fight, knowing full well that, like Susan B., she was a "martyr all my life not to what I won but to what was done."

By THE time Stein finished *The Mother of Us All* in early 1946 her condition was becoming serious. Rejecting the advice of her doctor, who told her to consult a specialist, she continued as if nothing were wrong, even buying a new car. In July, after nearly two years of continuous living in Paris, Stein and Toklas decided to retreat to the countryside once more. The imprisoned Bernard Faÿ had offered them his house in Luceau. A few days after their arrival, while on an excursion to the nearby town of Azay-le-Rideau, Stein became seriously ill with intestinal trouble. She and Toklas took a room at an inn and a doctor was summoned. Upon examining her, he ordered her immediate return to Paris. The next morning Stein and Toklas left by train; an ambulance met them at the station and took Stein to the American Hospital in Neuilly. After a series of examinations, the specialists recommended surgery once Stein had regained some strength. On July 23 she wrote her will, leaving nearly everything to Toklas.

A couple of days later Stein was suddenly informed that the doctors had decided not to operate after all, as it was unlikely she could survive the surgery. She, however, insisted that the doctors keep their word. According to Toklas, "Amongst the surgeons was one who said, I have told Miss Stein that I would perform the operation and you don't give your word of honor to a woman of her character and not keep it." On July 27 she was readied for surgery. "By this time," noted Toklas, "Gertrude Stein was in a sad state of indecision and worry. I sat next to her and she said to me early in the afternoon, What is the answer? I was silent. In that case, she said, what is the question? Then the whole afternoon was troubled, confused and very uncertain, and later in the afternoon they took her away on a wheeled stretcher to the operating room and I never saw her again."

RARELY HAS France had a foreign admirer as great as Gertrude Stein. From the beginning of her stay in 1903 until the end of her life in 1946, she continually championed France (versus the United States) as a place where creativity could flourish. In *Paris France*, published in 1940, she wrote: "Of course they all come to France a great many to paint pictures and naturally they could not do that at home, or write they could not do that at home either, they could be dentists at home because she knew all about that even before the war, Americans were a practical people and dentistry was practical." The legions of Americans who made their home in France in the twenties and thirties for the most part shared her view, as did those who, often following her advice and example, came after World War II. And while she "taught" Hemingway, Fitzgerald, and Sherwood Anderson in the flesh, from beyond the grave she continued to exert an influence on a generation who never had the chance to have tea *chez* Stein.

Chapter Four

The Chosen Exile of Richard Wright

WHEN, ON May 1, 1946, Richard Wright, his wife, Ellen, and their four-year-old daughter, Julia, sailed past the Statue of Liberty on their way to France, Wright felt only "relieved." The months preceding departure had been a bureaucratic nightmare. Wright's first application for a passport had been turned down, ostensibly because of the unsettled conditions in Europe. Undaunted, he appealed to the French cultural attaché in Washington, Claude Lévi-Strauss, who offered his assistance. In France, Gertrude Stein, who had written to Wright after reading *Black Boy* that "it is obvious that you and I are the only two geniuses of this era," also began working on his behalf. Eventually, through the combined efforts of Lévi-Strauss and Stein, he received an official invitation from the French government to visit France, all expenses paid.

Feeling that now a passport could hardly be denied, he sent the invitation, special delivery, to the State Department. After days of waiting for a reply, he telephoned the passport division in Washington. The staff claimed such an invitation had not been received. A duplicate was acquired, sent. Again, having obtained no response, he made another inquiry. The answer was the same as before. Enraged, Wright went to Washington. A doctor friend put him in touch with a State Department official, Evelyn Walsh McLean, who directed him to someone else. This person finally listened, and passports for Wright and his family were issued an hour later. The SS *Brazil*, on which he had already booked passage, was to sail in just a few days.

The episode was not atypical. The incident that precipitated his departure was similar. Wright had decided to move from New York to the countryside, and so he went house-hunting in New Hampshire. Within two days of searching he found his "dream house" and made a cash offer on it. But after a week of waiting he was informed by the broker that the owner had chosen not to sell his house to a black man. This refusal catalyzed his decision to go to France.

Although anger prompted Wright to leave the United States, it was a course he had contemplated for some time. In May 1945, he wrote to Stein that "maybe next year we will come to France and I hope Paris will be like so many have said it used to be. Will it? For a reason I don't know, I've always felt that France would mean something to me and that I'd live there. So I'm honor bound to see France." Stein wrote back encouraging him to come.

As Wright had long been an admirer of Stein, her support of his plan was important. She was one of the few white American writers then to speak out boldly on the "Negro problem," particularly in *Brewsie and Willie,* and he felt a curious kinship with her. He associated her ability to write genuine dialogue—most notably in *Melanctha,* an early novel with a black heroine—with remoteness from her source. Disconnected from the cacophony of other voices, he decided, a writer could hear in memory a certain manner of speaking more directly, clearly, without needing to filter out the speech of others which intruded daily into one's existence. He felt that detachment allowed for the creation of a perspective unavailable to the writer surrounded by the material he was attempting to transfuse into fiction. For Wright, too much energy was consumed in confronting that material, in which the constant battle against racism played too great a role.

In a 1945 journal entry, he wrote:

> [Stein] made me hear something that I'd heard all my life, that is, the speech of my grandmother who spoke a deep Negro dialect colored by the Bible. . . . Yes, she's got something, but I'd say that one could live and write like that only if one lived in Paris or in some out of the way spot where one could claim one's own soul. . . . All the more reason why I dream and dream of leaving my native land to escape the pressure of the superficial things I think I know. That's why I left the South, and now I want to leave the country, and some day I will, by God.

In Wright's mind, Paris was equated with freedom, freedom from "mob violence, blacklisting, character assassination, and the pressures of hysterical democracy."

When he arrived in France on May 8, 1946, he was not disappointed. Stein was on hand to greet him in Paris at the Gare St.-Lazare. In addition, to his great surprise, the American embassy had sent a public relations officer with two long limousines to aid in transporting him and his family to the two-room suite at the Hôtel Trianon that Stein had reserved for him. The first stop, though, after a brief tour of the city, was at Stein's for lunch. A few days later Wright learned the reason for the official American reception. "At a cocktail party a strange white American took me discreetly aside and whispered in my ear: 'Listen, for God's sake, don't let these foreigners make you into a brick to hurl at our windows!' " Wright did not heed the warning. At a news conference at his hotel he spoke out rancorously about race relations in the United States. He was not soon invited back to the embassy.

The headiness that he felt at being in Paris, however, soon began to overtake his anger with the situation in the United States. A week after arriving, he wrote his friend and editor, Edward Aswell: "Paris is all I ever hoped to think it was. . . . There is such an absence of race hate that it seems a little unreal. Above all, Paris strikes me as being a truly gentle city, with gentle manners." The longed-for detachment was also forthcoming: "One gets a good look at one's country from this perspective and one learns to see one's nation with double eyes, to feel what we have got and what we have not got. I've learned more about America in one month in Paris than I could in one year in New York. Looking at this country makes all the unimportant phases of the AMERICAN problem fade somewhat and renders the true problem more vivid."

The ease with which the races mingled in Paris was a major discovery for Wright. In an article about his first impressions of France, written shortly after his arrival for the French magazine *Samedi-Soir*, he focused on how Paris acted as a liberating force on black GIs. Wright reported a conversation with a black soldier and his French fiancée, and expressed his astonishment when his compatriot announced that he intended to take his girlfriend home to Missouri: "Had he forgotten the kind of city St. Louis was? Did he not know it would mean death to him if he took her there? . . . Then I knew! Ike, this nice black boy from America, *had forgotten.* He had lived in Paris for a couple of years and had learned to love and know its freedom. Despite Wright's enthusiasm for what he perceived as the GI's racial amnesia, it also concerned him: "I mused over how seemingly human it is to forget and yet how tragically inhuman it is. Wisdom comes not from forgetting, but from always remembering, and remembering is the only way to know not only one's history but one's self."

Although Wright always made it a point to remember, he also understood how easy it was, being in France, to forget the racism that had formed a daily part of his existence in his native country. In the United States, Wright felt, he was regarded as a black man first, a writer second. In France, he was an important *American* writer who happened to be black. It was distinctly new for him; never before had he experienced the sensation of being enfranchised on the basis of what he did, not judged on the basis of his color.

The welcome extended to him by the French, which surpassed even his grandest expectations, contributed a great deal to this

sense of belonging. At a reception hosted by the French government at the Hôtel de Ville, Wright was named an honorary
citizen of Paris. Gaston Gallimard, his French publisher, threw a
gala for him. Among those attending were notable members of
the French literary establishment: Roger Martin du Gard, Michel Leiris, Maurice Merleau-Ponty, Raymond Queneau, Jean
Paulhan, Marcel Duhamel. Other honors and invitations also
came his way: from the Paris P.E.N. club; from the Société des
Gens de Lettres, which presented him with a "Diplôme d'Amitié
Parisienne"; from the Club d'Essai, which devoted an entire
program to him and his work. To Wright, caught up in the whirl
of celebrations, "every day seemed like the night before
Christmas."

He was also grateful for the more personal and frequent invitations from Stein, who delighted in revealing Paris to him; she
took him on walking tours of her neighborhood, pointed out to
him where Shakespeare and Company had been located until
forced to close during the Occupation. In her apartment, Sylvia
Beach received him with the same warmth she had shown so
many expatriates before him. She had carried all of Wright's
books in her shop, had continually suggested them to her patrons, including Simone de Beauvoir, telling her, in relation to
Native Son: "You like violent books, well, here is a violent one, it
will hit you hard."

Wright also renewed his relationship with Jean-Paul Sartre,
whom he'd met in the United States the year before. The diminu-
tive, bug-eyed writer fascinated him, as did his companion, Beauvoir. Even more intriguing, though, was their existentialist
philosophy, which Wright had already been taken with before
going to Paris. With its emphasis on alienation, free choice, and
the absurd, this philosophic stance came naturally to Wright; it
seemed to describe the everyday existence of a black man in
America.

The turn toward the philosophy propounded by Sartre,
Camus, and others was therefore logical, an outgrowth of Wright's
own earlier cogitations on being black in white America. In many

ways he was an existentialist before existentialism formally existed. He had read a fair number of proto-existentialist writers—Kierkegaard, Nietzsche, Dostoevsky, Heidegger, Kafka—but unlike the Europeans, who developed the philosophy largely from books, Wright came to it simply from having lived in alienation, in absurdity, where often the only free act possible, such as defying Jim Crow laws, resulted in self-annihilation. Later Wright too would take in the same philosophers, would hone his own philosophy through careful analysis of European works, but the true impulse toward his embrace of existentialism was firmly rooted in his upbringing, in his personal observations of the absurd existence thrust on blacks in America.

Although not generally recognized as such, *Native Son*, published in 1940, can be read as a proto-existentialist novel. In Bigger Thomas, Wright created a character so profoundly alienated from society that freedom of choice becomes equated with freedom to kill. He is disaffected from society, from other blacks, from even his own family, and his perspective is decidedly skewed, "like I'm on the outside of the world peeping in through a knothole in the fence." But then he accidentally kills, and becomes inexplicably aware of how the murder of his white employers' daughter frees him from living a life of reaction. "Now that the ice was broken, could he not do other things? What was there to stop him? . . . Things were becoming clear; he would know how to act from now on. The thing to do was to act just like others acted."

His next major act is another murder, but this one is by design. Again he is empowered:

Out of it all, over and above all that had happened, impalpable but real, there remained to him a queer sense of power. *He* had done this. *He* had brought all this about. In all of his life these two murders were the most meaningful things that had ever happened to him. He was living, truly and deeply, no matter what others might think, looking at him with their blind eyes. Never had he had the chance to live out the consequences of his actions; never had his will been so free as in this night and day of fear and murder and flight.

Bigger's sense of engagement and absurd revolt, although used for negative ends, is nonetheless fully representative of what Sartre described as the essential existentialist situation, one in which "in the bright realm of values, we have no excuse behind us, nor justification before us. We are alone, with no excuses." Bigger's acceptance of the consequences of his actions, his recognition that he has chosen to act, frees him to become fully himself. "The existentialist does not believe in the power of passion," wrote Sartre. "He thinks that man is responsible for his passion. . . . Man, with no support and no aid, is condemned every moment to invent man." Thus Bigger, having escaped from living in relative existence to others, is now inventing himself.

It is not an easy perspective to maintain. Like Meursault, the protagonist of Camus's novel *The Stranger*, published two years after *Native Son*, Bigger accepts full responsibility for his actions, yet his legal defense rests on precisely the opposite. During his trial, his lawyer, Max, pleads his case by arguing that society, not Bigger, is to blame for his acts: "The hate and fear which we have inspired in him, woven by our civilization into the very structure of his consciousness, into his blood and bones, into the hourly functioning of his personality, have become the justification of his existence. Every time he comes into contact with us, he kills!" But as eloquent as the defense is, Bigger recognizes the inherent fallacy represented by that position. In the end, he is the true existential man: " 'I didn't want to kill!' Bigger shouted. 'But what I killed for, I *am!* . . . I didn't know I was really alive in this world until I felt things hard enough to kill for 'em.' " Neither religion ("that's for whipped folks") nor politics ("it's a game and they play it") is looked to for salvation. Bigger knows he is a man alone. So did Wright.

DESPITE THE warm reception in France, Wright decided to return to the United States. His decision was based in part on his inability to get much writing done amid the social whirl of Paris. More important, perhaps, he thought he belonged in America. "My life is over there," he explained to a journalist upon announcing his desire to repatriate after just eight months in Europe.

After a few months in New York, Wright realized that all the reasons that had inspired him to leave in the first place had not disappeared. His mixed marriage was as controversial as ever, often causing him to be harassed on the streets when walking with Ellen. He still had to go to Harlem to have his hair cut, was barred from certain restaurants, even in the Village, was addressed as "boy." At a midtown department store his daughter was denied use of the bathroom because of her "color." Wright needed no further proof of the inhospitableness of the United States. By August 1947, after less than seven months in New York, the Wrights were back in France. This time, the exile would be permanent.

Becoming a resident of Paris was different from being a visitor, however. Wright told his agent, Paul Reynolds, that he was unable to write much because his time was taken up with "getting the new apartment and moving into it, getting identity cards, rations, etc." While in correspondence he was careful to veil his frustration with settling, in actuality his love affair with Paris was often severely tested. His journal during the period of his return provides the best testimony of his ambivalence about France and the French. If he had a day largely free of obstacles he was quick to extol the pleasures of the city: "How lively and old Paris is. How like paintings the people are! What a deep serenity pervades everything here. What a pattern of living. The look of peace that shows on the faces of the people holds even in their suffering." But when thwarted, he lashed out against what he regarded as the French penchant for inefficiency. This entry comes a week later: "I love the French mentality sometimes, but not always. Not when practical matters are concerned. I see that most French stores are closed not only for two hours during lunch, but for longer periods. No wonder the men do not have suits to wear, the women are shoddy. I love leisure but not the kind of leisure that leaves a nation of beggars and cheats."

Wright seized on the lackadaisical habits of the French as a target for his wrath, but his deeper irritation was with his own inability to make progress on his new novel. Although he confessed in his journal that he felt uninspired, he did not probe the cause. To an outside observer, the reasons are fairly evident. First, Wright vastly underestimated what it took to settle in a new country, particularly France, which had not yet recovered from the war. The economy had slightly improved, but basic necessities were still in short supply. Seemingly endless lines formed daily outside shops where, using ration coupons, the citizens bought allotted quantities of food or fuel.

In addition, the first apartment the Wrights took in Paris, on the Rue de Lille, turned out to be unsatisfactory. Within a month they were searching for another. When they did eventually find one, on the Avenue de Neuilly, it took another month to get set up. Not long after, they moved again, to Rue Monsieur-le-Prince in the heart of the Left Bank. Another major problem was that Wright was continually besieged by visitors. Even though he welcomed the many sojourners who came through Paris that summer and fall, including Carson and Reeves McCullers, the full slate of social obligations did not leave him time to work without interruptions.

There is little to indicate, though, that Wright did much to ensure that his time was his own. He threw himself into the thriving French and international literary-political scene, continued to give talks at various forums, and involved himself with advising two new journals, *Présence Africaine* and *Les Temps Modernes*.

The association with the African and French West Indian writers who were forming *Présence Africaine* had begun on his initial visit, when he had met the Senegalese poet Léopold Sédar Senghor (later the country's first president) and through him the French West Indian poet Aimé Césaire. They, along with the Senegalese writer Alioune Diop, were then in the process of launching the magazine, whose mission was "to define the African's creativity and to hasten his integration into the modern world."

Now, upon his return, Wright was asked to join the list of sponsors, a group that already included Sartre, Camus, Gide, Michel Leiris, and others. Although he somewhat distrusted both Senghor and Césaire—Senghor because of his Catholicism, Césaire because of his membership in the French Communist Party—Wright nonetheless greeted the invitation with enthusiasm. The idea of an international magazine wholly run and staffed by blacks greatly appealed to him. Within a short time he became a major supporter of the journal, contributing his own work (the first issue contained Boris Vian's translation of Wright's story "Bright and Morning Star") and submitting writing by black American poets Gwendolyn Brooks and Samuel Allen. He also worked with Camus to establish a liaison with UNESCO and even solicited a loan from the Baronne de Rothschild to keep the review afloat.

Despite his firm belief in the importance of *Présence Africaine* as a forum for black writing from all over the world, Wright did not, or could not, strongly identify with the journal's underlying support of the *négritude* movement, which he viewed as primarily French-African in scope. As a non-African, speaking limited French, Wright could not comprehend what he considered the contradictory aims of the *négritudistes*. On one hand they advocated examining, rediscovering, and utilizing African cultural traditions as the basis for literary and political activity; on the other hand, individually, as members of the intellectual elite, they seemed more French than African, writing lyrical works in the best tradition of the French avant-garde.

The distance Wright felt as an American from African culture did not, however, translate into detachment from the aims of self-determination, which the review also advocated. For this reason, and because of a burgeoning friendship with *Présence Africaine*'s editor, Alioune Diop, who shared his more Western-oriented views on independence, Wright did not sever his ties with the magazine. Indeed, his interaction with the journal was far more positive than negative; despite certain ideological differences, his connection with the review helped him broaden his knowledge of the international dimensions of the racial problem. At the same time he realized that oppression was not the same matter for French Africans that it was for American blacks.

In France, the prevailing attitude was that colonial subjects, given a proper French education, which the French were willing to provide for the best and brightest, could become Frenchmen. The catch was that these enfranchised blacks had to be willing to play by French rules, that is, not espouse national liberation. "It's a desperate young black French colonial who resolves to return to his homeland and face the wrath of white Frenchmen who'll kill him for his longing for the freedom of his own nation, but who'll give him the *Legion d'honneur* for being French," noted Wright.

Given the contrasts between the treatment of blacks in France and in the United States, Wright was increasingly aware that racism was a far more complex matter in Europe. As a result, during his first few years in France, despite his growing knowledge of how the French used their "civilization" as a disarming tactic, Wright rarely spoke out against it. Instead, he used his position as the best-known black writer in the international community to focus on what he knew best: racism and oppression in America.

AT ABOUT the same time that Wright was becoming more involved with *Présence Africaine*, he became an unofficial advisor to *Les Temps Modernes*, founded by Sartre and Beauvoir in 1945. Unlike many other French journals launched after the war, *Les Temps Modernes* did not subscribe to a particular political, literary, or philosophical orthodoxy. The stated position of the editors was one of commitment to ideas, to open discussion of every current vital issue. Neither pro- nor anti-Communist, neither avant-garde nor conservative, *Les Temps Modernes* attempted to be an intellectual forum where a variety of views on virtually any topic could be freely exchanged. The intelligence, vigor, and nondoctrinaire position of the journal and its editors attracted Wright, who was becoming more interested not only in establishing himself within the European intellectual community but in expanding his own outlook. The journal, in turn, viewed Wright's association as an asset in strengthening its international focus. It was, for the most part, a happy and convenient union.

More important for Wright, however, *Les Temps Modernes* provided an opportunity to become better acquainted with Sartre. "How rare a man is this Sartre," Wright commented in his journal after an early meeting with the Frenchman. "His ideas must be good for they lead him into areas of life where man sees what is true." Another entry, written after an evening of conversation with Sartre and Beauvoir, goes further in showing the philosophical bond being created between Wright and Sartre: "Sartre is quite of my opinion regarding the possibility of human action today, that it is up to the individual to do what he can to uphold the concept of what it means to be human. The great danger, I told him, in the world today is [that] the very feeling and conception of what is a human might well be lost. He agreed."

Although he might have been expected to have seen in Camus a writer of similar sensibilities and concerns, Wright apparently did not find him as sympathetic as he did Sartre. Upon reading *The Stranger*, Wright noted in his journal that "it is a neat job but devoid of passion. He makes his point with dispatch and his prose is solid and good . . . [but] there is still something about this Camus that bothers me. Maybe because he is the artist and Sartre and de Beauvoir are not primarily."

Wright did not enter the already nascent Sartre–Camus imbroglio, which would break open publicly a few years later, yet he obviously felt much closer to Sartre, whose political views were more like his own, than to Camus. But it was not the case, as some have argued, that Wright was dominated by Sartre. While he certainly admired the French philosopher, he did not feel himself an acolyte. He saw Sartre as an ally engaged in a struggle similar to his own, namely, to liberate the individual through right action.

Of Sartre's play *The Respectful Prostitute*, Wright noted that Sartre, "above all modern writers, is seeking and preaching the integrity of action. . . . Let us be thankful for the eyes and mind of Jean-Paul Sartre who, in *La Putain Respectueuse*, is helping us to see ourselves." The last phrase is significant, for Wright felt that Sartre's existentialist outlook allowed him to see his own ideas more incisively, afforded him a perspective that, although born of alienation, enabled him to stand in solidarity with others.

This desire to belong to a community of like thinkers, as well as the belief, following Sartre's example, that the role of the intellectual was to speak out publicly on issues of the day, led Wright to become the only American actively associated with the Rassemblement Démocratique Révolutionnaire (RDR). Founded in early 1948, the RDR was not a political party but a political movement. Its basic goal was to unite the non-Communist left into a coherent force for political change, in Sartre's words, "to join all revolutionary claims with the idea of freedom . . . and to gather effectively the men of this country, whether producers or consumers, into neighborhood committees, town committees, factory committees, where they will find a concrete way to bring about the satisfaction of their demands." Originally the RDR confined itself primarily to French politics, but by late 1948, feeling it was impossible to ignore France's position in the international arena, the group began to address topics of world concern. It was then that Wright became involved with the RDR.

Although he was not officially a member (as a non–French citizen he could not be), Wright's support of the RDR was of considerable significance. First, it revealed the extent of his renewed political identity, a role he had been reluctant to play since quitting the Communist Party in the late 1930s. Second, it showed how involved (and accepted) Wright was in French intellectual circles; he had never really enjoyed this status in the United States, save in a very limited way.

Perhaps most important was the fact that as part of a group, even a group with as many divisions as the RDR, Wright could feel himself enfranchised. When he spoke, he was listened to; his views were quoted in the papers. In France he was no longer regarded as a black man clinging to fringe political views. Rather, he was a respected member of the intelligentsia; his opinions were sought on a variety of subjects, not only race relations. Indeed, at a forum in 1949, as an American concerned about the future of Europe, Wright spoke against the Marshall Plan and the formation of NATO. At another meeting, attended by more than four thousand people, on "L'Internationalisme de l'Esprit" (Internationalism of the Mind), Wright and fellow panelists Sartre, Camus, Breton, and others discussed the feasibility of unifying Europe intellectually.

At least part of the reason for Wright's enthusiastic acceptance in France was that he was echoing the prevailing anti-American feeling among the left, who were becoming increasingly concerned about the dominant position the United States seemed to be taking in European affairs. It would be wrong to suggest that he was used by the French, for the views he expressed were truly his own. But the nearly limitless opportunities given him to speak out would not have been so numerous had he not espoused an ideology that meshed with the current trend among left-leaning intellectuals.

In April 1949, however, Sartre, Wright, and others began to quarrel with the RDR; they thought that it had shifted too far to the right, as measured by the increasing criticism of the Soviet Union and decreasing admonition of the United States. The dissident faction felt that both superpowers should be equally mistrusted, even condemned. The focal point of the dispute was an invitation extended by the RDR to an American anti-Communist delegation. "Realizing that we had been had, [Maurice] Merleau-Ponty, Wright, and I refused to attend a meeting to which a few well-known American anti-Communists, such as Sidney Hook, had been invited, and during which some people praised the atomic bomb," wrote Sartre. An emergency meeting was called to try to effect a rapprochement; the attempt failed. Wright, Sartre, and Merleau-Ponty broke relations with the RDR.

This did not spell the end to Wright's public involvement in politics. He rarely missed an occasion, formal or informal, to speak out on issues of concern to him. He was active on the lecture circuit in Paris, and his talks, even if billed as literary, would inevitably turn political. At book parties given by his French publishers, Albin Michel and Gallimard, he would steer, or be steered, into giving lengthy observations on current topics ranging from the Marshall Plan to race relations in the United States.

ACTIVE INVOLVEMENT in politics left Wright little time to create literature. At first he made excuses (or alternatively, promises) to his agent for not producing the novel he had begun before settling in Paris. But by late 1948 he was not even mentioning the project in his letters to Paul Reynolds. Instead, he was preoccupied with the birth of a second daughter, Rachel.

In addition, Wright was directing Reynolds to buy back the movie rights to *Native Son*; these had been previously sold to John Houseman, Orson Welles, and Paul Green, who had successfully produced the dramatic adaptation of the novel on Broadway. He was eager to regain the rights, because a serious offer had come his way from the French filmmaker Pierre Chenal. He had several reasons for preferring Chenal over others, including Hollywood producers. First, Wright was clearly predisposed to having the film made by a Frenchman; second, Chenal had financial backing; third, Wright was offered a generous share of the profits; and finally, Chenal was willing to grant him artistic control—over both the script and the filming. He even was willing to let Wright star as Bigger Thomas. For Wright, who had received a prior offer from Hollywood with the proviso that Bigger's character be changed from a black to a white man (purportedly to make the film more universal!), the promise of artistic freedom was highly compelling.

By early 1949 the rights were once again the author's, but matters were far from settled. The French backers pulled out suddenly in February, "for reasons dictated by international policy." Wright and Chenal realized that "international policy" meant that the Americans, fearing the film would be nothing less than an indictment of American racism, had pressured the French to withdraw support. Chenal, however, was undaunted. During the Occupation he had made films in Argentina, and he quickly made a deal with an Argentine company, Sono-Films, to back the movie. Chenal himself would direct. Part of the film would be shot in Chicago, part in Argentina.

By late August, Wright was again back in the United States, where the old horrors of American life reasserted themselves. The company had difficulty finding a white actress who would appear on screen in a "Negro film," let alone in the arms of a black man; in contrast to Paris, Chicago was a divided city, with blacks confined largely to the South Side slums, where the garbage was not picked up, where trees did not grow, where human dignity was constantly suppressed; despite "official cooperation" from the city, bribes had to be paid to white policemen to film in white neighborhoods. After a costly month in Chicago, cast and crew, Wright, Chenal, and the Argentine producers left for Argentina.

Six months later—after a series of debacles, but ultimately with a finished film—Wright returned to France. *Native Son* opened in Argentina in March 1951 and was an instant financial success. In the United States, however, the situation was different. Censors demanded extensive cuts before they would allow its release; American distributors complied. To Wright's utter dismay, 2,500 feet of film were cut. Even so, in several states the film was still banned. On August 6, 1951, Wright told his agent that he did not want the American-edited version released in France: "My reputation is not being done any good by the film being shown. . . . People over here . . . will not be fooled into believing that the Negro problem in the USA is what the cut version of the film tries to pretend it is." Although the film was shown in Italy, with some original footage restored, it was never released in France.

Despite his knowledge of the deep roots of American racism,

Wright was surprised by the opposition in the United States to *Native Son* as a film. The book had been a best-seller; the play on Broadway had been critically acclaimed and financially successful. But he soon understood that for the masses in the heartland of America, ready-at-hand images were more immediately demonstrative than words; and America was the same America he'd left. As a writer in the satirical French newspaper *Le Canard Enchaîné* quipped, while Argentina was making a hit out of *Native Son*, the Americans were executing Willie McGee, the Mississippi black man convicted of raping a white woman who had in fact been his lover for many years.

Back in Paris, Wright reimmersed himself in the local literary and social scene, which he had acutely missed during his stay abroad. Again, political issues were foremost on his agenda. This time, however, Wright's attention was focused on forming the Franco-American Fellowship, whose aim was to forge bonds between the French and black Americans living in Paris. In an article Wright explained the reasons for starting the group.

France to [a black American] represents a state of humane civilization in which he is not coddled or singled out, but just simply "left alone." The U.S. Negro realizes, of course, that France is rent with social, political, and economic problems; he knows that France is no Utopia; but the difference in his life in France as compared with that [in] America is so vast and deep that there is in his heart a feeling of gratitude for being allowed to live as a man among men.

But something has begun to happen to the U.S. Negro in France; a new kind of anxiety has entered his consciousness; and this new worry has nothing to do with Frenchmen or their behavior towards him. With the advent of the Marshall Plan and the Atlantic Pact [NATO], the U.S. Negro has witnessed the spread and deepening of American influence in France. The constricting racial atmosphere which he had fled seems to be coming nearer to him across the Atlantic. For the first time since he landed in France as a refugee visitor, the U.S. Negro is asking himself: To what extent will some Frenchmen, eager to

please Americans, accept racial doctrines alien to French traditions and customs?

Among the Fellowship's activities were the investigation of racist hiring practices in American firms in France; support of the
Marxist French historian Daniel Guérin, who had been refused a
U.S. visa because of his critique of American society; and the
circulation of petitions condemning, and asking the U.S. Su-
preme Court to overturn, the "legal lynching" decisions in the
rape cases of Willie McGee and the Martinsville Seven, young
Virginia black men convicted on flimsy evidence of gang-raping
a white woman. In addition, the group sponsored cultural convo-
cations, bringing French writers and intellectuals such as Cocteau, Sartre, René Piquion, and Claude Bourdet to address the
membership.

Although the group never scored any major political or social
victories—American firms in Paris carried on their racist practices; Guérin was not granted a visa; McGee and the Martinsville
Seven were executed—it did succeed in creating a community of
black American exiles in Paris; such an alliance had not existed
prior to the formation of the Fellowship.

One black American expatriate who was reluctant to join the
group, although he did help with the early planning, was James
Baldwin. In his essay "Alas, Poor Richard," really an account of
his personal relationship with Wright, he disparages the Fellowship and remarks that on attending the first meeting he felt he
had been "trapped in one of the most improbable and old-
fashioned of English melodramas." Whether his comment was a
result of the actual meeting is difficult to determine, for Baldwin
and Wright had had, almost since the younger writer's arrival in
Paris in 1948, a stormy if not hostile relationship.

The matter was complex; the emotional entanglement, particularly on Baldwin's part, extreme. Wright had played a major role
in getting Baldwin started as a novelist. It was Wright, who after
reading sixty pages or so of what would become the twenty-year-
old writer's first novel, had successfully recommended him for
the 1945 Eugene F. Saxton fellowship, an award for fledgling

novelists. Upon Baldwin's arrival in Paris, Wright again worked on his behalf, obtaining for him a commission to write an essay for newly launched *Zero* magazine. The essay proved to be their undoing, for "Everybody's Protest Novel," which Baldwin submitted and *Zero* published, was construed by Wright to be a personal attack on him and on *Native Son*.

In some respects it was: "Bigger's tragedy," wrote Baldwin, "is not that he is cold or black or hungry, not even that he is American, black; but that he has accepted a theology that denies him life.... The failure of the protest novel lies in its rejection of life, the human being, the denial of his beauty, dread, power, in its insistence that it is his categorization alone which is real and which cannot be transcended." It is hard to read these words without sensing that Baldwin was offering a major critique of *Native Son* and of its author's literary-social intentions. Baldwin, however, did not feel then that he had publicly attacked Wright:

> On the day the magazine was published, and before I had seen it, I walked into the Brasserie Lipp. Richard was there, and he called me over. I will never forget that interview, but I doubt that I will ever be able to recreate it.
>
> Richard accused me of having betrayed him, and not only him but all American Negroes by attacking the idea of protest literature. It simply had not occurred to me that the essay could be interpreted in that way.... What made it most painful was that Richard was right to be hurt, I was wrong to have hurt him.... Richard was hurt because I had not given him credit for any human feelings or failings. And indeed I had not, he had never really been a human being for me, he had been an idol. And idols are created in order to be destroyed.

Their quarrel was never effectively patched up, although they did see each other from time to time. Wright even continued to lend Baldwin money, and when *Go Tell It on the Mountain*, Baldwin's first novel, was published, he publicly expressed his admiration. Baldwin, however, could not expel Wright from his psyche. In 1951, in another essay, "Many Thousands Gone," published in

Partisan Review, he again took on *Native Son* and indirectly Wright as well. Although the essay begins with Baldwin's expressing his admiration for the novel, the tone quickly turns: "*Native Son* finds itself at length so trapped by the American image of Negro life and by the American necessity to find the ray of hope that it cannot pursue its own implications." The core of Baldwin's critique, though, has really to do with his differences with Wright over the concept of the protest novel. For Baldwin, Wright's continual focus on racial injustice constricted his ability to create total, flesh-and-blood characters: "The reality of man as a social being is not his only reality and that artist is strangled who is forced to deal with human beings solely in social terms."

Baldwin was clearly onto something; he had perhaps perceived in its nascent form in *Native Son* what eventually would become a problem for Wright with the critics and with the public, namely, his almost obsessive involvement with his own rage. This was the catalyst for his work; protest, naturally, the form it took. Wright had reasons to be angry that Baldwin did not. Growing up nearly twenty years later, and in the North, Baldwin had not experienced the same degree of suffering as Wright. More significant, Baldwin did not share Wright's belief that the novel could (or should) be a vehicle for social change. This was for the younger writer an old-fashioned idea, a concept fully grounded in the proletarian-Communist fiction of the 1930s and no longer a viable form. Wright, despite his repudiation of the party, was still seeking an outlet for his anger and still felt it absolutely necessary to use his talent in the service of racial equality. The Europeans understood, he thought. The limitation was not his; if his American readers were bothered by what he had to say, that was good. If they rejected him, it was because they did not want to encounter the truth.

Wright never abandoned the concept, although he did attempt to probe the matter from a variety of angles. Remoteness from the daily indignities of living as a black man in the United States also allowed him to gain a larger perspective. "The break from the United States," he told fellow novelist William Gardner

Smith, "was more than a geographical change. It was a break with my former attitudes as a Negro and a Communist—an attempt to think over and re-define my attitudes and my thinking. I was trying to grapple with the big problem—the problem and meaning of Western Civilization as a whole, and the relation of Negroes and other minority groups to it." During his first years in France, Wright had turned the issue over and over, realizing in the course of his reading of existentialism and through his friendships with the leading proponents of the philosophy that the "big problem" was that of alienation. He had possessed this knowledge for years; rage was simply the expression of a profound sense of underlying alienation from "Western Civilization." It was this understanding that would form the core of his next novel, a book that had been in his head for years. It would be called, appropriately enough, *The Outsider*.*

The final form of *The Outsider* took a radically different turn from the first drafts. The six years of gestation, of grappling with the meaning of man alone, of encountering Europe and European ideas, left a profound mark on his creative psyche. From a crime story, the novel became a *roman à thèse* in the French existentialist tradition of Sartre, Camus, and Beauvoir, whose novels and philosophic outlook Wright had by now fully incorporated into his own thinking.

The Outsider is the story of Cross Damon, who at the beginning of the novel is employed as a postal worker in Chicago. Oppressed by a loveless marriage and an affair gone awry, by an overwrought, religiously obsessed mother whose legacy was "dread," and by a dead-end job, Cross suddenly is given a chance to start all over again when, through a case of mistaken identity, he is believed to have been killed in a subway accident. After surreptitiously observing his own funeral, he decides to set out for New York. His new "freedom," however, is almost destroyed when he

* Although it bore the same title as the British edition of Camus's *L'Étranger* (published in the United Kingdom as *The Outsider*), that was not completely Wright's doing. After months of indecisiveness, he had submitted a list of more than half a dozen possibilities to his publisher; from this list a salesman at Harper & Brothers finally selected the title.

bumps into an old acquaintance. But he quickly overcomes this obstacle by murder, then sets out for Greenwich Village. There he becomes embroiled with the Communist Party, who decide to use him, as a black man, to force a confrontation with the Fascist owner of an apartment building who has refused to rent to blacks. Cross allows himself to be installed in the apartment of a Communist leader and his wife. When the eventual dispute occurs, Cross kills both the Communist and the landlord. "I have killed two little gods," he notes after the murders. Pursued now by both the Communists and the police, he is found first by the Communists and shot down on the street.

This plot summary hardly describes the novel that Wright regarded not as a thriller so much as a "character study, dealing mainly with character and destiny." Cross, in Wright's vision, is an alienated, existential man, an individual outside of life. Imbued with Sartrean *mauvaise foi* at the book's beginning, by the end he has embraced a Nietzschean ethic of negation which he believes allows him to reject all received societal values. Separating himself from codified moral behavior, though, does not truly transform him into the overman. Despite Wright's attempts to cast Cross as the slayer of totalitarian dogmas through the murders of the Communist and the Fascist, the message in the end is not the triumph of the individual. It is instead one of horror: Cross's "absurd" freedom quest ultimately turns against him; his negation of values becomes self-negating.

In spite of its long, occasionally confused philosophical digressions, *The Outsider* cannot be dismissed, as Arna Bontemps suggested, as "an existentialist roll in the hay," for the issues Wright raised were not merely those of the French existentialists. His reference point was continually the black American experience; it was to this vision of reality, to this concern, that he welded the existentialist perspective. In a very real sense, Cross's antecedents were as much Bigger and Big Boy as Meursault and Roquentin. What Wright attempted to express in *The Outsider* was that alienation is the natural condition of blacks in white America. But rather than surrender to despair or dread, the black must own his alienation, must use this absurd knowledge to empower himself, to escape from seeing himself relative to society. By accepting this premise, he can, in fact, become a free individual. Cross's failure is that he never can escape his relativity to others, never can use his alienation for positive ends. In slaying the "two little gods" he sets himself up as a god, uses this freedom negatively and nonexistentially; he is always reacting rather than acting, and is incapable of seeing himself except in relation to others. Ultimately Cross is unable to make the necessary break with his past conditioning to create for himself positive freedom.

Wright's message (and implicit warning) did not play well in the United States. He was not surprised. Even before finishing the revision, he expressed his concerns about the book's American reception in a letter to his agent:

> I've been told that the atmosphere in America is hot and hysterical, and that no one wants to hear any point of view but the official one. The book is certainly not official yet I feel that it gets somewhere near what is happening in the world today. My hopes for it are not great; indeed I cannot conceive of anybody liking it, especially Americans. . . . It is not hopeful and it travels along a path that avoids popular conclusions.

The "hot and hysterical" atmosphere in the United States that Wright mentions was not an invention; it was the rise of McCarthyism. By the time *The Outsider* was published in 1953, the year after the letter was written, the terror was in full swing. The Senate Subcommittee on Investigations, chaired by Senator Joseph McCarthy, was interrogating ever-increasing numbers of leftists and liberals. Wright was so concerned that he would be forced to testify, as his friends Langston Hughes and Paul Robeson had been, that he refused to return to the United States to promote the book. An ongoing worry was that his passport would not be renewed in the Paris embassy and that he would be forced to return "home." Wright's movements were in fact being monitored, and had been since the late 1930s, by the FBI and perhaps the CIA. (The FBI dossier on him amounts to 228 pages.) Perhaps because the U.S. government feared an international incident, he was never denied a passport or subpeonaed to appear at the McCarthy hearings.

But Wright was visited on one occasion by Roy Cohn, chief counsel to the McCarthy-run Senate subcommittee, and his assistant, G. David Schine, who held the position of "chief consultant." According to Chester Himes, who was present, Cohn and Schine came to see Wright at his apartment for the purposes of gathering information on a former member of the John Reed Club in Chicago. When Wright denied knowing the person in question and claimed that he himself had not been a member of the club, a furious Schine began bullying him; he informed Wright that he and Cohn had coerced Langston Hughes into recanting his "un-American" activities and writings, and implied that they would force Wright to do the same. Wright remained defiant and ushered the two men out. After their exit an enraged Wright told Himes, "That stupid son of a bitch thinks he can threaten me; I'll never testify."

Although he remained largely immune from official harassment, Wright did feel the effect of the anti-Communist hysteria sweeping the United States: it came in the form of rejection of his work. *The Outsider*, despite its condemnation of Communism, was trampled on by the critics, and sales were poor; in addition, Wright began to find it difficult to publish work in the United States that was critical of American society. His long essay "I Choose Exile," written for *Ebony*, was deemed by the magazine's editors as too vitriolic a critique to print safely. When he resubmitted the essay to *The Atlantic Monthly* after receiving a request for just such an article, that magazine also rejected it. *Time*, meanwhile, launched what would amount to the first in a series of sustained attacks on Wright, marshaling (and manipulating) other black writers to denounce him: "While Wright sits out the threat of totalitarianism in Paris, an abler U.S. Negro novelist sees the problem of his race differently. Says Ralph (*Invisible Man*) Ellison: 'After all, my people have been here for a long time. . . . It is a big wonderful country.'"

In 1946, Wright had chosen exile; by 1953, he was being exiled. The difference was profound. It was not that his life in Paris was any less superficially satisfactory, but there was an underlying sense of having lost the premier existential value: choice. In addition, he was barraged from abroad by the numerous critics who complained that he had lost touch with present-day America. Even his staunch supporter and agent, Paul Reynolds, wrote him that he was "sort of worried about a man living in Paris and just writing novels laid in this country [the United States]."

Wright publicly resisted the idea:

> Any writer who has not, at the age of twenty, stored away the fundamental basis of his so-called subject matter will never do so. I took my subject matter with me in the baggage of my memory when I left America and I'm distressingly confident that race relations will not alter to a degree that will render invalid these memories whose reality represents one of the most permanent and distinguishing features of American life.

Despite this strident assertion, his next novel, *Savage Holiday*, although set in the United States, did not concern race. Written in less than six months immediately after he had finished revising *The Outsider*, it was the violent story of a psychopathic white man who kills his promiscuous female neighbor in order to take revenge on his mother, who had been equally promiscuous in his youth. Based on a true incident, the novel is severely flawed by its far too transparent psychology. Nonetheless, it revealed an attempt by Wright to create a work with different motivation and as such perhaps indicated his awareness of the need for new subject matter. To be sure, familiar themes were still present—violence and the fear of women, rooted in past events—but *Savage Holiday* marked a turn in Wright's development as a novelist.

In the United States few noticed the change from Wright's earlier preoccupations with black alienation and racism. When the book was published in 1954 as an Avon paperback (it had been rejected by Harper & Brothers, his usual publisher), it did not receive a single review, and sales were slight. In France, predictably, it sold well and was reviewed seriously, and Wright was invited to discuss the book on French radio.

ALTHOUGH GIVEN his involvement in Paris and the expatriate community there, it might have seemed logical for Wright to draw on France or Americans in France as subject matter, he did not, until nearly the end of his life. But the familiarity with the international realm of politics and ideas that he had gained by moving to Paris motivated him to attempt a radically new project, of far wider scope: a book about Africa. Paul Reynolds was enthusiastic about the idea: "I think your search for material, your going for a purpose, namely to find out, will be of great value to you." Harper this time agreed, and offered Wright a sizable advance.

Wright left Paris on June 4, 1953, bound for the Gold Coast (Ghana). Ten weeks later he returned to France, far wiser, far more critical of both the colonizers and the colonized. The resulting book, *Black Power*, is more than just an account of a country in transition; it is also a moving personal record of his daily reactions, of his own largely rebuffed quest for a common identity with Africans. "I was black, they were black, but my color did not help me," he wrote. In going to Africa, Wright discovered that he was intrinsically Western. He felt not a racial bond with Africans, but only a shared legacy of racial oppression. Wright's discovery of Africa was really a discovery of himself.

When it was published in the United States in 1954, *Black Power* sold reasonably well, but the reviews were mixed. Wright was becoming a major target of the American press, with attacks aimed squarely at him, and not so much at his product. In Europe circumstances were different. The book was immediately translated into French, German, and Dutch, and Wright was invited to talk at a variety of congresses. This pattern—official rejection in America, laudatory acceptance in Europe—would be more and more the case, deepening Wright's confirmed sense of exile. At this point in his life he was truly battling for his survival as an American writer. At the same time he had hardly become a French writer writing in English. The dilemma would occupy him for the rest of his life, drive him eventually to despair, perhaps even to a premature death.

By the mid-fifties Wright had nearly lost the battle for his reputation in the United States. His next three published books, *The Color Curtain, Pagan Spain*, and *White Man, Listen*, all nonfiction, did little to enhance his popularity in America. *The Color Curtain* was charged political reportage on an important conference on the Third World held in Bandung, Indonesia, but it was deemed hardly a matter of significance for most American readers. The error of estranging himself from the American reading public was compounded even more so in *Pagan Spain*, which was begun before the Bandung conference. Again, despite his insightful analysis of Spanish reality, religion, and the rise of Fascism, the book sold only 3,500 copies in the United States. Spain was not a subject that interested many Americans; fewer still had any interest in what a black atheist-Marxist American had to say about Catholicism and Fascism. *White Man, Listen*, a collection of sociopolitical speeches, served only to confirm that Wright was too "international" in his focus, too concerned with the Third World, too out of touch with contemporary America.

It was not just the American critics and the American public who began to question whether Wright still had much to say to them. His publishers and agent were becoming concerned as well. In a blunt letter responding to a new rejected outline for a novel, Paul Reynolds repeated his earlier assertion that Wright's exile had seriously affected his work:

> It seems to me—and of course I am only guessing now—that as you have found greater peace as a human being, living in France, and not been made incessantly aware that the pigmentation in your skin sets you apart from other men, you have at the same time lost something as a writer. To put it another way, the human gain has been offset by creative loss. So I think that

your present situation calls for some serious effort of reassessment, or re-evaluation, of discovering where you are and where you are going.

Although Wright could be rather thin-skinned when it came to taking criticism, he trusted Reynolds. His answer to his agent's concern was an outline for a novel that would return to a familiar theme: the story of a young black man growing up in Mississippi. Relieved that he had agreed to write a novel with a proven knowledge and interest base, Reynolds and Wright's editor, Edward Aswell, enthusiastically approved the idea that would eventually become *The Long Dream.*

There was perhaps another reason for Wright's decision to write novels again, namely, that the politics in which he had mired himself were beginning to become complex. As a spokesman for liberation and a strident critic of racial repression and colonialism, Wright found himself faced with a dilemma, the same one that faced all the French intelligentsia: Algeria. The majority of his friends and political compatriots had taken a decidedly pro-Algerian stance, and with his well-known position on the issue of national determination, Wright might very well have been expected to do so too.

He did not, the reason being that as a foreigner he was subject to immediate deportation for holding antigovernment views. Concerns about being repatriated dominated his instincts regarding the situation in Algeria, and his public position was thus one of neutrality. By neither condemning nor supporting the French government, his, and his family's, existence was not jeopardized. Indeed, he had always been careful not to criticize internal French matters, but as the Algerian war heated up, he became even more cautious.

While there can be no doubt that Wright's decision sprang from an overriding concern for security, this explanation does not reveal his entire thinking on the matter. Wright, however, had something of a blind spot when it came to France. He was either unwilling or unable to perceive that his adopted country might be as plagued by injustices and racist attitudes toward North Africans as his homeland was toward blacks. He firmly believed, despite mounting evidence to the contrary, that the French did not define their civilization in racial terms. This concept, even though based on his own experiences, obscured the reality of a France that was conducting an exceedingly brutal war against the Algerians and practicing a concerted policy of ghettoization against the North African population resident in France.

While his stance on Algeria did not seem to cost him friends among Parisian intellectuals, it did have an effect on his relationship with fellow black writers and intellectuals in Paris, a group from which he was becoming more and more detached. As Baldwin noted:

> He had managed to estrange himself from almost all the younger American Negro writers in Paris.... Gone were the days when he had only to enter a café to be greeted with the American Negro equivalent of *"cher maître"* ("Hey, Richard, how you making it, my man? Sit down and tell me something."), to be seated at a table, while all the bright faces turned toward him. The brightest faces were now turned from him, and among these faces were the faces of the Africans and the Algerians. They did not trust him—and their distrust was venomous because they felt that he had promised them so much. When the African said to me, "I believe he thinks he's white," he meant that Richard cared more about his safety and comfort than he cared about the black condition. But it was to this condition, at least in part, that he owed his safety and comfort and power and fame. If one-tenth of the suffering which obtained (and obtains) among Africans and Algerians in Paris had been occurring in Chicago, one could not help feeling that Richard would have raised the roof.

Baldwin's account of Wright's isolation was accurate, but his explanation was not wholly correct, for it did not take into consideration that a good deal of the animosity prevailing against Wright by the late 1950s was due to petty jealousy and rivalry.

Wright had succeeded, was an accepted member of the international intellectual establishment, was fairly secure financially. The struggle of the younger writers for identity as artists was no longer appropriately his; he had been through that twenty years earlier, before he'd written himself out of obscurity and poverty with *Black Boy* and *Native Son*.

Baldwin also failed to understand that Wright's earlier success did not necessarily leave him free from self-doubt or from anxiety about his current role as an artist. The repeated attacks on him, from abroad and from within the Paris expatriate community, compounded by more than a decade of not writing a work deemed of major significance, had begun to affect rather seriously his own sense of security. More and more Wright began to distrust nearly everyone who disagreed with him, interpreting a differing viewpoint as a vilification of him and his ideas. Even Chester Himes, a longtime friend and advocate, was placed temporarily on Wright's "enemies list"; Wright felt that Himes had portrayed him (or a character like him) unsympathetically in his novel *A Case of Rape*.

What most everyone, save perhaps Wright's close friends Himes and cartoonist Ollie Harrington, failed to perceive was that Wright was increasingly battling against despair and self-doubt. According to Himes, Wright confessed to him that "he had made a mistake writing only political books . . . and was then going to pick up the black oppression theme where he had dropped it." But even the new novel he was working on, *The Long Dream*, despite its having met approval with his editor and agent, was apparently a source of tension between him and his wife. Himes recalled that Ellen Wright accosted him on the street one day, claiming that he was the one responsible for her husband's return to writing about "poor oppressed black Americans when he had grown up to greater things." When Himes countered, asking what she thought Wright's subject should be, she replied, "I don't want him to wallow in the gutter like you."

Wright persisted with the novel, in spite of his own doubt in himself and that of others in him. The story he had begun, about a black Mississippi undertaker and his son, soon swelled beyond the scope of one novel. He decided to extend the saga into a trilogy. He concluded the first part, *The Long Dream*, with the undertaker's son, Fishbelly, fleeing to Paris, and thus set the stage for the second book.

Wright had already begun work on the next volume when *The Long Dream* was released in the United States. Book and author were soundly attacked. *Time* summed up the majority of reviews, stating that his writing had suffered immeasurably as a result of his detachment from his source: "By this time, Expatriate Wright should know that his picture is too crudely black and white. He writes as if nothing had changed since he grew up in Mississippi." A few weeks later, *Time* attacked again, this time inventing anti-American quotations to prop up its assertion that Wright had lost touch with America and American values. Wright threatened to sue but eventually dropped the matter publicly. Inwardly, however, he felt more and more that there was a concerted campaign afoot in the United States to discredit him.

While his books were no longer received as they had been, and the criticism was often hostile, there seems little evidence to suggest any conspiracy to destroy him as a writer. To some extent the critiques were justified; the American reality that Wright had known and observed so shrewdly nearly twenty years before had altered in the intervening decades. He was out of touch with American concerns; he had not been able to write a convincing book that could capture the American imagination in the way that *Black Boy* or *Native Son* had. Exile was taking its toll, if not on his actual writing, at least on his ability to understand the rapidly changing American consciousness and respond novelistically to the new challenges in the now (for him) largely imaginary country he had long since abandoned.

Despite the almost unanimous dismissal of his work in the American press, Wright continued on *Island of Hallucinations*, the next novel in the trilogy, which would recount Fishbelly's adventures in Paris. Now on familiar territory, he felt this might at least allow the critics to let go of the charge that he was out of touch

97

with his subject matter. He would never find out what their reaction would be, however, for he died before putting the novel into final form. It has yet to be published, although five episodes were excerpted posthumously in a collection of writings by black Americans.

WRIGHT'S DEATH, on November 28, 1960, has been written about extensively. Rumors still circulate about whether his heart attack was from "natural causes" or whether it was induced by an injection he was said to have received shortly before. If he had been killed, ran the rumors, then by whom? The CIA? The FBI? Perhaps the Soviets? Michel Fabre, Wright's diligent biographer, concludes that it is unlikely he was assassinated, but admits that the truth is elusive. The FBI files, naturally, are mute on the subject, containing only French obituary notices. What is certain is that in the last year of his life Wright was not well. Physically, he was suffering from a variety of stomach complaints. Psychologically, the continual downward spiral of his career had produced major outbreaks of anxiety. In addition, things were far from satisfactory in Paris. The prolonged conflict in Algeria, and the rise of de Gaulle and Gaullism, had resulted in increasing restrictions on personal freedom. Furthermore, Ellen had moved with their two daughters to England the year before Wright's death. (Wright himself had been denied an immigration visa.) In short, the complexity of assaults could quite easily have produced a heart attack.

Wright died nearly broke, alone, but in Paris. "I've found more freedom in one square block of Paris than there is in the entire United States!" He continued to believe this until the end. His legacy is tremendous, still felt. That much of the work is flawed is now a given; what is also a given is that in his work and in his life he was a model for a whole generation, particularly of black Americans, such as James Baldwin and Chester Himes, who decided likewise, at least for a time, to choose exile in the City of Light.

Chapter Five

James Baldwin: Equal in Paris

"BY THE time I was twenty-four—since I was not *stupid*, I realized that there was no point in my staying in the country at *all*. If I'd been born in Mississippi, I might have *come* to New York. But, being born in New York, there's no place that you can *go*. You have to go *out. Out* of the country. And I went out of the country and I never intended to come back." The year was 1948; the twenty-four-year-old was James Baldwin; "out of the country" was Paris.

He arrived on a cold, gray November day with "a little over forty dollars in [his] pockets, nothing in the bank, and no grasp whatever of the French language." What he did have was a tremendous amount of confusion in his head, but a sense as well that things could hardly be worse for him on the European side of the Atlantic. Contrary to his expectations, a friend met him at the airport, then whisked him to Deux Magots, one of the leading literary gathering spots among the Left Bank cafés. To Baldwin's astonishment, the Paris of his dreams, where great writers sat at café tables, sipping Pernod, discussing art and ideas, suddenly materialized. None other than Richard Wright was there, doing exactly that, as Baldwin recalled. " 'Hey, boy!' he cried, looking more surprised and pleased and conspiratorial than ever, and younger and happier."

This encounter would prove to be one of their last amicable meetings. It was here that Wright introduced Baldwin to his tablemates, the editors of *Zero* magazine; it was for *Zero* that Baldwin would write "Everybody's Protest Novel," his critique of *Native Son*, which ended any possibility of a friendship. Although for Wright the essay represented only an ungrateful and unwarranted attack on him and his work, for Baldwin it was a far more complex matter. It was an attempt to free himself from the imposing shadow of Wright, to establish his own sense of self as a writer. "I wanted Richard to see me, not as the youth I had been when he met me, but as a man," Baldwin wrote years later. "I wanted to feel that he had accepted me, had accepted my right to my own vision, my right, as his equal, to disagree with him."

Baldwin's need for acquiring his own vision had been responsible, in large part, for his coming to Paris. The earlier affirmation he had received from Wright had helped ignite his belief in himself as an artist. But the book he had begun and shown Wright four years before had been rejected by Wright's editor at Harper & Brothers and by Doubleday too. Another novel had stalled and Baldwin had come perilously close to losing the vision altogether.

Paris was supposed to work its magic, yet whom should he encounter first but Wright, his idol, the quintessential successful writer. The meeting could have been only bittersweet, the delight in seeing Wright mitigated by his belief that he had failed to live up to the older writer's expectations. There was thus a certain feeling of guilt, of shame, when he met Wright face to face for the first time since New York. But Baldwin's own pride did not allow him to talk about his doubts with Wright. Desperately wanting to be accepted on his own terms as a writer, he worried he might be patronized or, worse yet, pitied.

Wright's importance took on epic proportions in Baldwin's mind, for Wright was not just another famous writer: "His work was an immense liberation and revelation for me. He became my ally and my witness, and alas! my father." This is a heavy burden, even more so when the bearer is not aware of what's in the baggage he's intended to carry. Baldwin later admitted that it was not Wright's fault that he did not comprehend the complexity or depth of Baldwin's feelings: "I had identified myself with him long before we met: in a sense by no means metaphysical, his example had helped me to survive. He was black, he was young, he had come out of the Mississippi nightmare and the Chicago slums, and he was a writer. He proved it could be done—proved it to me, and gave me an arm against all those who assured me it could *not* be done. And I think I had expected Richard, on the day we met, somehow, miraculously, to understand this, and to rejoice in it."

Although Wright was aware that in no small way he had provided an example for a whole generation of young black writers, he could not fulfill Baldwin's expectations, even if he had known what it was the young writer was seeking. His actions on this cold November day were not the sort Baldwin so ardently desired. But in actuality, he was far from indifferent. He did introduce Baldwin to the *Zero* editors and gave him helpful advice on where to find a cheap hotel room. But this was practical assistance and, while perfectly in keeping with the situation, not the spiritual reunion Baldwin was after: "nothing less than that so universally desired, so rarely achieved reconciliation between spiritual father and spiritual son."

When reconciliation between father and son is not possible, its correlate, at least in Freudian terms, is spiritual patricide. Although this is admittedly a classic psychological interpretation, the record indicates that in Baldwin's case it is precisely what he set out to do. If he could not win Wright's acceptance, he would have to slay him. Chester Himes recalled that Baldwin used exactly these words in speaking of Wright, but Himes interpreted the remark somewhat differently: "At the time I thought he had taken leave of his senses, but in recent years I've come to better understand what he meant. . . . On the American literary scene, the powers that be have never admitted but one black at a time into the arena of fame, and to gain this coveted admission, the young writer must unseat the reigning deity." Baldwin's obsession with slaying or unseating Wright, regardless of the cause or causes, would in fact play a major role in *his* Parisian exile, and be a continuing theme in his essays for years.

BALDWIN WAS in almost continually desperate circumstances during his first few years in Paris. Unlike Wright, who had arrived to a hero's welcome and was financially secure, Baldwin was plagued by poverty, illness, and isolation. The myth of the artist is that dire experiences somehow foster creativity. As is usual, this was not true for Baldwin. What is true is that Paris gave him a sense of identity, of wholeness, that made penury worth enduring. The major initial gift for Baldwin was what it had been for Wright: freedom from racism; for while Paris was the same Paris for black and white Americans, black Americans did not feel by any means the same way they had felt at home: "I got over—and a lot beyond . . . all the terms in which Americans identified me. . . . And I realized I'd never be controlled by them *again.* . . . I felt that I was left alone in Paris—to become whatever I *wanted* to become. . . . I could *write,* I could *think,* I could *feel,* I could *walk,* I could *eat,* I could *breathe.* There were no penalties attached to—these simple human endeavors. . . . Even when I was starving, it was *me* starving. It was not a *black man* starving."

Starvation was for Baldwin not the abstraction it was for most of his fellow American expatriates. The forty dollars he arrived with represented his total cash reserves. When it was gone, as it was in three days, he had no other source of income. Fortunately he had a few friends in Paris, and he soon made many more. The first to come to his rescue was a friend from Greenwich Village days, Mason Hoffenberg, an American poet and student who later cowrote *Candy* with Terry Southern. Hoffenberg, in addition to lending Baldwin some money and buying him a meal or a drink or a pack of cigarettes, introduced him to his friends and acquaintances in the American community. Among those who became closest to Baldwin were Southern, novelist Herbert Gold, *Zero* editor Themistocles Hoetis, and writer Otto Friedrich. They too began to help Baldwin survive. Friedrich recalled that Baldwin "was . . . penniless in those days. He had no way of getting money. He scrounged, begged, and borrowed. He didn't pay his debts. He cadged his drinks." Or as Baldwin put it, "I floated, so to speak, on a sea of acquaintances." For Baldwin, living hand to mouth hardly constituted what some others liked to term "the Great Adventure." "There was a real question in my mind as to which would end soonest, the Great Adventure or me," he noted.

Insistent on staying, despite the hardships, Baldwin continued to "float." But the few francs he borrowed here and there, while they kept him from literally starving, were often not sufficient to pay for his room. On more than one occasion during his first months in Paris he returned to his hotel to find that he'd been locked out, his possessions confiscated. This would then mean a new, somewhat larger loan, from someone slightly better off than his fellow struggling writers. Wright could usually be counted on, as could a few other Americans who were actually employed in Paris.

This system obviously had its drawbacks, so Baldwin engineered a temporary solution to the rent problem: it was called the Hôtel Verneuil, owned by a generous Corsican woman who was not overly zealous about collecting the rent on time. This he had learned from fellow residents Gold and Southern, and he soon found out that he had not been misinformed. The test came shortly after Baldwin had moved in, when his privation life-style caught up with him and he became seriously ill. Rather than eject him, the owner nursed him back to health over a three-month period. "I will never know what made her suppose that I would ever be able to pay the rent or why she didn't simply call the American embassy and have me shipped home," Baldwin recounted years later. Instead, she climbed five flights of stairs twice a day to administer her folk remedies and feed him soup.

When Baldwin finally recovered he did pay her back, mainly by borrowing from others and with money earned from odd jobs.

He also apparently hustled in gay bars, picking up a "patron" now and then. According to Friedrich, "Jimmy was very gregarious. There were friends and admirers who liked to be seen with him, people who paid the bill. . . . He was always in love with someone and he had sex on the side with all kinds of people. He did it for fun, or just to impress people. He had a very active sex life apart from his romantic one. The two happened simultaneously." Later these experiences in the *milieu*, as the Paris gay scene was called, would form the background of *Giovanni's Room*, but for now the major focus in his fiction, when he could focus himself enough to write, was still New York.

At first, in fact, he was not finding writing at all easy: he "just tore up paper." Part of the problem was that writing, of necessity, was subordinated to survival. In a sense, scrounging meals and loans was tantamount to having a full-time job, but a job that was emotionally more consuming. Yet by the end of his first year in Paris Baldwin had begun to figure out how to get by with less difficulty.

It was not that his financial situation had much improved; he simply had learned how to make the most out of his contacts. Dinners, for instance, were available on a fairly regular basis at the home of fellow Americans Eileen Finletter and Stanley Geist. Southern and Hoffenberg, both students, would loan him their ID cards so he could eat at the low-priced university dining halls. To escape the cold in his unheated room in order to write, he found that he could, in the great French tradition, sit scribbling in his notebook for hours upstairs at the Café Flore over a single cup of coffee. And if he lingered long enough someone would invariably drop by and spring for another coffee or a drink, or at least replenish his cigarettes. Baldwin also discovered that the Arab cafés were far cheaper for meals than the cafés on the Left Bank. In addition, he developed the knack of latching on to visiting Americans who would take him out for a meal. It was, to be sure, a precarious existence, but it was an existence.

Of the alliances Baldwin made during his first year in Paris, one was of special importance. While cadging drinks at Deux

Magots one day, he struck up a conversation with a blonde Norwegian artist, Gidske Anderson. Her early impressions of him were of a man "intense, deep and serious . . . always dressed in black, a bit sinister in appearance." Both had recently broken off love affairs, and during their first few casual meetings they used this as the basis of conversation. Shortly after they met, Themistocles Hoetis invited Anderson and Baldwin to go to Tangier, and they readily accepted the invitation. When they arrived in Marseille, however, they learned that the next boat would not leave for a few days. Hoetis decided to wait; Anderson and Baldwin, short on funds, set off for Aix-en-Provence. Once there, they decided to hole up for a while.

Baldwin had brought along his typewriter, and now that he was removed from Paris he began to write ferociously. Suddenly, though, they were informed that the hotel owner, who was dying in the next room, was being disturbed by the incessant hammering of the keys. They were given a choice: they could leave the hotel, or Baldwin could stop typing, at least until the proprietor died. This presented them with a by now familiar dilemma, for they had already spent most of the little money they had. Baldwin stopped typing; Anderson prevailed on friends in Paris to send her money.

While they waited for funds, Baldwin fell ill with an inflamed gland and had to be hospitalized. When he didn't recover, the doctors performed a minor operation which though successful left him weak. The rest of the sojourn in Provence turned into an exercise in rationing their meager remaining resources to buy meals at a small restaurant, and waiting for money to free them from the hotel. When the check finally arrived they returned to Paris.

The trip, as silly as it may have seemed, was important for Baldwin in that he had been able to enjoy fully being with a white woman who was delighted to be in his company with no other motives than a genuine fondness for who he was as an individual. This was something of a breakthrough. Previously, because of a series of debacles, he had mistrusted white women: "The white girls I had known or been involved with—different categories—had paralyzed me, because I simply did not know what, apart from my sex, they wanted." With Anderson it was not at all like this, and that fact confirmed again for Baldwin that there really was a profound difference between the freedom accorded him (and everyone) in Europe and the bondage he continually felt on home ground. On another level the experience also marked a security in his own identity.

He had not been back in Paris long when an incident occurred that shook his newly acquired sense of freedom and well-being: he was arrested for possession of a stolen bed sheet. According to Baldwin, he had met a fellow American in a bar and, hearing that he was dissatisfied with his hotel, had arranged for him to get a room in the place where Baldwin had recently moved—the Grand Hôtel du Bac. The American moved in the next day, bringing with him a sheet from his former lodgings. As Baldwin's linen was filthy, he borrowed the sheet from his compatriot. Shortly thereafter, the police arrived and, to Baldwin's total astonishment, arrested them both. Over the Christmas holiday of 1949, Baldwin and his acquaintance were interrogated, fingerprinted, and kept locked up in a series of freezing cells. Finally, after eight days of harsh captivity, and thanks to the assistance of an American patent attorney Baldwin knew in Paris, the charges against them were dismissed.

As usual, Baldwin turned the unpleasant episode into a learning experience. The major lesson was that he was not treated "as a despised black man," but rather, to his surprise, as an American: "And here it was they who had the advantage, for that word, *Américain*, gave them some idea, far from inaccurate, of what to expect from me. . . . The question thrusting up from the bottom of my mind was not *what* I was, but *who*." This was the dawning of a tremendous awareness, namely, that the color of his skin, which had divided him consistently from others in the United States, did not prevail in Europe: "In my necessity to find the terms on which my experience could be related to that of others, Negroes and whites, writers and non-writers, I proved, to my astonishment, to be as American as any Texas GI."

This revelation was also linked with the growing realization that in many ways it was easier for him to associate with white Americans or Europeans than with fellow blacks—a pattern he discerned operating for many of his black countrymen. The explanation, for Baldwin, was that the black American in Paris was attempting to sort out for himself his own identity and not accepting, indeed was even refuting, the role and identification based on color thrust upon him in the United States.

In an early essay on the subject, Baldwin wrote: "It is altogether inevitable that past humiliations should become associated not only with one's traditional oppressors but also with one's traditional kinfolk. Thus the sight of a face from home is not invariably a source of joy, but can also quite easily become a source of embarrassment or rage. The American Negro in Paris is forced at last to exercise an undemocratic discrimination rarely practiced by Americans, that of judging his people, duck by duck, and distinguishing them one from another."

These early years in Paris were a period of intense discovery, of real formation of the individual who was James Baldwin. By far his most important realization, though, was that, as was not true at home, he did not have to apologize for being a writer. The distrust of intelligence that characterized American society did not apply in Paris. In Europe the artist had respect, did not have to pretend, as Baldwin put it, that he was really a "regular guy." "This lack of what may roughly be called social paranoia causes the American writer in Europe to feel—almost certainly for the first time in his life—that he can reach out to everyone, that he is accessible to everyone and open to everything. This is an extraordinary feeling. He feels, so to speak, his own weight, his own value."

This status was in no small part responsible for Baldwin's being able to remain, for as long as he did, virtually dependent on the kindness of strangers. In the States, he would have been disdained, as a freeloader, as someone who was not "contributing to society." But in France, the regard with which the French held their artists rubbed off as well on the foreign community, and allowed him to exist, not only materially but also psychically. His compatriots, mostly fellow writers, believed that he (and they) were doing something important. There was no sin attached to poverty, to cheating the landlord to pay the muse. In the United States, continually plagued by self-doubt, Baldwin really felt that he might go crazy, kill or be killed. In France, despite the precariousness of his material life, his mental life was nourished, affirmed. For the artist in Paris, "it is as though he suddenly came out of a dark tunnel and found himself beneath the open sky. And, in fact, in Paris I began to see the sky for what seemed to be the first time."

This new self-confidence, this liberation, kept him working. He even began to make a little money from writing. *Partisan Review* took two essays from him during his first years in Paris, "Everybody's Protest Novel" (first published in *Zero*) and "Many Thousands Gone," both about Richard Wright. *The Reporter* published "The Negro in Paris," later retitled "Encounter on the Seine: Black Meets Brown." He also managed to sell a short story, "The Outing," actually a reworked section from his first, rejected novel, to the Paris-based *New-Story* magazine.

Baldwin's major literary efforts during this period were spent on two novels. The first, at that time entitled *Crying Holy* (later *Go Tell It on the Mountain*), was a further reworking of the book for which he had been awarded the Eugene F. Saxton fellowship. The second was a very early version of *Giovanni's Room*.

Among the major difficulties he was having with *Crying Holy* was that the autobiographical quality of the novel was opening up serious old psychic wounds, particularly those concerning his relationship with his stepfather, whom until adolescence he had believed was his father. The book was functioning on one level as a purge for the resentment, anger, and fear he had long felt for the man he called his father; on another, it was bringing all of those emotions to the surface, forcing him to confront them and, what's more, transform them into art. Since his "father" was now actually dead, there was no way he could effect any sort of reconciliation. As for the other novel, it too had its share of psychological entanglement: its theme was homosexuality, and thus Baldwin was forcing himself to "go public" with his sexuality. He also had doubts about its publishability; homosexuality was still not commonly a subject dealt with openly. Despite the difficulties, he could not give up on either book. But going forward was not easy either.

Part of the difficulty, according to young fiction writer Truman Capote, who was passing through Paris at the time, was that Baldwin was concerned that his eventual book be neither a protest novel nor a problem novel. Capote, who had heard plot summaries of both novels, told Baldwin that one of his ideas, a book featuring a homosexual in love with a Jewish woman could be only a problem novel. He then apparently advised Baldwin to concentrate on his Harlem family novel, *Crying Holy.*

Although Baldwin later denied that Capote pointed him in the right direction, what is clear is that form was a concern of Baldwin's. He had in fact denounced Richard Wright for writing "protest novels." This, in turn, led to another difficulty: the lack of a model he could make his own. Having embarked on a mission to unseat Wright, he could hardly use him as a guide for his own writing. Faulkner, whom he also avidly admired at this time, was too artistically unique an author to imitate. Baldwin described his dilemma thus: "As a writer I needed a box to put thoughts in—a model. I couldn't use D. H. Lawrence, for example (I was too much like him). I had to find someone else."

Baldwin's quest took various turns, but through the urging of fellow Americans Stanley Geist and Otto Friedrich he discovered Henry James, an author whom he had tried to read earlier but who had not inspired him, for he simply could not relate to James's universe. "It might have been in a foreign language for all it meant to me then," Baldwin recalled about his attempt to read *The Portrait of a Lady* as a teenager. But now in Paris, he could understand James as one exile understood another. Just as James was able to write most convincingly about Americans when he did not live among them, Baldwin used the detachment of living abroad to gain a perspective on himself and on the situation of being a black man in America.

The nightmare that America had been for Baldwin, while it had fueled his literary imagination and provided ample material for his creative self, had also nearly consumed him spiritually and physically. "I didn't know what was going to happen to me in France but I knew what was going to happen to me in New York," he commented. "If I had stayed there, I would have gone under." In the relative security of Paris, however, he could look at his own past and his own country without fearing that the present would overtake him: "The French gave me what I could not get in America, which was a sense of 'If I can do it, I may do it.'"

In the United States, the daily struggle to survive precluded Baldwin's understanding of his own predicament in terms broader than that of individual reaction against the forces bearing down on him. In Paris, still obsessed with the experience of American culture, but freed from participation in it, he could start to unravel how the personal was connected to the public. Like James, he began to see that the small actions of the individual within a culture had metaphoric implications, could be read as a reflection of the society itself. Identity within society, whether James's upper-class Americans or Baldwin's disenfranchised souls inhabiting the lower depths, is the central dilemma around which the work of both writers turns. Both James and Baldwin wrote novels of manners; the manners were simply different.

Baldwin did not appropriate James's style; instead he adopted a Jamesian optic. "The means to order and describe something that had happened to me in the distance—America—was James," he noted and added that "James became, in a sense, my master. It was something about point of view, something about discipline. And something about the silence in which I myself was living began to help me because I was able to go back to something in myself in that silence—the silence of living in Paris— which allowed me to write."

In real terms this translated into a direction to take with his novel. About his debt to James in providing him with the perspective to transform *Crying Holy* into *Go Tell It on the Mountain*, Baldwin observed: "The book was very hard to write because I was too young when I started, seventeen; it was really about me and my father. There were things I couldn't deal with technically at first. Most of all I couldn't deal with *me*. This is where reading Henry James helped me, with his whole idea about the center of consciousness and using a single intelligence to tell the story. He gave me the idea to make the novel happen on John's birthday."

IF BALDWIN was rescued by James through literature, he was aided in the spirit by a tall, thin, pale seventeen-year-old Swiss painter, Lucien Happersberger. They met one night in early 1951 at La Reine Blanche, a bar in St.-Germain-des-Prés run by a woman from Brittany who allowed Baldwin to drink on credit. As Happersberger had just arrived in Paris from Lausanne, Baldwin decided to introduce him to the local scene. That night, they formed an almost instant alliance; within a short time they were sharing their meager resources, concocting stratagems to cadge a drink or meal. Happersberger was unlike the men Baldwin usually met in bars. Not only was he considerably younger than Baldwin, he was also just as indigent. What they had in common, though, was admiration and concern for one another as individuals. In Happersberger, Baldwin found the emotional support he had been lacking in his first years in Paris.

A few months after they met, Happersberger realized that between the difficulties with the novel and the continual hustle to survive, Baldwin was becoming anxious and despondent. What his new American companion needed, he decided, was the typical European cure: a rest in the mountains. In this case the country was Switzerland, where Happersberger's family owned a chalet in the tiny, remote village of Loèche-les-Bains (Leukerbad). For Baldwin, it was an introduction to a totally different world. In his essay "Stranger in the Village," he recounted the reaction of the locals at his appearance: "If I sat in the sun for more than five minutes some daring creature was certain to come along and gingerly put his fingers on my hair, as though he were

afraid of an electric shock, or put his hand on my hand, astonished that the color did not rub off. In all of this, in which it must
be conceded there was the charm of genuine wonder and in
which there was certainly no element of intentional unkindness,
there was yet no suggestion that I was human: I was simply a
living wonder."

Despite his profound sense of feeling exotic, the two-week
vacation during that summer of 1951 allowed Baldwin a welcome
respite from the daily struggle of life in Paris. Nearly consumed
by the city, which seemed now even more overwhelming, by
autumn he was seriously wondering whether to scrap the novel
he'd been working on for almost ten years. He made an important decision: to return for the winter to Loèche-les-Bains. There,
in the snowy isolation of the village, typing to the accompaniment
of Bessie Smith records, he finished the book in three months.
On February 26, 1952, he walked down from the mountain to a
larger town below, and mailed the manuscript to his agent, Helen
Strauss, at the William Morris Agency in New York. The title was
now *Go Tell It on the Mountain*.

THE NOVEL is ostensibly the tale of the Grimes family, yet in
telling the story, Baldwin weaves an exquisite and complex tapes-
try in which the Grimeses serve as vehicles for illuminating a
particular society—that of Harlem. But by virtue of the univer-
sality of the concerns and themes, the resonating significance is
far broader; the Grimeses, like characters in a biblical story (or in
a Henry James novel), illustrate the human predicament, not just
the specific problems besetting a black American family in the
1930s. This is not to imply that the characters are pasteboard
figures; rather, it is the reverse. Baldwin's characters are so vivid,
their struggles so authentic, their hatred and suffering so recog-
nizable that they transcend the social milieu of the novel.

Although written in the third person, *Go Tell It on the Mountain*
is highly autobiographical, not only in incident but in emotional
and psychological substance as well. Like John Grimes, the book's

central figure, Baldwin grew up in Harlem, surrounded by a half
brother and sisters. His own mother, like Elizabeth in the novel,
was the suffering shield, acting (though often ineffectually) as a
buffer between the children and her violent, vicious preacher
husband. Baldwin, like John, underwent a radical transformation
in his life at the age of fourteen, when he became a young
minister. Perhaps most significant, though, John's quest for identity is Baldwin's own.

John's attempt to come to an understanding of himself, in
relation to the past, present, and future, forms the central drama
in the book. The past and present he is dealing with are inextrica-
bly entwined with the larger question of family relationships. His
struggle is in coming to terms with himself as a product of the
twisted series of psychic and physical upheavals undergone by
the older members of the Grimes family, while charting an escape from the dark, pervasive forces that have so ensnared these
figures. The most compelling problem is the animosity he feels
toward his stepfather, Gabriel, whom he ardently wishes to overcome, perhaps even murder. In addition, he is battling against
the lures of the street: worldliness, sexuality, idleness, sin, even
freedom. But the bigger obstacle is guilt at wanting to sin, to
murder Gabriel, to follow his own desire to succumb to the
wayward impulses of the "world."

The temporary resolution to the dilemma is his conversion on
the threshing floor, a powerfully hallucinatory, profoundly visionary experience. Emerging from his ecstatic delirium, John feels
"saved," filled with joy. But despite his own immediate sense of
having dispatched the forces pulling him "downward," he is also
aware that the triumph is not complete. The Avenue still exists;
his stepfather's menacing presence still confronts him; he is am-
biguously stirred by the kiss the beautiful boy Elisha bestows on
his forehead.

"The province of art is all life, all feeling, all observation, all
vision," wrote Henry James in *"The Art of Fiction."* In *Go Tell It on
the Mountain*, Baldwin followed the "master's" dictum, allowing
himself to use his own past as ready-at-hand material for his

fiction. The incidents in the novel, so closely paralleling his own, were there from the first draft. What took him almost a decade to write was the "feeling," the "vision." In doing so, Baldwin outgrew the role of "Frog Eyes," the abused preacher's son and boy minister, and became James Baldwin, novelist.

WITHIN A few weeks of receiving Baldwin's manuscript from Switzerland, Helen Strauss happily notified the young writer that Knopf was quite interested in the novel and wanted to discuss it with him as soon as possible. Baldwin was alternately elated and chagrined. Although delighted at the possibility of publication, he was without funds to make the trip to New York. As he had already borrowed money from almost everyone with whom he was acquainted in Paris (and repaid little), he could hardly expect anyone to provide him with the boat fare. Then, just as desperation was beginning to overtake him, an old friend from the States turned up in Paris, an actor with whom he'd been chummy in the mid-forties and who had since made it big: Marlon Brando. He responded immediately to Baldwin's request, loaning him $500. Baldwin was a passenger on the next ship out of Le Havre.

The day after his arrival in New York, he went straight to Knopf only to learn that his novel had not yet been accepted. In fact, the house was divided over whether to publish it or not. One major objection was that it contained too much "come to Jesus" rhetoric; another was that the end was too explicit in detailing John's homosexual leanings. Baldwin was crushed when Knopf editor Philip Vaudrin detailed what he saw as the novel's faults. "I gagged literally and began to sweat, ran to the water cooler, tried to pull myself together and returned to the office to try to explain the intentions of my novel," Baldwin remembered.

Later that afternoon he talked with William Cole, publicity director and an editor at the firm, who was far more enthusiastic about the book than Vaudrin. Although he apparently made suggestions similar to Vaudrin's, he did so in a more sympathetic way, assuring Baldwin that he did not have to tinker with the plot or remove all of the church scenes, but should just focus them more sharply. Baldwin agreed to make further revisions; Knopf in turn gave him $250, with another $750 to be paid on acceptance of a final manuscript.

Baldwin's stay in New York was brief. Once he had the Knopf check, he immediately booked return passage to France. He would later remark that the trip was "a nightmare. I'd been away just long enough to have lost all of my old habits—all my old friends, all my old connections. . . . I came back into a kind of limbo." In a story written years afterward, "This Morning, This Evening, So Soon," he described, through the voice of the narrator, the difficulty he had experienced being "home." " 'I *had* to get back here [to Paris], get to a place where people were too busy with their own lives, *their private lives*, to make fantasies about mine, to set up walls around mine. . . . That's what it's like in America, for me, anyway. I always feel that I don't exist there, except in someone else's—usually dirty—mind.' "

Back in Paris, Baldwin immersed himself in revising *Go Tell It on the Mountain*; he finished it in two months. This time the manuscript was accepted at Knopf; publication was scheduled for May 1953. Although inwardly he felt his situation had changed—he was now about to be a published novelist—outwardly it seemed to make little difference. The $750 received from Knopf, to be sure, would keep him afloat for a while, but his newly earned status did not translate into a comfortable physical existence. There was a difference, though: he now knew that he could write commercially publishable work. Reinvigorated by this knowledge, over the nine months between acceptance and publication of the novel, he worked prodigiously, turning out a play, *The Amen Corner*, and getting yet another start on what would become *Giovanni's Room*.

The Amen Corner was essentially a dramatic adaptation of *Go Tell It on the Mountain*. The setting was again a storefront Harlem church, the theme that of religion as a force in the black community. But where the novel was filled with dark tension and poignant beauty, the play, despite some excellent scenes, was superficial, less convincing. Seen in the context of Baldwin's development, however, *The Amen Corner* allowed him to finish off the experience of his youth and served as an ultimate testament to his distant Harlem past. He had hoped, when he sent the play to Helen Strauss, that it would prove to be "Broadway material," representing perhaps a big financial break, but it did not. She could not find a producer; and even though it did have a production at Howard University in the mid-1950s, it would take about ten years before it would be performed on Broadway, and even then it was not terribly successful. Indeed, financial success would elude Baldwin for some time.

By the spring of 1953 he had again run out of money and had moved to Gallardon, a small town near Chartres, where he lived in a communal house with Gidske Anderson, the Norwegian woman with whom he'd journeyed to Provence several years before, and two other artists. On a rainy morning in early May he set out for Paris, to see if by chance a small check from family or friends awaited him at American Express. Because of a transit strike he had to walk in the downpour from the outskirts of the capital to the office in the Place de l'Opéra. By the time he approached the mail window, he was completely soaked. To make matters worse, there was no check. There was, however, a package from Knopf containing ten copies of *Go Tell It on the Mountain*. That afternoon he sat in a café, slowly drying himself out, hoping that the contents of his sodden parcel, dripping water onto the floor, were not ruined; hoping too that someone he knew would drop by so that he could show off his triumph; but hoping most that that someone would lend him enough money to get back to the countryside. At nightfall he was still waiting and had to go back out into the rain, to another café, to find a benefactor.

The poignant absurdity of his situation was not lost on Baldwin, but it did not deter him from continuing to work. Yet more and more he was feeling that France, and Paris in particular, were no longer as enchanting as they had been. Part of the problem was that Baldwin was finding it increasingly difficult to ignore the French treatment of the Algerians, especially now that the Algerian war was beginning to heat up considerably. Although he agreed with Richard Wright that for them Paris was the "city of refuge," he quickly noticed (as Wright was not so keen to see) that it was not the same for the Arab population: "It would not have been a city of refuge for us if we had not been armed with American passports." For Baldwin, incidents such as the brutal beating by the police of an old, one-armed Arab peanut vendor began to change his attitude.

What bewildered him most was the way in which the French managed to maintain a double standard as far as race was concerned. When he challenged them to explain why they could treat him well while derogating Arabs, they would respond, "*Le noir Américain est très évolué, voyons!*" (The black American is very evolved, you see) and tell him that "the Arabs were not like me, they were not 'civilized' like me. It was something of a shock to hear myself described as civilized, but the accolade thirsted for so long had, alas, been delivered too late." The difference in attitude was clearly demonstrated to him one evening when he was stopped by the police while walking through the streets in Paris. Suspecting he was a North African, they asked him to show his identity papers. He did not have his passport, but he did have a copy of *Go Tell It on the Mountain* with him. He produced the book, with his photograph on the back jacket. The menacing attitude of the police immediately changed: "*Ah! vous êtes écrivain! Vous pouvez partir, Monsieur.*" (Ah! you're a writer. You may go, sir).

But it was not just the political situation that was plaguing him. His personal life was in turmoil. Despite the arrival in Paris of a longtime friend and mentor, painter Beauford Delaney, Baldwin felt unconnected, lonely, depressed. The main reason was that Lucien Happersberger had returned to Switzerland and was now married. Finally, after months of doubt and despair, he journeyed to Loèche-les-Bains. To his relief, he discovered that although his relationship with Happersberger had changed, the deep friendship endured. Baldwin was consoled but also was wise enough to realize that his lingering presence there would serve neither of them well. He left Switzerland, eventually settling for a while in Les Quatre Chemins, a hamlet near Cannes. It was there that he began to disentangle *Giovanni's Room* from his later novel, *Another Country*.

According to Baldwin, the genesis of *Giovanni's Room* was in a novel begun before he had even left the United States: *Ignorant Armies*. This early version, now lost, was modeled on the true story of a young Columbia University student, Lucien Carr, who in 1944 killed David Kammerer, an older man with whom he had been long acquainted and who had attempted to assault him sexually. Baldwin followed the case in the papers, fascinated by the grisly story. What he did not know at the time was that the story actively engaged three of America's (then unpublished) major writers: Allen Ginsberg, Jack Kerouac, and William Burroughs. For them the murder was not a tabloid abstraction: Kammerer had been a friend of Burroughs from his St. Louis days; Carr was a classmate of Kerouac and Ginsberg; Carr confessed the slaying first to Kerouac, then to Burroughs, and both were subsequently detained briefly by the police as material witnesses, after Carr, following Burroughs's advice to get himself a good lawyer, did exactly that. In the end, to the immense relief of all, Carr received an eighteen-month sentence for manslaughter. But for Baldwin his fate was immaterial; the daily newspaper accounts of the crime and trial had fueled his imagination sufficiently to lay the groundwork for what some ten years later would develop into *Giovanni's Room*.

While the Kammerer incident provided Baldwin with the basic plot, it was his own experiences in the *milieu*, including an affair with a young Frenchman that gave the book its detail and emotional intensity. Baldwin's short novel is the story of a young white American, David, who has come to Paris. There he meets Hella, an American woman, with whom he believes he has fallen in love. But his real attraction is toward the *milieu*. Although he did have an adolescent homosexual experience, David at first fancies himself not a participating member of that scene: "I was intent on proving, to them and to myself, that I was not of their company. I did this by being in their company a great deal and manifesting toward all of them a tolerance which placed me, I believed, above suspicion."

When Hella leaves for Spain, to think over her relationship with David, he reimmerses himself in the gay scene, mainly because he is broke and knows that Jacques, an older Belgian-American businessman, will lend him some money, as he has frequently done before. After David gets a loan from Jacques, the two head to a local gay bar run by a Frenchman, Guillaume. There David meets Giovanni, an Italian immigrant who is working for Guillaume. They connect immediately and end up spending the night together: "He pulled me against him, putting himself into my arms as though he were giving me himself to carry, and slowly pulled me down with him to that bed. With everything in me screaming *No!* yet the sum of me sighed *Yes.*"

For the next few months David and Giovanni have a rapturous, tender love affair, but when Hella returns David abruptly breaks it off, leaves Giovanni without even telling him. Now abandoned, Giovanni is forced into relying on Jacques and Guillaume. Meanwhile David is trying to convince himself that he really is in love with Hella and wants to marry her. Finally, after acquiescing to Guillaume's demands for sex, Giovanni, enraged over the degradation that has befallen him, kills his patron. After a week he is arrested; at his trial he is condemned to death. David and Hella leave for southern France, but there, again realizing his own true sexual orientation, David betrays Hella; she in turn leaves him and goes back to America. As the book ends (and begins, for the story is told in a series of flashbacks), David is returning alone from Provence to Paris on the morning of Giovanni's execution.

This synopsis of the novel does not explain Baldwin's deeper motivations for writing it. First, following James's dictum that "there is no impression of life, no manner of seeing it, to which the plan of the novelist may not offer a place," Baldwin was attempting to write an impression of his own life in the *milieu*. At this, he clearly excelled, for *Giovanni's Room* conjured up a view of Paris that defied the tourist brochures, offered the spectatorial reader an insight into the machinations of a world largely hidden, even closed to casual observation. Moreover, in presenting a genuine homosexual love story as filled with compassion, complexity, and cruelty as any conventional tale of lovers, Baldwin was stating unequivocally that a man could have as fulfilling a relationship with another man as with a woman. But Baldwin's vision also encompassed the inherent difficulty of such an affair and acknowledged that for most American males the choice was beset with anxieties. What was acceptable in the *milieu* was not so easily accommodated outside of it, even in Paris.

Furthermore, despite his attempt to portray the relationship between Giovanni and David as a natural matter, Baldwin was also clear-eyed about the predatory nature of the gay underworld. Guillaume and Jacques are repulsive creatures, vile "benefactors" who exploit innocence for their own ends. That Baldwin understood all these dimensions of the gay experience is evident from his own life. With some men, such as Lucien, Baldwin did encounter the sort of tenderness and purity that existed between David and Giovanni. But as a poor, gay man in Paris, he also on occasion allowed himself to rely on people like Jacques and Guillaume, who were only too ready to offer a meal, a drink, and a few francs for the privilege of having a young man in their company and, they hoped, in their bed.

But these aspects of the novel represent only one of the dimensions that Baldwin was writing about with such candor. On another level, *Giovanni's Room* mirrored the quintessential situation encountered by so many of Henry James's Americans abroad who discovered themselves in the process of discovering Europe. Following in the long Jamesian line of Roderick Hudson, Christopher Newman, Isabel Archer, and Lambert Strether, David is searching in Europe for an identity, although he suspects, and rightly so, that "the self I was going to find would turn out to be only the same self from which I had spent so much time in flight." But at the outset this knowledge is opaque to the protagonist. He therefore plunges himself into experiencing all he can, thinking, like Strether in *The Ambassadors*, that experience will equate with self-knowledge. And to some extent it does; but as in the case of

James's hero, it comes too late to erase the mistakes of the past. Nor is the wisdom gained from Europe necessarily happy or even useful: "Americans should never come to Europe," Hella says. "It means they never can be happy again. What's the good of an American who isn't happy? Happiness was all we had."

Giovanni's Room is an ambitious novel, a book that turns the usual order of things inside out: the possibility of true homosexual love; Europe as a source not just of knowledge but of bitter truth; happiness as a false concept. All that is missing in the inversion is race, but as Baldwin explained, "I certainly could not possibly have—not at that point in my life—handled the other great weight, the 'Negro' problem. The sexual-moral light was a hard thing to deal with. I could not handle both propositions in the same book. There was no room for it."

Although Baldwin did not complete *Giovanni's Room* in Les Quatre Chemins, he did ascertain which elements to keep and which to discard from the amalgam of this novel and his next, *Another Country*. At first he thought of turning the Giovanni segments into a short story, but as he began to work on the piece, it lengthened, the story and theme becoming too complex to treat adequately in a shorter form. "*Giovanni's Room* came out of something I had to face," Baldwin remarked. And again, just as *Go Tell It on the Mountain* had allowed him to come to an understanding of his adolescence, religion, and his relationship with his stepfather, *Giovanni's Room* represented a coming to terms publicly with his own sexual identity.

BY THE spring of 1954, Baldwin's financial situation had improved. Not only had he made some money from the sale of paperback and British rights to *Go Tell It on the Mountain*, but he had received the good news that he had been awarded a Guggenheim grant. Yet curiously, now that he was actually able to support himself in France, he was becoming, as he put it, "out of kilter in Paris. . . . I couldn't get along with the bulk of the American colony, especially the American *Negro* colony who, so far as I could see, spent most of their time . . . sitting in bars and cafés, talking about how awful *America* was." This disjointedness, in combination with his growing awareness of the prevailing French attitude toward Algeria, made him decide to return, at least for a while, to the United States. He admitted, however, that he was unprepared psychologically for what he knew would await him.

By the summer of 1954 he was back in New York. This time he felt on surer ground, for Happersberger had accompanied him on the first part of the stay, thus providing him with a bridge to Europe. A stint at the MacDowell Colony also helped. There he nearly finished *Giovanni's Room*; in addition, Sol Stein at Beacon Press contracted with him for a collection of essays. Despite his misgivings, America was finally according him the consideration he deserved. The highlight of his stay, though, was Howard University's production of *The Amen Corner*, as this translated into recognition from the black community and proved to him that he was still speaking to those who had engendered him.

With *Giovanni's Room* he did not fare so well. Knopf rejected it, apparently because of its explicit theme of homosexuality. Other publishers also turned it down. Finally it was accepted by his English publisher, Michael Joseph, but no one in the United States seemed willing to touch it. The bad news from New York publishers was mitigated somewhat in the spring of 1955, when Beacon Press issued, to great acclaim and lively sales, *Notes of a Native Son*. By then, however, Baldwin was planning to return to France, feeling that in his year at home he had gained whatever he could from the States.

He had not been back in Paris long when Helen Strauss informed him that she had sold *Giovanni's Room* to Dial Press. Dial had been persuaded to acquire the novel by Philip Rahv, a long-time supporter who had first published Baldwin in *Partisan Review*. Baldwin's editor at Dial, though enthusiastic about the book, felt it still needed revisions. On this occasion Baldwin did not take the criticisms of the novel as judgments on himself, as he had initially with *Go Tell It on the Mountain*. He complied with his editor's critiques, taking the opportunity to revise the novel completely over the next several months.

At about the same time, he accepted an assignment for the

British magazine *Encounter* to write an article on an international conference of Negro African writers and artists held in 1956 in Paris. Among the luminaries attending were Léopold Sédar Senghor, Aimé Césaire, and naturally, Richard Wright. Baldwin found himself suddenly having to confront, from a new angle, his own identity: that of a black man with no memorable ties to Africa, no sense of the African experience. Two years earlier he had felt a similar apartness when asked by an African man where he was from. "I am an American," he had replied. The African pressed him: "And your parents?" "Americans also." "But," responded the African, "you obviously have African ancestors. What country were they from?" Baldwin admitted he had no idea. At this the African was shocked; he accused Baldwin of denying his ancestry, of joking with him. Baldwin could reply only that if it were a joke, it was shared by millions of his black American compatriots.

Now, at the conference, he experienced a similar sense of his separateness. Intellectually he could relate to the calls for national autonomy, but in his soul he could not feel a real connection with the aims of his African "brothers." Neither could he adopt Richard Wright's attitude that the Africans should take advantage of their colonizers' dethroning of the old tribal ways to enact a true liberation—from Europe and from their own past. Although he was confused about what to make of the conference itself, it did catalyze in Baldwin a feeling that the black struggle for liberation was also his struggle, but that the role he had to play was at home, not in the international arena. While not able to find a true identity in his African heritage, he did rediscover a sense of self as a black American. Sweeping over him was a feeling of necessity to act from this knowledge, to use his talent toward achieving more than just being James Baldwin, exiled writer. This powerful realization hit him during a break from the conference, when he was walking with Richard Wright and several Africans up the Boulevard St.-Germain:

Facing us, on every newspaper kiosk on that wide, tree-shaded boulevard, were photographs of fifteen-year-old Dorothy

Counts being reviled and spat upon by the mob as she was making her way to school in Charlotte, North Carolina. There was unutterable pride, tension, and anguish in that girl's face as she approached the halls of learning, with history, jeering, at her back.

It made me furious, it filled me with both hatred and pity, and it made me ashamed. Some one of us should have been there with her! I dawdled in Europe for nearly yet another year, held by my private life and my attempt to finish a novel, but it was on that bright afternoon that I knew I was leaving France. I could, simply, no longer sit around in Paris discussing the Algerian and the black American problem. Everybody else was paying their dues, and it was time I went home and paid mine.

Baldwin's decision to return "home" was different from the choice he had made nearly a decade earlier to escape the United States. After years of struggle to create himself as an artist in France, he had finally succeeded, and could easily have remained among friends in a country that not only suited him but respected him. He also did not have any illusions about what to expect at home. And yet he felt a responsibility to use his growing prestige as an artist in service to his people and to his country. Or as Baldwin stated: "One is responsible to life: It is the small beacon in that terrifying darkness from which we come and to which we shall return. One must negotiate this passage as nobly as possible, for the sake of those who are coming after us." Just as the church had earlier called little "Frog Eyes" to be its witness, the racial muck that had mired him, that had forced him to flee, now summoned him back in the summer of 1957 to face with courage and nobility "the fire this time."

Chapter Six

The Rebirth of Paris English-Language Publishing: Little Magazines, Literature, and D.B.'s

DURING THE 1920s and 1930s, twenty significant English-language publishers were turning out memorable literature in France, in response to the influx of English-speaking expatriate writers and readers. By 1940 not one of these presses was still operating. Although the war did have an impact, in reality only Obelisk Press was forced to close because of the Occupation; the others had disappeared gradually, in part as a result of the willingness of London and New York to publish a number of expatriate writers, such as Joyce, Pound, Stein, Hemingway, Kay Boyle, Djuna Barnes, and Henry Miller, who had formed the authorial nucleus of the imprints. There had been as well, by the middle to late thirties, a gradual but decided drop in the number of exiles in Paris, either through repatriation or general global scattering.

The legendary English-language literary magazines—among them *transition, Contact, The Little Review, The Transatlantic Review, This Quarter, The New Review,* and *Tambour*—had also ceased to exist, some well before the beginning of World War II, largely for the same reasons as had the publishers. For the reviews, however, it was the usual plague of little magazines, chronic lack of funds, that also contributed to their demise.

After the war, with Paris once again inundated with anglophone expatriates, it naturally followed that there would be a resurgence of publishing in English. And just as the little magazines of the twenties and thirties had often served as vehicles for first-time writers, so did the literary journals that came into existence in Paris in the late forties and early fifties. In many instances, these magazines were the first to publish emerging writers who would later make significant contributions to American and international letters. Perhaps even more daring than their predecessors, the Paris-based reviews of the postwar era provided a forum for an array of talent ranging from the highly conventional to the thoroughly experimental. It was in the pages of these journals that writers tested their wings and, in many cases, ascended to full flight.

THE FIRST of the literary magazines to spring up after the war was *Points*, founded in late 1948 by Sindbad Vail, son of Peggy Guggenheim and Laurence Vail. No grandiose pretensions were behind its inception; rather, it was conceived "to give the editor or editors and his pals an outlet for their work plus an egotistical desire to acquire 'fame' or 'notoriety.' " According to Vail, the idea of starting a magazine came to him in the summer of 1948 while visiting his mother in Venice. Twenty-five at the time, he was thinking he ought to find something to do. His first inclination was to open an art gallery in Paris, but as he knew "even less about art than literature," he was discouraged by the prominent collectors in his family. "What else to do," remembered Vail, "than turn to literature?"

Back in Paris that fall, he decided to test the literary waters by seeking submissions through an ad in the *Herald Tribune*. Under the heading "Attention Young Writers," he proclaimed that a new review was being conceived that "welcomed young writers and ideas." The response was so overwhelming that Vail was forced to cancel the original three-day ad run after just the first day. The next step was to set up business. For this, he discovered, he needed a French partner. After one false start, with a French businessman who apparently tried to cheat him, Cyril Connolly, editor of the English review *Horizon*, put Vail in touch with a young French writer and editor, Marcel Bisiaux. Bisiaux was at that time running a literary magazine, *84*. The two hit it off at once and agreed to join forces. The cognate *Points* was chosen as a title, and a decision was made to publish half of the journal in French.

Through Bisiaux, who was also connected to Les Éditions de Minuit, they set up an office at the vanguardist publishing firm and waited for quality submissions to arrive. For Vail this proved more difficult than he had imagined; while a great deal of material did arrive over the transom, little of it was publishable. (Bisiaux, who already had a number of contacts in the French literary community, did not have this problem.) Eventually, however, Vail felt he had enough English-language writing, of at least some quality, and *Points* went to press. "In our innocence," he recalled, "we printed 5000 copies of POINTS No. 1, and we feared that might not be enough. We had no advance publicity, no agent and no means of distribution. . . . Naturally we sent copies to everyone we knew, but after three or four hundred that gave out." These copies amounted to nearly the entire circulation of that first issue. About ninety-nine percent of the other copies distributed to booksellers and newspaper kiosks were returned.

It was hardly a propitious start for Vail's enterprise, but he doggedly kept on with it, learning rapidly how to edit and sell a magazine. In retrospect it is easy to see why the first issue did not make much of a splash. Aside from Vail's general naiveté about the business of running and distributing a literary review, *Points* No. 1 suffered for two main reasons: first, the English-language work was of rather poor quality; and second, another magazine appeared on the scene almost simultaneously, *Zero*.

Zero's debut was far more successful than that of *Points*. Its editor, Themistocles Hoetis, not only had done far more advance work in terms of distribution but had had the foresight to include name writers among his contributors. Its premiere issue, in the spring of 1949, featured work by Christopher Isherwood, Kenneth Patchen, William Carlos Williams, and Richard Wright, as well as the controversial essay on Wright by the young James Baldwin. But what *Points* lacked in terms of good writing, *Zero* lacked in funds. Vail later admitted that a *New York Times* correspondent in Paris suggested to him quite seriously that he give Hoetis his money and let *Zero* do the work. In the end, Vail's cash prevailed over Hoetis's literary acumen; after just three issues in Paris, *Zero* moved to Tangier and then Mexico, where despite an attempted revival it succumbed to its ever-mounting financial woes.

Two other, very short-lived magazines saw the light of day in the early summer of 1949, *Janus* and *ID*. Although *Janus*, a half-French, half-English poetry journal, had a stirring manifesto, the poetic contributions did not match its rhetorical flourishes. *ID* printed stories, comparably as atrocious as *Janus's* poetry. After a few issues the two magazines merged, but then folded after just one composite number. Not everybody writing in Paris was destined for fame.

Points, meanwhile, continued for nearly a decade, noticeably improving with each number. After a few issues and the discovery that not many Frenchmen bought the journal, the French-language contributions were cut by half; eventually they were purged altogether. Vail reduced the number of issues from six to five to four a year and settled on a print run of a thousand copies, the majority of which he was actually able to sell.

Curiously, *Points* got better as the competition increased, as it noticeably did in the early 1950s with the advent of two remarkable little magazines: *New-Story* and *Merlin*. Part of the reason was that many of the contributors to these magazines also sent their work to Vail. *The Paris Review* was begun around this time as well, but with its consistently high-quality, often international writing by name authors, its advertisements and capable distribution, it quickly entered a different echelon and could not really be construed as competition.

New-Story, a monthly that premiered in March 1951, although Paris-based, relied heavily on contributions from Britain and the United States. Originally edited by David Burnett, the magazine immediately distinguished itself with its eclecticism. Aside from contributions by prominent French writers (in translation), however, the majority of the work was by American writers—such as Alison Lurie, James Baldwin, Terry Southern, William Goyen, and Ray Bradbury—who were young and relatively unknown. Despite the excellence of its short stories, editorial disputes and lack of funds destined it to a short print life. By 1953 it had ceased publication.

Of all the little magazines that began during the postwar era, *Merlin* was by far the most experimental. Founded in the spring of 1952 by Scottish-born Alexander Trocchi and an American, Jane Lougee, it also included on its international editorial board Americans Richard Seaver and Austryn Wainhouse, South African Patrick Bowles, and Englishman Christopher Logue. Besides being gifted writers and editors, they were a colorful group, as passionate about living as they were about literature. Trocchi and Logue were "true bohemians, Beats before the Beats officially existed," remembered bookstore owner George Whitman. "Christopher was the scruffy poet, quite down and out most of the time. He definitely fancied himself as Baudelaire or somebody like that. Alex was always haranguing about something or other, usually the government or puritan society. He and Jane were a real contrast: the angry young man and this sweet, pretty girl from Maine whose father was a banker."

Writer Eugene Walter also recalled the group, in particular Logue: "He liked to propagate the idea that he was a somewhat shady character; he told wondrous wild tales to further the effect. . . . When Christopher's mother visited Paris, he tried to keep her under wraps, finally brought her to the [Café de] Tournon. Everybody thought she'd be at least a red-haired Polish gypsy, or a Tunisian midwife, but she was a pink-cheeked little

English lady with a silk print dress and a cameo." As for Seaver, Wainhouse, and Bowles, they were quite different from Logue and Trocchi. Noted Whitman, "They were more reserved, every bit as intense, but not so ostentatious about it."

Merlin's inaugural issue, which hit the stands in the fall of 1952, featured a manifesto by Trocchi which proclaimed that "MERLIN will hit at all clots of rigid categories in criticism and life, and all that is unintelligently partisan. To say that MERLIN is against obscurantism in criticism is not to say that it is against obscurity in poetry. MERLIN is for innovation in creative writing which renders creative writing more expressive."

Later, less bombastically, Trocchi remarked that *Merlin*'s primary objective had been to create "a vital meeting ground for the thought and work of American and English writers on the one hand and Continental writers on the other." A glance at the contents of the quarterly over the three years of its erratic existence reveals that the editorial objective was clearly met. Along with numerous works by the editors, particularly Logue, Wainhouse, Trocchi, and Seaver, and other English-language authors in Paris, it also featured prominent European writing, usually in superb translations, including work by Genet, Henri Michaux, and Eugène Ionesco. The acquisition of these Continental writers was made possible by an arrangement with Sartre and Beauvoir's *Les Temps Modernes*, whereby *Merlin* was granted rights to reprint in translation any of the writing appearing in the French magazine. But one name that did not appear in Sartre's journal dominated *Merlin*'s pages, in quantity if not also in quality: Samuel Beckett.

Beckett's inclusion in practically every issue of the quarterly was not coincidental. He was, at least in the minds of the *Merlin* editors, their "discovery." Actually it was Richard Seaver who first brought Beckett's work to the attention of the *Merlin* group, but they all quickly latched on to the writer as if each had personally discovered him. According to Seaver, in early 1952 he came across Beckett's work in the display window of Les Éditions de Minuit: "I remember looking in the window a dozen times and reading the titles [*Molloy* and *Malone Meurt*], vaguely recalling the author's name. He was Irish and I associated him with Joyce." Seaver finally bought the books. After the second reading he was convinced that *Molloy* and *Malone Meurt* were "miracles, two stunning works."

Through further inquiries at Minuit he learned that the third volume in the trilogy, *L'Innommable*, was forthcoming and that an earlier novel, *Murphy*, had been published five years before by Bordas. (Although Seaver did not know it then, *Murphy* had been published in English in 1938, but to no acclaim.) Seaver, by now a Beckett fanatic, rushed to Bordas, hoping that the novel was in print. Not only was it still available, but as Seaver noted, "by the look of the stock in the back of the shop, the original printing was virtually intact." At the same time he learned that French radio was about to record an unproduced play of Beckett's, *En Attendant Godot*. He managed to finagle his way into the studio in the hope of meeting the great unknown author. His wait was as much in vain as that of Vladimir and Estragon, but he did hear Roger Blin, who would later perform innumerable Beckett works, read the part of Lucky for the first time.

Meanwhile Seaver associated himself with *Merlin* and for its premiere issue wrote the first substantial essay in English on Beckett. A copy was sent to Seaver's literary hero. Silence. Then Seaver learned through Jérôme Lindon, publisher at Minuit, that Beckett had a manuscript in English that he had written during the war. Seaver wrote to Beckett asking if he could publish excerpts from the novel in *Merlin*. Again, no response. Then, one rainy afternoon, months later, "a tall, gaunt figure" appeared at Seaver's door, handed in a manuscript in a black binder, and disappeared. That same night, recalled Seaver, "a half-dozen of us—Trocchi; Jane Lougee, *Merlin*'s publisher; two English [*sic*] poets, Christopher Logue and Pat Bowles; a Canadian writer, Charles Hatcher; and I—sat up half the night and read *Watt* aloud, taking turns till our voices gave out, until we had finished it."

In a note accompanying the manuscript Beckett had specified which section from *Watt* they could use in *Merlin*: Mr. Knott's inventory of his possible attire, and possible positioning of furniture in his room, hardly an easily excerptible passage. "I believe," remarked Seaver, "that Mr. Beckett was testing *Merlin*'s integrity by that demand, for he tended to denigrate all his work, we were later to learn, and perversely chose a section which, taken out of context, would, he deemed, have to be rejected."

Naturally, *Merlin* published the extract. The response from the small readership was almost completely negative. "Avant-garde, all right," replied an angry reader, ". . . but let's draw the line at total absurdity." Five percent of the subscriptions—that is, five— were canceled. "We knew we were on the right track," remembered Seaver. "Thereafter not an issue of *Merlin* appeared without something by Beckett."

The continual inclusion of work by Beckett had other negative repercussions—this time from the French postal authorities from whom *Merlin* had been trying to obtain magazine-rate postage. After numerous requests for the cut-rate mailing privilege had been turned down, *Merlin* finally secured a personal interview with a postal bureaucrat to appeal the case. The meeting was short, the appeal denied. Mailing privileges were not given to "organs of propaganda," the postal authority explained. "We were stunned," recalled Seaver. "We pressed for a clarification. 'Messieurs, who is Samuel Beckett?' A writer, a very fine one; we have published several of his works, we said. 'And this Mr. Beckett, does he not finance your magazine? . . . Because, gentlemen, it appears to our examiners that your magazine is an organ of propaganda dedicated to furthering the fame of Mr. Beckett. I'm afraid your case is closed.' "

Undaunted by reader or postal authority reception, the *Merlin* group continued to push Beckett's work. Amazed to learn that *Watt* had been rejected by a number of publishers, *Merlin* decided in the autumn of 1953 to launch a publishing house in order to issue the novel. As Seaver explained: "Having lost relatively little money on the magazine, we determined we would expand and see if we could lose more money more quickly by publishing books." Beckett was paid an advance of 50,000 francs ($100), double the amount paid by Minuit for *Molloy*.

The matter was not so easily settled, however. To their dismay the *Merlin* group learned that under French law they needed to form a company to go into publishing and for that they needed a French manager (*gérant*). This law, they also discovered, applied to *Merlin*, which now, having come under scrutiny by the authorities, was being threatened as well. In addition to the legal woes, there was the small problem of money. In their initial enthusiasm they had contracted for several more books, counting on getting credit from printers around Paris, only to be informed categorically that printing jobs had to be paid up front. The difficulties seemed nearly overwhelming, and serious consideration was given to pulling out of both the magazine and book enterprises, when an unlikely angel appeared on Seaver's doorstep: the dapper and flamboyant Maurice Girodias.

Girodias, then in his mid-thirties, was no stranger to publishing. His father, Englishman Jack Kahane, had founded and run the legendary Obelisk Press in Paris, which published Henry Miller, Anaïs Nin, Lawrence Durrell, Radclyffe Hall, Frank Harris, and D. H. Lawrence. After his father's death in 1939, Girodias began his own publishing firm, Les Éditions du Chêne, specializing in art books. (Continuing Obelisk Press under German occupation would have been impossible. Girodias also deemed it wise to begin using his French mother's last name to avoid persecution as a Jew.) Since Les Éditions du Chêne did not publish work that could be construed as at all critical of the occupying forces, it actually flourished during the war.

In 1945, while continuing his French imprint, Girodias revived Obelisk Press, reissuing Miller's *Tropic of Cancer* among other titles. But the next year his legal troubles began. First he was sued for libel by Félix Gouin, French Socialist Party leader, for publishing a pamphlet by Resistance leader Yves Farge critical of collusion between the government and big business. Girodias no sooner won the case than he, along with two other French publishers, was prosecuted by the government for publishing obscene books: Miller's *Tropic of Cancer*, *Tropic of Capricorn*, and *Black Spring*. This was the first obscenity trial in France since the celebrated cases involving Flaubert's *Madame Bovary* and Baudelaire's

Les Fleurs du Mal in 1857. The French intellectual establishment rallied to his defense, but for two years *l'affaire Miller* continued. Ultimately, the government dropped the case. By now Girodias was nearly broke. A short time later, through a bad business deal made with a creditor, he lost all of his publishing businesses.

For nearly three years Girodias lived in what he described as "near-complete bumhood." Devastated by the loss of his publishing houses, embittered against what he saw as the government's enfranchisement of bourgeois morality, he felt desolate, unable even to contemplate rising above his circumstances. Then, in the spring of 1953, he founded Olympia Press, in order to "escape complete social and economic annihilation." He reasoned that "publishing books in English, in Paris, books that would sell easily because they would belong to the 'not to be sold in USA and UK' category, appeared . . . the only possible way for me to make money and build up a new publishing business in spite of my lack of capital." It was at this point that he learned from *Merlin* editor Austryn Wainhouse that Collection Merlin, as the magazine's book-publishing enterprise was called, needed a French partner. Thus his appearance in early spring 1953 at Seaver's lodgings; thus the birth of Collection Merlin–Olympia Press.

The deal Girodias offered the young expatriates was simple: He would agree to act as *gérant*, would put up the money for the books, would allow Collection Merlin total editorial autonomy. In exchange, the *Merlin* group would let Girodias publish under his own imprint several of the books, besides *Watt*, for which Collection Merlin had already contracted. These included English translations of Jean Genet's *The Thief's Journal*; the Marquis de Sade's *La Philosophie dans le Boudoir*, and Georges Bataille's *Histoire de l'Oeil*. Additionally, Girodias wanted to sign up Seaver and other bilingual Paris residents as paid translators, perhaps even as writers of erotica. "He was eloquent, suave, compelling," Seaver recalled. The arrangement was quickly concluded, both sides ecstatic. For Girodias, it meant a fixed stable of translators and writers; for the expatriates, the deal represented not only an end to *Merlin*'s legal and cash-flow difficulties, but also improvement of their generally precarious personal financial situations, because of the expected commissions for translation and writing. Amazingly, the agreement was actually what it seemed, benefiting both parties for a good long while.

Soon after the joint venture was formed, the *Merlin* group took Beckett to meet Girodias. They went en masse—Seaver, Trocchi, Logue, and other members of the *Merlin* group—parading "their writer" up the Boulevard St.-Germain, exuberantly chattering, forcing a wondrous Beckett to turn his head continually from side to side to catch the reverential, ponderous, as well as mundane, remarks being thrown his way. But once at 13 Rue Jacob, Olympia's headquarters, Beckett became silent. According to Girodias: "There was nothing you could say or do to get Beckett to enter into any conversation, to utter any opinion or to make any statement. We went ahead with the book because of the *Merlin* enthusiasm. By then I had read it, and I knew we had no hope of selling the book to tourists—they were only interested in porno."

Deirdre Bair points out in her biography of Beckett that the author's reticence may have been due to concern over being published by Girodias. In 1938, Beckett had refused a commission from Girodias's father to translate Sade for Obelisk, not because he was unenthusiastic about Sade but because he did not want his name associated with a press that published primarily erotica. Now, however, he did not object. There were at least three reasons: first, he genuinely appreciated the enthusiasm of the *Merlin jeunes*; second, after several rejections, he was eager to get *Watt* in print in English, as it might result in foreign sales in Britain and the United States; and third, the book would be issued under the dual imprint Collection Merlin–Olympia Press, and thus would be separate from the main Olympia enterprise—pornography.

As Beckett refused to make any changes to the text, the printing of *Watt* was accomplished promptly. In May 1953, the first Merlin–Olympia title appeared. According to Girodias, although only 2,000 copies were printed, it took five years for the first edition to sell out. The publication of *Watt* ended neither the Merlin-Olympia collaboration nor the relationship with Beckett. Over the next few years Merlin-Olympia brought out a number of other works including a stunning first novel by Wainhouse, *Hedyphagetica*; a book of poems by Logue, *Wand & Quadrant*; and in the spring of 1954, *Molloy*, in an English translation by Patrick Bowles in collaboration with Beckett.

The *Merlin* group's move into translating Beckett came about simply because they wanted to publish more of his work, but as he had ceased writing in English, he would not give them anything new. As for the older work, aside from *Watt*, Beckett was disinclined to have any of it issued. Translating Beckett, however, proved to be a monumental undertaking.

According to Seaver, who took on translating Beckett's story "La Fin," the process was excruciating. Each day they would meet for about five hours at La Coupole. At the end of the first week, Seaver tallied up the number of pages brought into English and discovered that despite thirty to thirty-five hours of work they had managed to render only four or five pages of the original. "Every word, every phrase, was gone over with meticulous care," remarked Seaver. "Sam is the most polite as well as the nicest of men, so that whenever a word had to be changed, he prefaced it with how much he liked what I had done, 'but . . . ,' or else he would say of his own French, "That's impossible, it can't be translated,' as if what he had written wasn't any good." What Beckett wanted, Seaver realized, was not so much a translation as a re-creation of the work in English, but one that was wholly faithful to the French. In the end they achieved just that. The final product was, in Seaver's words, "a complete redoing of the original."

With *Molloy*, Beckett decided a different approach was needed. He asked Bowles for a draft of the entire novel, which he would then revise. But he cautioned that Bowles should not merely translate the book, but "write a new book in the new language." In the meantime, Beckett had been translating *En Attendant Godot* himself, as Barney Rosset, then starting up Grove Press, had offered him a contract for the book in English.

Despite Rosset's attempts to sway him to move swiftly on the translation with promises of large sales and an American production of the play, Beckett could not be persuaded to produce the re-creation quickly. He had stated to Rosset at the outset that it would take him six months to a year to reinvent *Godot* in English, and he refused to be hurried. Rosset waited. As Seaver noted, the only benefit Beckett had really received from him on "La Fin" was that Seaver made the process go faster. "Otherwise he would have agonized over it." But with *Waiting for Godot*, Beckett would not let anyone remove the agony. In fact, from then on he always did his own "translations," in his own time frame, his own way.

As SERIOUS as the members of the *Merlin* group were about literature, they managed to indulge themselves from time to time in the pleasures of Paris. *Paris Review* editor George Plimpton remembered going one summer with Trocchi, Lougee, Logue, and others from *Merlin* to the famous Quat'zarts Ball, the wild all-night party hosted by French art students. The Quat'zarts began with a raucous half-naked procession through the streets. Next, the revelers entered the Théâtre Wagram, where at ten the doors to the packed hall were locked, and not opened until dawn. Music and dancing started, followed at around midnight by the "spectacles." These consisted of "living statue" tableaux performed by different ateliers in the boxes and on specially rigged scaffolding in the balcony. A spotlight moved from spectacle to spectacle, illuminating the participants. A grand prize was given for the most spectacular.

Plimpton's hosts had not prepared a tableau, but only fifteen minutes before the spotlight would hit their box, Trocchi announced that he and Lougee would present a spectacle no one would ever forget. Not only that, it was guaranteed to win first prize: Trocchi and Lougee would copulate on the velvet balustrade of the box while the others would stand in attendance and fan them with palm fronds. "All of this came as somewhat of a surprise to the French student-hosts, and also to Alex's [Trocchi's] friends, especially Jane [Lougee]," recalled Plimpton. "But such was the excitement of the moment—the booming from the military bands, the frenzied movement of the dancers, the searchlight in the darkness—that the scheme seemed inspired."

Lougee undressed and got into position. The others, meanwhile, gathered up sheaves of straw to serve as palm fronds. In response to shouts from above that Trocchi needed to make his entrance, he came charging up the stairs. But in his haste he hit his head on an overhang and knocked himself out. "When the searchlight reached the 'tableau' it illuminated the back of a naked girl half-reclining on the balustrade, her head turned away looking back, as if expecting someone, into the recesses of the box where in the shadows, a single figure [Plimpton] was discernible waving a stalk-like sheaf of straw. No one knew what to make of it." They did not win the grand prize but were rumored to have been favorably mentioned for having the spectacle with the most "symbolic effect." Upon reviving, Trocchi expressed his fury: "Why didn't one of you take my place?" he queried. "No one was quite sure how to answer that," remarked Plimpton.

IN BETWEEN such wild antics as these, the *Merlin* group kept up its publishing enterprises. Although none of the Merlin–Olympia titles was helping Girodias pay even the printers' bills, the *Merlin* group, as translators and "d.b." (dirty book) writers—the term was Girodias's—were contributing substantially to Olympia's coffers. At the same time, the young writers profited from the arrangement, as Girodias paid them, often in advance, between $500 and $1,000 per manuscript. While by no means a sizable amount, such a sum could keep a nonextravagant expatriate in food, drink, and lodging for a good many months in the early fifties, when a room could be had for about $15 a month, a café meal for well under a dollar.

Of those associated with *Merlin*, everyone but Jane Lougee contributed to Olympia's output of d.b.'s. Richard Seaver translated Apollinaire's erotic novel *Les Exploits d'un Jeune Don Juan*; Austryn Wainhouse rendered Sade's *La Philosophie dans le Boudoir* and Bataille's *Histoire de l'Oeil*. Christopher Logue, as Count Palmiro Vicarion, authored an erotic espionage tale called simply *Lust* and another potboiler entitled *White Thighs*. Patrick Bowles, writing as Marcus van Heller, contributed *Roman Orgy*. Iris Owens, another talented writer associated with *Merlin*, as Harriet Daimler wrote a number of books, including *The Woman Thing*.

Alexander Trocchi, though, was by far the most prolific of the group. He translated Apollinaire's *Les Onze Mille Verges*, reading aloud at a café each night the parts of the translation he had completed that day. He was also turned into Frances Lengel and wrote the novel *Helen and Desire*, which according to Girodias "was to become the model of a new brand of erotic writing." Later, under the pseudonym Carmencita de las Lunas, he wrote *With Open Mouth*, another profitable title. Trocchi also authored a serious novel under his own name for Olympia, *Young Adam*. No sooner had the novel been published in France than Trocchi learned it had been accepted by an established publisher in the States. To his chagrin, he had to inform the American house that it was no longer available. George Plimpton also sent Olympia some sample chapters of a porn novel, but to his surprise they were rejected. Girodias "had never turned down anything anybody in the literary colony wrote for him," noted the *Paris Review* editor, "but two chapters of this thing ... were quite enough."

The contributors to Olympia, Girodias observed, "usually were genuine writers and even the most one-sided and single-minded creations of that time often reveal attractive talents." They did indeed. Trocchi later wrote a startling, extremely good novel, *Cain's Book*. Logue, when he returned to poetry, produced some excellent verse. Seaver went on to become an editor at Grove Press and other houses, where he distinguished himself as a discerning champion of the avant-garde. Another of Olympia's authors, Alfred Chester, who was also on the *Merlin* fringe, wrote the powerful and disturbing novel *The Exquisite Corpse* and a number of superb short stories.

* * *

GIRODIAS ALSO found talent (and profits) beyond the *Merlin* group. Henry Miller sent him *Plexus*. Through association with French publisher Jean-Jacques Pauvert, with whom Girodias shared an office for a time, he acquired the English rights to the now classic sadomasochistic novel *Histoire d'O*. Mason Hoffenberg, longtime Paris hanger-on, repeatedly tried to sell Girodias his work, convinced that "his manuscripts were glorious achievements and that they were thick enough to be converted into books," remembered Girodias, who disagreed with Hoffenberg's assessment. One day Hoffenberg appeared with his friend Terry Southern. "I had never met Terry before," Girodias recalled, "although I had heard about his wild sense of humor, and I sensed that working with Terry would help bring out the constructive aspects of Mason's submerged talents. We agreed that the story should be about sweet, blue-eyed, curvaceous Candy." *Candy*, by "Maxwell Kenton," was one of Girodias's all-time hits, and a best-seller in the United States as well when it was reissued by G. P. Putnam's Sons.

Within a year or so of its founding, Olympia Press was beginning to turn rather handsome profits. Part of the reason for Girodias's early success was his publishing stratagem, which he vigorously maintained for most porn titles through the press's first five years. It was extremely simple, and extremely lucrative. Rather than publish a book first and then sell it, he would invent titles and authors, then write imaginary blurbs for the d.b.'s to stir the libidos of his subscribers (mostly in England), to whom his catalogue of new books would be sent. According to Girodias, "They immediately responded with orders and money, thanks to which we were again able to eat, drink, write, and print. I could again advance money to my authors, and they hastened to turn in manuscripts which more or less fitted the descriptions."

This process was reserved solely for Olympia's pseudonymous erotica. A number of titles arrived completed, most of them unpublishable. But one manuscript in particular proved to be an exception. It was by a Russian émigré professor who taught at Cornell University, Vladimir Nabokov. The book was *Lolita*.

Through Nabokov's Paris agent, Girodias learned that the book had been sent to a number of American presses but had been rejected by all of them. Girodias, "struck with wonder, carried away by this unbelievable phenomenon: the apparently effortless transposition of the rich Russian literary tradition into modern English fiction," signed up the book immediately.

Initial reaction to *Lolita*'s publication, in September 1955, was hostile—not from the critics, who didn't even bother to review it, but from his subscribers: "Why are you publishing junk like that?" "You're giving yourself a bad name." "Trash like this is a sheer waste of time." "Any more like the last one and you can strike my name from your list." Then, more than a year later, eminent English novelist Graham Greene, in an interview with the *Times Literary Supplement*, pronounced *Lolita* one of the "three best books of the year." This, quite naturally, stirred up a great deal of commotion in England. Critics took sides. Public debates were held. Sales soared. Girodias thought he might have a best-seller in the making.

And he would have had, save for the intervention by the French authorities. As a result of the novel's new celebrity, *la brigade mondaine* (the worldly brigade), as the French vice squad was charmingly called, arrived at his office and seized twenty-five titles, including *Lolita*, for inspection. A couple of weeks later, all of the books seized were banned in France. Meanwhile, in an ironic turn, American customs had deemed the book not obscene, thus clearing its way for sale of rights in the United States. This was now, Girodias figured, his best shot at getting the book back in print, but in the interim he appealed the French decision. In the end, Girodias triumphed on all scores. *Lolita* was sold to G. P. Putnam's Sons in the United States and to Weidenfeld & Nicolson in Britain. The French ban was lifted. Not long after, Girodias and Nabokov finally had a best-seller.

Success, however, was still not quite as unfettered as it should have been for Girodias. He had become embroiled in a major struggle with Nabokov, who felt that the 17.5 percent due Girodias on all American sales (as called for in the Olympia–

Nabokov contract) was excessive, if not dishonest. The "Lolitaga-tion," as Nabokov termed it, dragged on for years, but Girodias prevailed, earning by some accounts more than $300,000 on the deal.

This was not the last of Girodias's problems with authors. J. P. Donleavy, whose book *The Ginger Man* was published the same year as *Lolita*, and eventually to great acclaim and large sales, also sued Girodias, claiming that he had been cheated out of a portion of his royalties. He kept up litigation for fifteen years, finally winning, at least in principle, and not in the courts but by buying the press at a bankruptcy auction in 1972. Unfortunately for Donleavy, his strategy backfired. Not only did he no longer have a case, as he now owned the press he was suing, but the debts so outstripped the assets that there was no way to relaunch Olym-pia without a considerable investment.

Nor was *l'affaire Lolita* the end of Girodias's problems with the law. *Lolita* was banned again in 1959, then unbanned after Gir-odias agreed to drop his suit against the government. In other cases, though, he was not so lucky. By the late fifties a concerted effort was mounted against Olympia, the charge *outrage aux bonnes mœurs par la voie du livre*—outrage to propriety by way of books. By 1965 he had been indicted and acquitted twenty-five times, had racked up fines totaling $80,000, and had been banned from publishing books in France for eighty years. He eventually won against the government, but the continual litiga-tion, in combination with other bad business deals, including an absurd adventure in running a nightclub, culminated in finan-cial disaster.

At the same time, the gradual lifting of restrictions on "ob-scene" literature in the United States and Britain resulted in greatly increased competition for Olympia; its status as premier pornography publisher was reduced and its sales adversely af-fected. In a sense, Girodias's mission, to attack the priggish estab-lishment, was completed. "The first shock was over, and formerly obsessed readers had become used to the notion that their clan-destine world was open to all, that the secret was a fake, that nothing was reprehensible or forbidden," Girodias commented. "Those literary orgies, those torrents of systematic bad taste were quite certainly instrumental in clearing the air, and clearing out a few mental cobwebs." But as in all successful revolts, victory disarmed the revolutionary. By the early 1960s Girodias had nothing much left to fight for; in winning the war, he essentially put himself out of business.

Yet when the barricades were still up, the struggle was glorious. Not only did Girodias's enterprise make him, for a while at least, a considerable amount of money. More important, the little porn press that could also managed, as a sideline, to catapult into prominence some of the most important writers of the latter half of the century, among them Beckett and Nabokov. Others, like Trocchi, Southern, and Donleavy, were launched in their careers. And more than a handful of expatriates paid the rent thanks to Girodias's d.b. mill. In the end, Olympia's fostering of distinguished international literature in the mid-fifties set a record that any major publisher could envy.

The magazines too not only provided expatriates in Paris a forum for publishing but also brought new French writing to the attention of American editors. Barney Rosset's Grove Press, which had first published Beckett in the United States, hired Beckett's "discoverer," Richard Seaver, in the late fifties. With his arrival, the house increased even further its already substantial investment in French writing, adding Genet, Duras, Robbe-Grillet, Robert Pinget, Albertine Sarrazin, Pauline Réage, and many others to its list. Among those Grove did not publish, such as Sartre, Nathalie Sarraute, Claude Mauriac, and Claude Simon, George Braziller generally did. In Britain, John Calder performed a similar service.

A great many of these French writers had made their English-language debuts in *Merlin* or *The Paris Review*. *Evergreen Review*, in some ways *Merlin*'s logical successor, was first published in New York by Rosset in 1957 and continued to bring international writing to the American public. That an American-based review could now do what formerly was the province of the little Paris magazines reflected the growing interest in contemporary European literature and, moreover, the impact these magazines had made on discovering for English-language editors and readers new literary trends in France. This is not to say that these authors would not have eventually appeared in print in English translation, but certainly the pioneering efforts of *Merlin* and of Seaver (who also assumed a major responsibility at *Evergreen Review*) hastened their arrival on American shores. In sum, the Paris-based reviews gave opportunities to the young expatriate writers and contributed to promoting awareness of some of the most impressive and influential European literature of this part of the century.

Chapter Seven

The Paris Review

THE EARLY history of *The Paris Review* is in many ways the story of the Parisian expatriate literary community itself. Almost every anglophone writer and would-be writer in Paris in the early to middle 1950s seemed at one time or another to be involved with the review, as contributor, advisory editor, or playmate. In short, *The Paris Review* was the dominant English-language literary magazine in Paris in the 1950s. From its inception, it was a major presence, an event.

The magazine was originally the idea of Peter Matthiessen and Harold (Doc) Humes. The two had met at Le Dôme, in Montparnasse, in the spring of 1951. Humes was at that time publishing a magazine, the *News-Post*, part gossip column, part guide to restaurants and nightlife. Matthiessen had recently arrived in Paris and was working on his first novel, *Race Rock*.

Humes was "a remarkable figure," Matthiessen recalled: "burly and curly ... with a deep laugh ... aggressive, warm-hearted, curious, yet with convictions on every subject ... all of which made him impossible." As for Matthiessen, "he was young, suave, inquisitive, quite handsome. He and his wife, Patsy, were *the* attractive young couple around Paris, possessing something of the same sort of allure . . . as did the Crosbys [Harry and Caresse] in the twenties."

After a few meetings Humes offered Matthiessen the unpaid position of fiction editor at the *News-Post*, as he had decided to include a short story in each issue of the magazine. Matthiessen agreed, acquiring as his first story "The Sun and the Still-Born Stars" by the then unknown Terry Southern. But Southern's short story, according to Matthiessen, "was so much better than [Humes's] magazine that I persuaded him to put to death the . . . *News-Post* and start a new literary magazine, using Terry's story all over again."

Humes, never one to be timid, began planning how the new venture would be organized and what kind of writing would be featured. He also decided that he would naturally be editor in chief. Matthiessen could edit the fiction. "It didn't take long to realize that the magazine just wasn't going to work with Doc in charge," Matthiessen remembered. "Lovable and intelligent though he was, he couldn't work with people. So I got in touch with [George] Plimpton, who was at Cambridge in England. I knew he had run the Harvard magazine [*The Harvard Lampoon*] and I asked him to come over to Paris and run this one. He said sure—can't imagine why—and it ruined his whole life."

From conception to reality, that is, from Matthiessen's summoning of Plimpton to the publication of the first issue of the new magazine, took a while—almost two years. Meanwhile, Humes and Matthiessen had joined forces with several others, including William Pène du Bois, Thomas Guinzburg, John Train, and William Styron. Styron, at twenty-six, was the only one in the group who could actually claim to be a writer, having just published his first novel, *Lie Down in Darkness.* Their usual meeting place was a little bar in Montparnasse, Le Chaplain. Styron recalled the scene vividly:

You could carve your name with an outstretched forefinger in the smoke of the place, but the refreshment was not too expensive, and in its ambience—quiet enough for conversation yet lively enough to forestall boredom, gloom, self-conscious lapses—it seemed to be a fine place to sit and work up a sweat about new magazines and other such far-fetched literary causes. . . . The young *patron* of Le Chaplain, named Paul, by his own proclamation loved America almost as much for "*ses littérateurs*" as for "*ses dollars*" (winks, knowing laughter, toasts in beer to two great nations), and if *The Paris Review* were to celebrate a patron saint, it would possibly have to be this wiry, tough, frenetic Algerian with the beneficent smile, who could vault over the bar and stiff-arm a drunk out into the night in less time than it takes to say Edgar Poe, and return, bland as butter, to take up where he left off about Symbolist imagery. Try starting a little magazine at Toots Shor's. *Les américains en Amérique!* indeed.

By the late spring of 1952, the midnight sessions at Le Chaplain had actually begun to produce results. A real planning meeting, as distinguished from the brainstorming sessions at the bar, was scheduled one afternoon at Matthiessen's light-filled studio apartment on an "Utrillo-like back street," the Rue de Perceval in Montparnasse. Train, Styron, Humes, Matthiessen, du Bois, and Guinzburg had been glumly trying out names for some time when Plimpton arrived bearing two bottles of absinthe. "Everyone was at a low ebb," remembered Styron, "and it is quite probable that once again the group would have broken up had it not been for Plimpton's absinthe." Whether it was really the absinthe that hastened the birth of the review is still questionable in the minds of the participants, but whatever the reason, by that evening the new magazine had a name and a fledgling identity. The simple title, *The Paris Review*, suggested perhaps by Matthiessen, perhaps by Train, met with unanimous approval.

Launching the publication, however, took more than a couple of bottles of absinthe and a name. There were complications: Plimpton was still a student at Cambridge and not actually on the scene except during holidays; Humes, who with his "experience" publishing the *News-Post* was expected actually to manage the magazine, chose instead to spend his time reading and working on his own writing, explaining that it was better for the others to learn for themselves; in addition, in order to comply with French law, they needed a French partner.

The lack of adequate capital was also an obstacle. During one early discussion Plimpton announced he had hit on a scheme to raise funds. He would offer the Paris *Herald Tribune* a literary page that would run in each issue. This would make so much money that the new venture could be not only safely launched but bankrolled for years. When a question was raised as to how the newspaper would fit the "literary page" into its already packed format, Plimpton explained that the *Trib* could simply eliminate the stock market pages. "After all, none of us read the stock pages, did we?"

Needless to say, the *Herald Tribune*, if ever approached, did not take Plimpton up on his grand scheme. All the same, enough money (around $1,000) finally was found to print, ship, and distribute the inaugural issue. The rather conservative established French journal *La Table Ronde* agreed to sponsor the new venture and allow the *Review* reprint rights (in translation) to work appearing in the French journal. The French magazine also provided the *Review* with tiny office space at its headquarters at 8 Rue Garancière.

Now that technical and business matters were settled, the group resumed discussions of what the magazine should (and should not) be. On this point, they were fairly united. According to John Train, "We wanted to get away from the style of most of the other American literary quarterlies, with *Partisan Review* in the lead, which were steeped in literary and political theory, as were our French counterparts." Translated, this meant no excursions into politics or polemical critical essays, "just the prime matter, except perhaps for occasional newsy pieces on what was brewing on the European literary and artistic scene."

Although almost from its inception *The Paris Review* saw itself in relation to American and British literary magazines, setting up offices in New York and London and arranging for distribution in the United States and the United Kingdom, it attempted as well to steer a middle ground between its more immediate competition, the Paris-based *Points* and *Merlin*. As Plimpton saw it, *Points* was dedicated to publishing the work, nearly exclusively, of generally unknown writers; *Merlin* was an English-language ver-

War correspondent Ernest Hemingway conferring with a young member of the French Resistance shortly before the liberation of Paris.

Not content to sit out the war in Paris, Hemingway attached himself to the U.S. Twenty-second Infantry commanded by Colonel Charles (Buck) Lanham (*right*) for the push into Germany.

TOP: PFC Irwin Shaw (*reading map*) was assigned to the army's Signal Corps. The former Hollywood screenwriter was now responsible for writing scripts to accompany the official newsreel film footage shot by, among others, cameraman Philip Drell, who sits behind Shaw in the jeep. BOTTOM: Outside Paris, Shaw and Drell pass out candy, gum, and cigarettes to a thankful group of newly liberated citizens. French writer Simone de Beauvoir noted that for her the GIs were "freedom incarnate."

Mary Welsh, Time-Life correspondent, at about the time she began her tumultuous affair with Hemingway.

Gertrude Stein, Alice B. Toklas, and their dog, Basket II, surrounded by American soldiers. "The American army is delightful I like them so much, and it is all every day just that way," wrote Stein.

Stein, Toklas, and Basket II in their Paris apartment on the Rue Christine.

Richard and Ellen Wright, who left the United States in 1946 to take up permanent residency in Paris.

Richard Wright in his newfound role of European intellectual. As his fame rose in Europe, his star fell dramatically in the United States. By the time of his premature death in 1960 he had largely been abandoned by American readers.

James Baldwin, struggling young novelist during his early Paris years. "Which would end soonest," he wondered, "the Great Adventure or me?"

sion of the French *engagé* reviews. *The Paris Review*, on the other hand, intended to accept and encourage submissions (and subscriptions) from abroad.

From the start, the editors also actively sought out the famous, first as subjects for the now legendary "Writers at Work" interviews, and subsequently as contributors. The interview strategy, in Plimpton's words, "was done in part so as to be able to put a famous writer's name on the cover to entice readers to buy the magazine and by indirection, having read the interview, to wander on and read the work of someone just starting off and with no reputation at all." (For the first published interview Plimpton approached one of the most renowned literary personages at Cambridge, E. M. Forster, who enthusiastically agreed to contribute his thoughts on writing.)

Unlike *Merlin* and *Points*, which eschewed any attempts at commercialization, the *Paris Review* editors were savvy enough to realize from the beginning that noncommercial literary and artistic work would not be undermined by using commercial devices to get the magazine read and distributed. A phrase from Malcolm Cowley, "Enterprise in the service of art," was Plimpton's motto. It did not hurt either that the highly talented editors were well connected with a number of very impressive writers, albeit many of them just emerging. They had as well the critical acumen to recognize artistic excellence and the courage to publish the work of these writers.

During the fall and winter of 1952, despite the fact that Plimpton was still spending most of his time at Cambridge, the magazine was finally put together. Styron was asked to write a preface. "After a while," recalled Train, "he produced a laborious piece wrestling with his own particular literary theories. It was my task to edit this effusion, and I blue-pencilled it with vigor. Styron, nettled, fired back a rejoinder which unlike the original submission had feeling and strength."

It was this "Letter to an Editor" that they decided to print, as well they should have, for Styron's remarks were exactly in keeping with the feeling behind the *Review*: "Let's by all means leave out the lordly tone and merely say: Dear Reader, THE PARIS REVIEW *hopes* to emphasize creative work—fiction and poetry—not to the exclusion of criticism, but with the aim in mind of merely removing criticism from the dominating place it holds in most literary magazines and putting it where it belongs, i.e., somewhere in the back of the book." Other ruminations of Styron's focused on the question of whether this generation would produce writing of any note. This apparently had been a major part of his earlier, rejected preface, but here, after a defense of Norman Mailer and James Jones, he stated simply that if a writer did not think he could create literature worthy of himself, his place, and his time, "then he'd better pack up his Underwood, or become a critic."

The first issue of the magazine was evidence that Styron's remarks reflected the prevailing philosophy of the editors. Literature and art dominate. The fiction in the first issue included a story by French writer Antoine Blondin (in translation) and pieces by three then unknown writers: Peter Matthiessen, Eugene Walter, and Terry Southern. The poetry offerings featured works by Donald Hall (poetry editor), Robert Bly, and F. George Steiner (who would drop the "F." and become a distinguished critic). Art was represented in a portfolio of drawings by a Paris resident, American designer Tom Keogh; the essay form, by Henry de Montherlant. The interview was with Forster, conducted by two of Plimpton's Cambridge acquaintances, scholars P. N. Furbank and F. J. H. Haskell. In their proper place, "in the back of the book," were translated literary commentaries by French writer C. Chesnaie and Italian critic Giacomo Antonini as well as a piece on Paris by the *Review*'s own John Train.

BY THE time the first number of *The Paris Review* appeared, in February 1953, Humes had returned to the States to take up graduate studies at Harvard. Train took over as unofficial managing editor and Humes was "demoted" to advertising and circulation manager, at least on the masthead. In reality, he had nothing to do with these departments, but the editors did not feel it right to eliminate this founding father's name altogether. Humes, however, became enraged and rushed down to New York to intercept the copies of the magazine destined for the United States. At the dock he broke open the packing crates and, with a red rubber stamp bearing his name and an editorial title, began stamping each issue of the *Review* just above the masthead. He managed to get through five hundred copies or so until his arm gave out. When the next issue appeared, his name had been reinstated at the top of the masthead, appearing along with that of editor Plimpton, who was now back in Paris; fiction editor Matthiessen; art editor du Bois; and poetry editor Hall, who was studying at Oxford. Humes was removed, by the fourth issue, to advisory editor, despite his nonadvisory role.

ASIDE FROM the rebellious and eccentric Humes, the founders of the new magazine were very different from the literary renegades who had started up *Merlin*. Most of them came from money: both Train and Plimpton had attorney fathers; Guinzburg's father was cofounder and president of Viking Press; du Bois was the son of established artist Guy Pène du Bois. All were well educated at prestigious institutions: Plimpton and Train at Harvard; Matthiessen and Guinzburg at Yale; Styron at Duke. Even Humes had earned a degree from MIT. More like Henry James's Americans abroad than Henry Miller's, the *Review* founders were members of the upper crust, not terribly interested in straying too far from their roots.

As a result, Paris never represented a refuge from the United States. It was simply a great place to dawdle in for a while, to expand one's living experiences. This is not to imply that the group did not gain a great deal from being in France. But there is a significant difference between feeling exiled, as did Wright, and to some degree Baldwin, and being on an extended holiday. Writer Evan Connell, Jr., speaking of the *Paris Review* crowd, observed that "no one really thought of himself as an expatriate.

I mean, we all figured that we'd be in Paris for a while, but not permanently. As it was, we were all running off to other places—Barcelona, Florence, London—to see what the rest of Europe looked like."

Paris, however, was not absent from *The Paris Review*. Indeed, the early issues were imbued with a sense of France and French life and letters, and in both scope and substance the journal was far more Eurocentric than any comparable literary magazine published in the States. Every issue included work by French or European writers (usually in excellent translations) and like *Merlin* served as an important conduit for younger French authors to become known in America. In addition, a fair amount of the fiction and poetry by the Americans abroad had France as a backdrop, and in some cases as a focus. The editors profited (and appropriated what they could) from the literary scene surrounding them in Paris.

At the same time, they were shrewd in their assessments of what their major constituency—American readers—wanted to read and know, always ensuring a balance between known and unknown writers, generally avoiding highly experimental work. Or as one observer put it, "*The Paris Review* was quite adept at publishing not the real avant-garde, but the mainstream avant-garde." There is, of course, nothing wrong with such a position. The avant-garde *Merlin* lasted but a few years; *The Paris Review* is still a major force in literary publishing. Over its nearly forty years of existence it has consistently offered its readers quality writing and has played a major role in establishing a great number of literary reputations.

THE EARLY days of the review were marked by tremendous enthusiasm, hard work, a fair amount of chaos, and a great deal of fun. The work involved not only editing the magazine but promoting it as well. To this end, hundreds of posters were printed up and pasted on the walls of buildings, on light poles, in café toilets, and on the sides of open-air *pissotières* on the street.

Plimpton recalled that this was usually done late at night, "in flying squads." Hawkers were also employed (on commission) to sell the magazine on the streets and in bars and cafés; subscription salesmen were hired to go door to door to garner an 800-franc [three-dollar] commitment for a year's worth of the review from unsuspecting English-speaking housewives. Among the subscription sellers was the young English writer Colin Wilson, who also helped out in the office for a while. Although later tremendously successful as an author, how well he sold subscriptions is unknown: he reportedly absconded with the receipts one day and returned to England.

Besides these immediate attempts to sell the magazine, the editors made a concerted effort to distribute the journal as widely as possible in France, the United States, and Britain by hooking up with established distributors. The strategy worked well: within a year of its appearance *The Paris Review* had increased its circulation by a third. In addition, the editors actively sought out advertisers, in Paris, New York, and London, and here too they met with success. The press took an interest in the new review, which contributed greatly to furthering subscriptions, sales, and advertising. "A lively and stimulating venture," wrote *The Sunday Times* of London. The *New York Herald Tribune* described the magazine as "a promising reminder of the old days when the Left Bank was headquarters for a whole department of world letters." A long, glowing article in *Newsweek* noted that the *Review* was "the first really promising development in youthful, advance guard, or experimental writing in a long time."

But the editors hardly spent all their time focused on "enterprise in the service of art." In the great tradition of the Lost Generation of the twenties and thirties, they seemed as dedicated to enjoying Paris as to issuing and promoting a quality magazine. Rather than cloister themselves in their headquarters, they extended their editing and discussion sessions into bars and cafés. As a result, *The Paris Review* was a very public enterprise, enmeshed with the vibrant life of the Left Bank. This exuberance comes through particularly in the magazine's early issues, when it was still more Paris-centered.

There was a practical reason as well for removing the editorial functions to the cafés: the stolid, austere atmosphere at the *Table Ronde* offices, described by Plimpton as "the kind of silence one associates with clerking in nineteenth-century London," was in decided contrast to the buoyant, bustling energy of the new magazine and its editors. And there was an additional problem: at six o'clock sharp, the *Table Ronde* offices were locked. As none of the *Review* staff was entrusted with a key, anyone working after this hour was forced to descend through the windows, dropping some six feet onto the Rue Garancière below. Occasionally, Plimpton remembered, "this exodus—which must have looked like the flight of second-story men surprised in mid-job— coincided with the return of the mounted Garde Républicaine from an official function." Apparently this elite guard never bothered even to inquire why several young people were plum- meting down the façade of the adjacent building. Perhaps, as Plimpton surmised, they felt it was "beneath their dignity to do anything about it."

Around the corner from the nominal office was the real head- quarters of *The Paris Review*, the Café de Tournon, just in front of the Palais du Luxembourg. There, on any given evening, could be found the magazine's staff mingling with myriad other ex- patriates. One of the regular habitués, novelist Eugene Walter, who became an advisory editor of the *Review*, perhaps in part because of his frequenting of the Tournon, remarked that the café "developed into a scintillation center, a firebox, a winter garden, a zoological park. . . . Everybody turned up sooner or later." "Everybody" included the *Merlin* group: Trocchi, Lougee (often with her Siamese cat), Logue, Bowles, Wainhouse, Seaver. Neither group viewed the other in terms of competition. The *Review*, in fact, quickly turned the *Merlin* editors, particularly Logue, Bowles, and Trocchi, into contributors, and after the demise of *Merlin* gave Bowles a job as editor.

Other Tournon regulars were often *Paris Review* contributors, or destined to be: Max Steele, Evan Connell, Jr., Alfred Chester, and John Phillips (J. P. Marquand, Jr.), who became, like Steele and Walter, an advisory editor. Animated conversations, occasional arguments, proclamations of various sorts filled the air until two A.M., when the café's proprietor ousted the convocation. "It was all immensely young and stimulating and fun," reflected Walter, "and now seems beyond belief innocent and productive, in this establishment which was literary salon, permanent editorial board meeting, message center, short order eatery, debating club, study hall. Four literary reviews in English, one in French; who knows how many books and other works springing forth from this noisy, smokey, clattery, raunchy, beat-up café?"

As Walter noted, far more than just chitchat went on in the cafés. Connell remembered a memorable lunch with Christopher Logue:

> None of us had any money to speak of, and Christopher was reputedly the poorest of us all. I heard a story that he was living on the equivalent of six dollars a month. I liked Christopher a lot and so I asked Max [Steele] if he thought Christopher would be offended if I took him to lunch, at least [feed] him for one day. Max suggested that I make a business proposition to Christopher: lunch in exchange for his criticism on a story. Christopher agreed, and I brought along a little five-page story. I thought he'd skim through it and talk about it for a couple of minutes and then we'd have a nice lunch. Not at all. He took this thing apart—he must have talked for an hour—not paragraph by paragraph, or sentence by sentence, or phrase by phrase, but word by word. He'd say, "This word is useless. Move this word up here." It had never occurred to me that the structure of the prose could be so important. I just sat there horrified for about an hour. For better or worse Christopher has affected the style I use more than anybody else. . . . At Stanford, [Wallace] Stegner and those people would point out that too many words ended in "ly" or something. But Christopher was just ferocious about style and the structure of English prose. That sort of exchange went on between writers.

Terry Southern rarely stopped by the Tournon or other cafés where such literary discussions took place. He preferred the much seedier Old Navy, where, at least to the Ivy Leaguers, he always seemed surrounded by "bizarre companions talking a strange—'hey, man,' 'ho, man,' 'aw, man,' 'man!' patois. Not the speech of Archibald MacLeish or E. M. Forster who were friends of the *Paris Review*." To the *Review* crowd, Southern personified the hipster, the true expatriate desperado. John Phillips recalled that, at least initially, Southern maintained a distance from the largely clean-cut group, even when they ventured into the Old Navy. This aloofness only strengthened in their eyes the dangerous true-bohemian persona he so actively cultivated. "If after many evenings of being solemnly scrutinized by Terry in those cramped premises one tried to acknowledge his presence with an overture of any form—an innocent wave or friendly nod, or wink or mere 'hi there'—which could be construed as collegiate and uncalled for, it was mercilessly ignored. There was no penetrating that Texas cool."

The contrast between Southern and the magazine staff is exemplified by an incident that occurred around the time of the publication of Southern's story "The Accident" in the first issue of *The Paris Review*. In the original manuscript Southern had written a line of dialogue that read: "Don't get your shit hot." Plimpton, who had grown up in a straight-laced New England family, decided that "shit" was too strong a word. Also, he was worried that U.S. Customs, notoriously sensitive in those days, would confiscate the issue in New York. He changed "shit" to "crap"; then, just as the magazine was to go to press, he altered it again to read simply, "Don't get hot." When the review hit the stands, Southern was enraged enough actually to abandon his table at the Old Navy and storm into the office. His protest was so vehement, remembered Plimpton, that at one point the editor found himself telling Southern, "Terry, don't get so hot!"

After this encounter Southern wrote a fifteen-page letter of protest, demanding that it be printed in the magazine. Matthiessen was called in to try to straighten out matters, as he was Southern's link with the review and the only one who knew where the Texan lived. When Matthiessen arrived, Southern refused to open the door. After they had shouted at each other for a while, Matthiessen trying to explain that the protest letter was much too long to print and Southern adamantly refusing to cut a word of it, Matthiessen left. Back at the office he threw away Southern's blast and composed a brief erratum note: "Terry Southern is most anxious that *The Paris Review* point out the absence of two words from his story 'The Accident' (issue one): The sentence 'Don't get hot' *should* have read 'Don't get your crap hot'—an omission for which we apologize to all concerned." Art Buchwald, then a columnist for the Paris *Herald Tribune*, thought the notice the funniest he had ever read, and wanted to write about it in the paper. But convinced that his editor would not print the word "crap," he abandoned the idea. Such were the times.

Southern, however, neither mollified nor, apparently, amused, broke off relations with Matthiessen for a number of years. Nonetheless, he did allow the *Review* to print another story in the fourth issue (the one Matthiessen had originally acquired for Humes's *News-Post*) and remained a fairly regular contributor for the next dozen years.

BY THE end of its first year *The Paris Review* had established itself as a solid literary quarterly, not by any stretch of the imagination avant-garde, and yet on a certain cutting edge, namely, in being willing to take a chance on young, even unpublished, writers. While its interview subjects, naturally, were the famous—E. M. Forster, François Mauriac, Graham Greene, and Irwin Shaw—its fiction, besides Southern's stories, was almost consistently by emerging writers. Among the excellent stories were works by Evan Connell, Jr., Alfred Chester, and James Leo Herlihy. The poetry department, perhaps because Hall was at Oxford, tended to favor his British contemporaries—Geoffrey Hill, Thom Gunn, George Barker—and American formalists such as Richard Eberhardt, Richard Wilbur, Howard Moss, and John Simon (later better known as a critic).

What perhaps set the *Review* apart from other literary journals, though, was its innovative use of illustration (to accompany stories) and its reproduction of artists' portfolios. The inclusion of art came about largely because the review was begun in Paris, where artists, like writers, both established and unknown, abounded. The more well-known artists were featured in the portfolio section, a visual counterpart to the interviews; the unknowns were employed to "illustrate" the fiction and embellish the blank spaces.

Certainly the biggest artistic coup of the quarterly's early years was the reproduction of line drawings from the *livres d'or*, the large-format guest books kept by Paris restaurants. Ordinarily these books were simply signed by distinguished patrons, with perhaps a comment or two hailing an establishment's cuisine, but when these patrons were artists, they almost always illustrated their remarks. Knowing this, du Bois, the art editor, and Plimpton spent several weeks going from restaurant to restaurant, particularly those known as artists' haunts, and somehow persuaded the managements to allow them to photograph their cherished guest books. Among the drawings the *Review* reproduced were contributions by Picasso, Matisse, Braque, Cocteau, Raoul Dufy, André Derain, Leonor Fini, Saul Steinberg, Jacques Villon, even Toulouse-Lautrec. Such were the rewards of editing a review in Paris.

Financial rewards, however, at least for authors, were a bit more difficult to obtain. Connell recalled that in the early days "everybody knew that *The Paris Review* didn't pay if it could get away with it. The publishers didn't have much money, of course, but what they did have they wanted to stretch as much as possible." After having appeared in the *Review* a few times without being paid the promised 5,000 to 10,000 francs ($10 to $20) per story, he decided to press the issue.

> I finally went up to the office, as that was a lot of money in those days. Some girl was sitting behind the desk and I said, "Is George here?" She kind of froze and her eyes darted into this

other room. Then she looked at me and said, "No, George is not here." A few weeks later I ran into George on the street. As it was around noontime, he suggested we have lunch. When the bill came—it was probably around sixty-five cents or so—George hesitated, then said, "Ah, let me take you to lunch." I was about to say yes, but then I realized that if George bought my lunch it would be another six months before I'd get paid. So I insisted on paying for my own meal. I still had to wait a while before I finally squeezed some money out of him, but I did finally get what was owed.

The solvency of the magazine, and hence its record of payments to writers, greatly improved when, in the summer of 1954, Plimpton managed to talk Prince Sadruddin Aga Khan, a recent Harvard graduate, and second son of the Aga Khan, into becoming the *Review*'s first publisher. Although his financial commitment was not large, had he not come forward (at Plimpton's urging) when he did, it is unlikely the quarterly could have continued for much longer.

But for Plimpton the major highlight of 1954 was seeing Ernest Hemingway buy a copy of *The Paris Review*. The event took place at the Ritz. Hemingway was on a return visit; Plimpton happened to be at the hotel attending a wedding reception for Joan Dillon, daughter of the U.S. ambassador to France. As Plimpton recalled, he was walking with other wedding guests through the corridor connecting the hotel to the Rue Cambon when he spied Hemingway at the bookstall. Astonished to see the famous author, he threw out his arms to keep anyone from going forward. All eyes fixed on Hemingway, who nonchalantly drew money out of his pocket and bought the magazine. It was, according to Plimpton, the only time he saw anyone buy a copy.

Later Plimpton was introduced to the writer in the Ritz bar and after some hesitation nervously asked him if he would consent to be interviewed. Hemingway agreed, but he balked at Plimpton's idea to conduct the interview while walking through Hemingway's old Paris haunts. He would give an interview, he told the young editor, but he was damned well not going to tramp around Paris to do it. In reality, it took the enterprising Plimpton a considerable effort finally to conduct the promised interview: two weeks of watching bullfights in Madrid, and later a trip to Cuba, where more time was spent fishing than interviewing. The result, however, which appeared in issue 18, was worth the pleasant trouble. A relaxed, thoughtful Hemingway truly talked about himself as a "writer at work."

DESPITE THE adventures, community, and romance of being in Paris, the original editorial contingent began to drift away from the city by the mid-1950s. Humes, the first defector, had departed before the premiere issue of the magazine went to press. Matthiessen left for the States in late 1953. Another cofounder, Guinzburg, went back even earlier in order to run the New York office. Styron had gone to Italy shortly after the founding, and he too was in the United States by 1954. Plimpton stayed on in Paris until 1956 but made frequent visits to the States throughout the 1950s. Upon Plimpton's departure, Robert Silvers (later a founder of *The New York Review of Books*) took over as Paris editor, running the magazine for a while with the experienced assistance of John Train and later Blair Fuller.

But with Plimpton's return to America the magazine's Parisian focus was noticeably altered. More and more, the work being published was written by Americans living at home. To be sure, Europeans were featured (as they still are), but fewer expatriates made their way into the pages of the *Review*. Part of the reason, according to Fuller, later the Paris editor, was that by the mid-1950s, "France, with a sharply inflating currency, already at war in Algeria and soon to experience Dien Bien Phu, was scarcely as attractive to artists as it had been. The resident American writers were relatively few, and [they] were in Paris for practical reasons."

* * *

THE PARIS Review is still flourishing under George Plimpton's steadfast editorial supervision. It still has its Paris editor, novelist and poet Harry Mathews. Everyone who played a major role in its history, including Humes, who dropped out of sight some years ago, is listed on the masthead. Gone, however, is an office for aspiring Americans abroad to pop into on an afternoon. (The magazine's current Paris headquarters is Mathews's home.) But in a sense it lost its true Paris identity long ago with the major repatriation of the founders. Just as they had turned their attention in the early 1950s to the Paris writers and artists among whom they lived, once home they focused their energies on those who formed their stateside literary nucleus. But the *Review* has kept the vision that Styron advocated in the preface to the first issue, that of welcoming "the good writers and good poets, the non-drumbeaters and non-axe-grinders. So long as they're good."

Chapter Eight

"In Paris in a Loud Dark Winter"

AT DAWN, on D Day, June 6, 1944, a young U.S. Navy lieutenant stood attentively on the bow of the submarine chaser under his command. Behind him the big guns boomed. Above, hordes of Allied aircraft crisscrossed the sky, their high-pitched drones mingling with the cacophony of exploding bombs and small-arms fire. A hundred yards ahead, Normandy Beach was littered with spent shells and spent soldiers. This was not the France the officer had known briefly in childhood, not the France he had dreamed of so often, not the land of poets and painters and cafés and beautiful women and good cheap wine. This was an inferno, a nightmare without an ounce of romance. He could not dwell long, though, on the "abstract landscape of blasted trees." A dead soldier, afloat on the waves, was spotted. The lieutenant pulled out his manual and performed his first and only burial at sea.

The lieutenant's name was Lawrence Monsanto Ferling. A few years later he would reclaim his father's name, Ferlinghetti, which had been shortened after the older Ferlinghetti had arrived in the United States. A graduate in journalism from the University of North Carolina, Ferling had enlisted in the Navy shortly before the Japanese attack on Pearl Harbor. A model sailor, he had risen rapidly in the ranks and had been in command of his own ship for the last eighteen months. The outsider poet, painter, political activist, bookseller, and publisher he would become was almost as far off as his name change.

ON AUGUST 25, after a brief hiatus in England, where repairs were made to his ship, Ferlinghetti was again off the coast of France, this time near Cherbourg. Suddenly the incredible announcement came over the ship's radio that Paris had been liberated. Other news followed; the crew was given forty-eight hours of liberty. Ferlinghetti wasted no time in disembarking. In Cherbourg the lieutenant and his second-in-command found an abandoned but seemingly serviceable jeep. Amazed at their good fortune, they decided to drive to Paris. But the jeep soon broke down and the two ended up touring Brittany instead.

In the town of St.-Brieuc they wandered into a café. In the process of eating real food and drinking wine, Ferlinghetti noticed that the paper tablecloth had a poem written on it. Examining it carefully he discovered that it also bore a signature: *Jacques Prévert*. He was astonished. Here in a humble café, in an out-of-the-way place, a poem had been written on a tablecloth by an important poet. For Ferlinghetti, this was the France of which the legends had been made. On leaving the café he took the tablecloth with him. The incident was prophetic. Fourteen years later City Lights would issue Ferlinghetti's translations of Prévert's *Paroles*.

BY CHRISTMAS 1945, after having seen further action in the Pacific theater, a decorated ex-Lieutenant Ferlinghetti was back in New York. For a time he pursued employment as a journalist, but the closest he could come to an editorial office was a job in the mail room in the basement of the Time-Life building. He thought he might be able to work his way up in the organization, but he quickly discovered that if one didn't start out in the copy room, the doors were shut to editing or writing. After eight months he quit, and in the fall of 1946 enrolled as a graduate student in English at Columbia University under the GI Bill.

At Columbia, Ferlinghetti immersed himself in literature, both within and beyond the curriculum. In class he studied Joyce, seventeenth-century English literature, American modernism, and the usual range of prescribed courses. In the end, he settled on Victorian literature as his specialty, feeling that to understand the modern movement it was essential to be grounded in the writing of that era. For his thesis, he chose to concentrate on John Ruskin's art criticism, in particular his work on the English painter J. M. W. Turner. The eventual title was "Ruskin's Turner, Child of Light." He received his M.A. in 1947.

While the reading he did for classes helped ground him in literature, the books he discovered on his own had perhaps an even greater influence on his ultimate formation as a writer. All were by expatriate Americans: Pound, Stein, Miller, Eliot, and Elliot Paul. Paul, the least well-known of these literary figures, had been an editor, with Eugene Jolas, of *transition*, an avant-garde little magazine published in Paris in the late twenties and thirties. His book *The Last Time I Saw Paris*, a memoir of Paris during the days of the Lost Generation, had a profound impact on the young Ferlinghetti. Its evocation of that era brought back distant memories of the France where he had lived with his French great-aunt (and foster mother) between the ages of two and six. This book, along with his enthusiasm in general for the Paris expatriate writers—especially Miller, Hemingway, Pound, Wolfe, and Joyce—and his more recent experiences in France during the war, led Ferlinghetti to think seriously about studying for his Ph.D. in France. "I was very conscious of living out the Lost Generation myth—the Hemingway myth of *The Sun Also Rises*—and fancied myself at the Dôme writing something, being a part of that tradition," he recalled. "At the time that myth was very near, very important to me, and had a great deal to do with my going over."

With his M.A. in hand and three years of support left on the GI Bill, Ferlinghetti made the decision: he would go to the Sorbonne for his doctorate. "The requirements for an American Ph.D. were so academic," he explained. "You couldn't do your dissertation on a living author. And you had to do all these courses that I wasn't interested in." In January 1948, the young scholar, who still had a fair command of French (the language he had actually spoken before English), set sail for France. He knew he would not find any of the Lost Generation there, but thought he might be part of a new wave of American writers in Paris, who would, like their older counterparts, create a viable new literature of expatriation in the City of Light.

It snowed the day Ferlinghetti arrived in Paris. He didn't care. The cafés were open, the streets aswarm with fashionable pedestrians. It was as magical as he had envisioned. That first morning he walked and walked through the city, from Left to Right Bank, saw the Louvre spread out along the Seine, saw Notre-Dame spiraling upward. As he approached the Tuileries, he paused now and then to take in the sights, or to peruse the old books for sale from the *bouquinistes* along the Seine. Near the Tuileries, he boarded a bus. Despite the falling snow, he stood in the open-air platform at the back, not wanting to have a steamed-up bus window come between him and the streets of Paris. At Place Voltaire (now Place Léon Blum), "between Bastille and Père Lachaise," he alighted. On a slip of paper was the address of the Edgar Letellier family, who let out rooms at 9 Place Voltaire.

Here he was greeted warmly. "Monsieur Letellier was a music teacher who looked like Beethoven—wild hair and all. He tutored pupils in his home. . . . His wife was a jolly lady, very hospitable. They had two young daughters as well." Ferlinghetti was shown the room—spacious and light-filled—he could occupy. When told the price, approximately $50 per month, with two meals included, he committed himself on the spot. As the GI Bill gave him a living allowance of $65 a month, he decided that the remaining $15 was certainly enough spending money. He was also glad to be living with a family, because he felt it would greatly aid his French.

Ferlinghetti enrolled at the Sorbonne at once and was delighted to discover that French graduate school was all it was cracked up to be, namely, that the emphasis was on research for the dissertation, not on attending classes. The only requirement was that he meet with his *rapporteur* (academic advisor) twice a year to discuss his readings and the progress he was making on his thesis. Nonetheless, he did unofficially attend a few classes at the beginning in order to improve both his French and his knowledge of French literature.

In a letter home to Anna Bisland, his adoptive mother, who with her husband, Presley, had brought up Ferlinghetti from the age of ten, he noted that he had "hardly made a dent in French Literature." He then went on to say: "At present I am translating Flaubert, Proust and French Romantic poetry." Although he continued to read these and a great many other major French writers, he soon abandoned formal study. Instead he used the abundant amount of undirected time to explore literature on his own, perfect his French, and reconnoiter Paris. "I'd walk the streets for hours, poems in my head," Ferlinghetti recalled. "I thought I was a symbolist poet at first, since I knew their work when I was first there: Baudelaire, Rimbaud, [Émile] Verhaeren. . . . Then, after I started reading the surrealists, I thought I was a surrealist poet—a *Nadja* surrealist, not a *Manifesto* surrealist." He also remembered various other personae he took on, depending on what writers he was reading: "I was Apollinaire and [Blaise] Cendrars, and of course I was Stephen Dedalus, Joyce's eternal young hero who sets forth to forge in the smithy of his soul the uncreated conscience of his race, and also to do battle with the world, in the classic tradition of young heroes since the beginning of time, or at least since the beginning of literature."

He began to write as well. At that time for Ferlinghetti, this meant writing a novel, which he began doing shortly after settling in at the university. With his head filled with the prose rhythms of Joyce and Wolfe, with Paris arrayed in all its postwar glory before him, he started to create what he later described as "a conventional novel inspired by Thomas Wolfe, particularly the Wolfe of *Look Homeward, Angel.*" The story, predictably enough, was about a young man discovering himself in the French capital. Its working title, borrowed from the "East Coker" section of Eliot's *Four Quartets*, was *The Way of Dispossession.*

The novel promptly became his major priority: "I'd get up in the morning. Madame would bring me a *café au lait* and a *tartine,* and I'd write all morning." In a letter he noted that "I am most interested at the moment in my novel in English, which I have now extended to over 10,000 words." Part of the reason for his ardor (and word counting) was that he had learned from a friend back in the States that Doubleday, Doran was sponsoring a contest for first novels. He decided to enter. In a letter to Anna Bisland, he explained: "The minimum number of words to be turned in is not [10,000] but 20,000 plus a complete synopsis of the rest of the novel, and there is no deadline, so that I am well-started and have plenty of time. As for the idea of getting an 'immediate' income from it, that is not my plan at all, since it is not *now* that I need money, but in about a year."

In the afternoon Ferlinghetti would go out and sit in a café, read, write in a notebook, "just watch Paris." The city was endlessly fascinating, everything was of interest. It was also relatively poor. "What few realize," noted Ferlinghetti, "was that it took Paris a long time to recover from the war. Outwardly it didn't show so much. Nothing had been bombed as in the country, but the [Parisians] really were having a pretty hard time of it. The $65 a month I had was twice what most students had, even as much as many workers had to support families." Even when the Parisians had money to buy goods, the situation was not that much improved, as supplies of basic commodities were hardly abundant. According to Ferlinghetti, "There were lines for everything. You'd see people lined up at the *laiterie* with their ration coupons to buy two liters of milk. There were lines for bread, lines for petrol. There were, of course, far fewer cars then. Gasoline was still rationed and expensive, but you'd see lots of bicycles."

DURING THAT first winter Ferlinghetti spent most of his time alone. When he did socialize it was primarily with the Letelliers. "There were a lot of Americans around, studying on the GI Bill," he recalled, "but because I wasn't really taking classes I didn't meet any of them." In the spring of 1948, however, he decided to look up the brother of a young woman he'd known at Columbia, Mary Whitman. Her brother George had gone to France in 1946 to work as a volunteer in a resettlement camp for war orphans. When this closed, he stayed on in Paris and attended classes in French language and culture at the Sorbonne. "I had moved into the Hôtel de Suez at 31 Boulevard St.-Michel and started up a little lending library consisting mostly of old American and English books I bought up at the Sorbonne," Whitman recollected. "One day this tall, well-dressed young man walked into the room and handed me a note, saying that he'd known my sister at Columbia. He was still Ferling then. We got on well from the first, talked about writers and Paris and I don't know what else. After that, he'd come by all the time. If I wasn't there, he'd just sit and read."

Ferlinghetti too remembered his first encounter with Whitman: "George was seated in an armchair in the middle of his tiny room in his third-rate hotel. Books were piled from floor to ceiling on all four sides. He had something cooking over a can of Sterno." A year later, having run out of room for the books, Whitman separated the library/bookshop from his living quarters and opened the Librairie Franco-Américaine at the Paris City Club on the Boulevard de Courcelles. Ferlinghetti also frequented Whitman's new establishment. Whitman, who was doing a booming business as the anglophone expatriate population increased, soon outgrew the new space. In 1951, with money from an inheritance, he purchased an old Arab grocery store on the Rue de la Bûcherie, on the Left Bank directly facing Notre-

Dame, and transformed it into the Librairie Mistral. Renamed Shakespeare and Company in 1964, in honor of Sylvia Beach, it is still thriving under Whitman's care.

Whitman's example as a bookseller had a direct impact on Ferlinghetti. Although at the time he had no intention of opening a bookshop himself, he liked the idea of making a living from books. In 1953, when he started up the City Lights bookstore in San Francisco, it was with Whitman's model in mind. He in fact has called his bookstore the "sister shop" of Whitman's Shakespeare and Company.

BY THE spring of 1948, Ferlinghetti had finished his novel and sent it off to Doubleday. It was rejected, but a New York agent, Margaret Christie, discovered it and offered it to Simon & Schuster. This second house turned down the book, but not without writing an encouraging note to Ferlinghetti via Christie: "We all agree that here is a writer, perceptive, sensitive, and a weaver of tales. We want to see anything else that he does, even if it is only a few pages." Ferlinghetti was heartened by the response, although discouraged by the outcome. He did, however, accept the dual verdict. Rather than continue trying to sell *The Way of Dispossession*, he began to make notes toward another novel.

He also started working on a series of poems in the form of cantos—following Pound's model—which he called *Palimpsest*. The title, like the form, was borrowed, this time from H.D., whose novel of the same name Ferlinghetti acquired that spring in the original 1926 Paris Contact edition, "a purple book, with ivory paper." Although the poems Ferlinghetti was writing had nothing much in common with H.D.'s work, save perhaps the underlying motif of the palimpsest, in which one story is imposed on another, her imagistic prose had a far more lasting influence on him than did Pound's poetics. In his novel *Her*, begun the next year, he attempted to follow H.D.'s example of careful craft, "clean and hard as Greek lettering on a lintel."

At the time, however, he was under the spell of Pound's "poem, including history." This in itself was a departure from Ferlinghetti's earlier poetry, which had been heavily influenced by Eliot. Although he continued to work sporadically on the *Palimpsest* manuscript for another year before abandoning it, he was becoming increasingly aware that these poems reflected less his own voice than they did those of others. The discovery was important: in realizing the need to reject the diction, theme, and phrasing of Pound and Eliot, he was making significant steps in the development of his own poetic style and vision.

It would be a while before Ferlinghetti fully understood and accepted the transformation, but the transition from poet-imitator to poet did not take long. That spring, while on a trip to southern France, he began to jot down in his notebook the first poems (or notes toward poems, as he has described them) that are genuinely his own, that reflect what would become the distinctive Ferlinghetti voice and eye:

> low red tile roofs
> and the tin charley on the Mairie with
> a rusty tin flag and a sword
> . . . .
> Its burnt steeples are a part
> of the sky and do not hold it up

Here, the immediate visual impression of place, a hallmark of Ferlinghetti's early work, is paramount. Impression, though, is not description: the steeples are not really burnt, are not really part of the sky; the town hall does not actually display a tin flag and sword. This is the surrealist legacy speaking in American English, and precisely because the poem fragment is written in English and not in French, its echoes of another tradition, while evocative of its forebears, are far less imitative. In a sense what Ferlinghetti had learned from Pound was to "make it new." Surrealism in American English is different from surrealism in French.

It is not coincidental that on that same trip Ferlinghetti discovered the work of French poet René Char. While Char's poetry makes use of surrealist juxtaposition of inchoate imagery, in which fragment is set against fragment, his concern, particularly in the late thirties and forties, was to reveal, through the impossible commingling of elements, the mysterious essence of things, events, human interaction. In particular, Char's concept of poetic illumination through "lightning instants" appealed tremendously to the young American, who, already imbued with the Joycean notion of the epiphany, found in Char a poetic counterpoint by which the epiphany could become the basis for a poem itself. Once Ferlinghetti had deciphered what the French poet was about, he began to transpose Char's poetics onto his own. This was the essential breakthrough. He was now appropriating no longer a voice but a method.

In one of the few poems subsequently published from that period, Ferlinghetti recorded his debt to Char, both in name and in the power of the imagination to transport the poet far beyond the immediate, to conjure up an entire scene from one small event. His style, direct and concrete, is not that of Char, however. If there are debts in diction or form, they are owed to Prévert:

> In Paris in a loud dark winter
> > when the sun was something in Provence
> when I came upon the poetry
> > of René Char
> I saw Vaucluse again
> > in a summer of sauterelles

DURING THE summer of 1948, Ferlinghetti returned briefly to New York. His adoptive father, Presley Bisland, was seriously ill and not expected to live. Although he felt distinctly out of place back in the United States, Ferlinghetti actually contemplated remaining for a while out of concern for Bisland. But neither Bisland nor his doctor wanted Ferlinghetti to stay: "If you stuck around," the doctor advised Ferlinghetti, "it would make him feel that you realized he didn't have long to live." After a few weeks, Ferlinghetti was again bound for France.

On the ship back he met two women, Mary Barrett and Marie Birmingham (later Marie Ponsot). According to Ferlinghetti, they were among the first intellectual women that he got to know well. Extremely well-read, they shared Ferlinghetti's literary interests in modernism. One object of their enthusiasm, though, was a writer unknown to Ferlinghetti: Djuna Barnes. They were so taken with Barnes, in fact, that when they arrived in Paris they looked for—and found—an apartment on the Rue du Cherche-Midi, the street on which Barnes had lived and which figured prominently in her novel *Nightwood*. They also gave their new American friend a copy of the novel.

"*Nightwood* was a major discovery for me," remarked Ferlinghetti. "I filled up notebooks with scribblings that were very imitation *Nightwood*. When I wasn't imitating, I was jotting down quotes from the novel." Later these "scribblings" would form the basis of his first published novel, *Her*, which Ferlinghetti readily admitted was descended from Barnes. "*Her* is a direct heterosexual appropriation of *Nightwood*."

Barnes's work, in which Paris is a protagonist, also began to catalyze a greater awareness in Ferlinghetti that since the late nineteenth century, cities had been a major subject for writers. Already familiar with Hart Crane's *The Bridge*, Eliot's *The Waste Land*, Whitman's *Leaves of Grass*, Baudelaire's *Les Fleurs du Mal*, and Verhaeren's *Les Villes Tentaculaires*, he began exploring the way in which images of the city figured in modern poetry. By the next year, the theme became so compelling that he decided to adopt it as the topic for his thesis.

At this juncture, however, Ferlinghetti was more concerned with how the city intersected with his own life. Drawn more and more to the Left Bank scene, particularly around the Sorbonne, with its all-night cafés, seedy bars, theaters, and continual array of interesting characters, he decided at the end of the summer to leave the Letelliers in their less dynamic Right Bank location and move to his own apartment somewhere in the heart of the action.

Finding an apartment was fairly difficult, since few were available. As a result of the shortage there was a thriving black market; rents were much higher than the actual value of apartments. Even if an apartment was located, key money usually had to be paid, which often equaled five or six times a month's rent. But Ferlinghetti got lucky. Through George Whitman he met a plumber who lived with his wife and three children in a two-room basement apartment on the Rue de Vaugirard. Aside from being much too small for the family, the place was quite damp. This was a real problem, as the whole family had incipient tuberculosis. The plumber wanted to move to the country, but because he owed money to many in the neighborhood he couldn't see his way clear to leave. Ferlinghetti offered him a deal: he'd settle the plumber's debts, which amounted to about $100, in exchange for the apartment. The plumber happily agreed. "None of this was legal," noted Ferlinghetti, "so I had to pretend that I was only temporarily living there."

Once ensconced in his new quarters, Ferlinghetti was not so sure he'd made such a great deal. The apartment's two main advantages were "its location—in the heart of 'Hemingway country' in Montparnasse—and the prewar fixed rent of [the equivalent of] $26 a year. The apartment itself consisted of two small rooms, only one of them with light. There was one large piece of hollowed-out stone that must have been there from the Middle Ages: that was the sink, with one cold-water spigot above it. The toilet, a stand-up john [Turkish toilet], was halfway up the stairs. You had to be very careful to be outside when you flushed, or else you'd get soaked. For bathing, I used the public baths nearby, like most of the other Parisians then."

Despite the drawbacks, the apartment offered definite advantages. Because of the negligible rent, he could spend more money on books and leisure activities, could even travel more outside Paris. But above all, because of both the convenient location and his greater financial resources, he could spend much more time in local cafés. In the grand Parisian tradition, he quickly claimed one café, the Mabillon, for himself. When this closed, sometime after midnight, if he was in the mood to stay away longer from his "hole," he could move across the street to the Pergola, which stayed open all night.

As the autumn chill began to set in, Ferlinghetti discovered that it was not only somewhat romantic to sit in the café to write, but also far more comfortable. "The apartment was very damp, and unheated," he remembered. "But at the Mabillon, you could sit on the terrace even in winter. They had these canvas flaps that came down to the ground, and potbellied stoves."

That October, Ferlinghetti acquired a roommate, a friend from the Navy, Ivan Cousins. He had been lured to Paris by Ferlinghetti's letters; the reality was not what he had expected. In a letter to Anna Bisland, Ferlinghetti reported on Cousins's dissatisfaction: "Ivan is doing much of nothing, since he hasn't found a position as yet. In fact, he doesn't like Paris. This is mostly because of his lack of creature comforts. I doubt whether he stays here longer than this spring." Ferlinghetti's prediction was not wrong. By the summer of 1949 Cousins had returned to the States.

The contrast between the two lay in their respective interests rather than in their tolerance for substandard living conditions. For Ferlinghetti, Paris was not equated in the least with his two-room "cave" or his meager living allowance. Life in the capital was elsewhere. Paris was mythical and magical, the city of poets and painters, of intelligence, of beauty; it was the place that was allowing him the opportunity to create himself as an artist, and which was enfranchising him on this basis. As he firmly believed that Paris had given him life, it was easy to overlook the practical difficulties.

During that winter of 1948–1949, Ferlinghetti continued to pursue both his scholarly and his artistic interests. Academically, he closed in on a definitive subject for his thesis: the city as symbol in modern poetry. To the authors with whom he was already familiar, such as Whitman, Eliot, and Baudelaire, he added a few others, including Mayakovsky, García Lorca, and Francis Thompson. Artistically, he kept on writing poetry and began working on what would become the novel *Her.*

There was a close link between his academic and creative activities. The reading he was doing for his thesis was directly related to the novel he was trying to write; the focus of both was on the city as poetic symbol. The novel, however, proceeded faster than his thesis. By the spring of 1949 he had finished the first draft. Although *Her* was not published until a decade later, it was not altered significantly in the intervening years.

Her is a novel, in the form of an interior monologue, about Andy Raffine, a young American in Paris in search of himself and in pursuit of "her," a sculptor with whom the narrator/protagonist has become obsessed. Although in the tradition of Breton's *Nadja*, Aragon's *Le Paysan de Paris*, and Barnes's *Nightwood*, with liberal evocations of (and even quotations from) Joyce's *Ulysses* and *Finnegans Wake* as well as H.D.'s *Palimpsest*, Ferlinghetti's novel is not a clone of these earlier works. Its originality lies in the individuality of Andy Raffine's quest itself, in which "all propaganda to the contrary the hero [is] not searching for something like his father mother sister brother who will always and forever be only ghosts by the wind ungrieved and the hero is not looking for them and he is looking for himself instead as he goes walking on."

In spite of its Parisian backdrop and largely European antecedents, this search for the self is something quintessentially American, in the spirit of Henry James, Wolfe, the young Hemingway, the Fitzgerald of *Gatsby*, the Kerouac of *The Town and the City*: namely, the quest for identity within the American fabric, whose heritage is complicated because of its heterogeneity. For Andy Raffine, a true victim of literature, the task is even more complex, because he is in Paris attempting to become himself while surrounded by the ghosts of his literary heroes of the Lost Generation. While wanting to be like them, he is also seeking to overthrow them in order to gain his own identity.

At the Café Mabillon, the protagonist falls into conversation with a waiter, Lubin, "a bent character out of those Twenties books, one of those Americans-in-Paris books, still hanging on to haunt another generation." As the exchange progresses, Lubin's drunken spiel takes a serious turn. From talking picturesque nonsense, the waiter suddenly zeroes in on Raffine and in a few rambling sentences reveals what is at the heart of the young American's dilemma—his inability to sort out his past in order to create his present:

> "Is it my own past swimming up before me, or isn't it? An American like you with a label like Raffine! Dung of Europa, aren't we the lost tribesmen, and me your wandered father come back again? The same wash, in a different bundle, sent to be laundered in America. The long return! . . . Born by inadvertence, Master Raffine, you pulled up your drawers and came out, only to find yourself in another country, wandering around lost between nowhere and here, neither fish nor whore, with no holy water stoup to call your own."

Within an already autobiographical novel, this is one of the most revealing autobiographical moments, for the speech applies also to Ferlinghetti. But unlike his protagonist, he was able in Paris to resolve much of his rootless past, to overcome being a victim of literary myth and become a maker of literature. By the time he left Paris, Ferlinghetti was on his way to seeing that in order to free himself from the specter of the Lost Generation, he had to make his own myths. More than a quarter-century later he would express it most definitively in his "Adieu à Charlot (Second Populist Manifesto)":

> Sons of Whitman
> in your 'public solitude'
> bound by blood-*duende*
> 'President of your own body America'
> Take it back from those who have maddened you
> back from those who stole it
> and steal it daily
> . . . .
> You Whitmans of another breath
> there is no one else to tell
> how the alienated generations
> have lived out their expatriate visions

here and everywhere
The old generations have lived them out
Lived out the bohemian myth in Greenwich Villages
Lived out the Hemingway myth
in *The Sun Also Rises*
at the Dôme in Paris
or with the bulls at Pamplona
Lived out the Henry Miller myth
in the *Tropics* of Paris
and the great Greek dream
of *The Colossus of Maroussi*

Despite the large amount of creative work that Ferlinghetti was doing, aside from the novel he sent to Doubleday, he did not bother to submit work to little magazines, not even those in Paris. "I read *Zero* and *Points*, of course, but I never sent them anything," he explained. "They were, as far as I was concerned then, much too far above me. I never dreamed I could get anything printed in those magazines." Ferlinghetti's creative work, in fact, would not appear in print in any form until 1955, when he published a collection of poems, *Pictures of the Gone World*, as the first in City Lights's Pocket Poets series.

In addition to writing, reading, and working on his thesis, Ferlinghetti took up drawing in 1949. Both the Académie Julien and La Grande Chaumière had open studios, where anyone armed with charcoal and paper could come in and draw from live models. The opportunity seemed too good to pass up. He also continued his critical study of art, begun at Columbia, but in Paris he vastly expanded his awareness of contemporary painters. He got so wrapped up in Picasso that he began to dream about the artist. In poem 24 of *Pictures of the Gone World* he directly transcribed such a dream:

Picasso's acrobats epitomize the world

. . . .

but that night I dreamt of Picasso
opening doors and closing exits
opening doors and closing exits in the world

> I dreamt
> > he painted a Picasso
> > > in my room
> > shouting all the time
> > > *Pas symbolique!*
> > *C'est pas*
> > > *symbolique!*

During the summer Ferlinghetti returned to the United States for another brief visit. His adoptive father had died during the winter, and Ferlinghetti was concerned about Mrs. Bisland, who was not in good health. This would be the last time he would see her; Anna Bisland died the following year. Although he enjoyed his visit, Ferlinghetti again felt somewhat estranged from life in the United States. He was decidedly relieved when, after just two weeks, he was again Paris-bound.

On the return voyage he ran into a woman who had been in the same class with him at Columbia, but with whom he'd never really talked. Her name was Selden Kirby-Smith. Kirby, as she was called, was on her way to study at the Sorbonne; she had recently earned her M.A. from Columbia. On board ship they discovered they had a number of interests in common, and spent a lot of time together. They continued to see each other fairly frequently in Paris. He took her around the city, introducing her to his friends and to Paris itself—its cafés, museums, theaters, clubs. By the spring of the following year the friendship had blossomed into a romance.

During that academic year Ferlinghetti's main focus was on writing his thesis, now officially entitled "La Cité: Symbole dans la Poésie Moderne: À la Recherche d'une Tradition Métropoli-taine" (The City as Symbol in Modern Poetry: In Search of a Metropolitan Tradition). Although he found it rather easy to come up with ideas to write about, the writing itself, which had to be done in French, was more difficult. By the late spring of 1950 he was nearly finished. Concerned that he had not expressed himself in perfect Académie French, he sought out a professional translator, a Frenchwoman, to correct any errors in the text. "I used to visit her once a week," recalled Ferlinghetti. "She lived in a big old elegant flat on the Boulevard des Italiens. I took to her somehow. Nothing happened with it except that I used her as the basis for two poems, number 12 and number 13 in *Pictures*."

The major revisions and corrections to the thesis, now 224 pages long, were completed by the early summer. Ferlinghetti also finished a short subsidiary thesis, another requirement for the Ph.D. This paper, on Ruskin and the nature of the gothic, he had adapted in part from his M.A. thesis. As his oral defense was not scheduled until September, he found himself with a few months of true leisure. Inspired by Henry Miller's *The Colossus of Maroussi*, he decided to head for Greece via Spain. In Madrid he was captivated by the art in the Prado and in the small museum devoted to the works of the Spanish impressionist painter Joaquin Sorolla y Bastida. He hastily jotted down his reactions to Sorolla's work. Later, these lines became Number 8 in *Pictures of the Gone World*. Perhaps more important, this poem inaugurated a continuing and fruitful trend in Ferlinghetti's work: poems about painting and painters.

From Madrid he made his way to Majorca. His original intention was to stay on the island for a time, then hire himself out on a yacht bound for Greece. Not really to his dismay, he never got beyond Majorca. While he was there, Kirby and her mother visited for a week. By now the relationship had become fairly serious and Kirby was hoping for a marriage proposal. Ferlinghetti, however, was not sure he was ready to take such a dramatic plunge. "I cried all the way through Italy," Kirby remembered. "Then finally in Florence there came a telegram which said, 'Will you marry me?' . . . I wired back 'yes,' in fourteen languages." But shortly afterward Ferlinghetti changed his mind. They did eventually marry, but not until April 1951.

At the end of summer 1950, Ferlinghetti returned to Paris and began preparing for the public defense of his thesis. "I made notes for it," he recalled, "as you had to speak perfect Académie Francaise French and I didn't feel I could afford to make a mistake. I then got even more nervous when I learned that one of the judges had written a paper about the city in poetry. I hadn't read it. I could just hear him saying, 'You've spent all these years of research and you haven't read my paper?' I thought it would be the finish of me. But fortunately it wasn't brought up."

Indeed, the defense went very well. Before a large crowd, including George Whitman and Kirby, Ferlinghetti responded persuasively to the questions. Despite his *rapporteur's* admonition not to read from his notes, Ferlinghetti persisted, feeling on safer ground. The only awkward moment occurred when he stumbled in a translation of lines from *The Waste Land*. One of the judges looked at him quizzically and demanded how he could make such an error in translation. Unfazed, Ferlinghetti responded: *"Je voudrais citer un vieux adage français: Une traduction est comme une femme. Quand elle est belle, elle n'est pas fidèle. Quand elle est fidèle, elle n'est pas belle"* (I would like to quote an old French adage: A translation is like a woman. When she is beautiful, she is not faithful. When she is faithful, she is not beautiful). The hall (and judges) burst out laughing. Ferlinghetti was awarded his Doctorat de l'Université *avec mention* (with distinction).

Ferlinghetti remained in Paris until the end of 1950. He had originally contemplated staying on indefinitely, but with his funds from the GI Bill cut off when his studies ended, and with no "practical" reason to linger, he packed up and made preparations to return to the United States. In Paris a friend of his, Robert Payne, had talked up the West Coast, particularly San Francisco. His descriptions of the cosmopolitan city intrigued Ferlinghetti: it sounded more like a European locale than an American one. As a result, Ferlinghetti felt less sorry about leaving Paris. Perhaps there was a place in America where he could live; he would at least visit, in early 1951. The visit, of course, turned into a lifelong residency.

FERLINGHETTI HAD gone to Paris as a scholar. "I figured that I'd get my Ph.D. and then get a job in some school like the University of North Carolina, where I'd gone as an undergraduate. You know, live the life of the professor." But it was not to be. For one, when he got back and started looking for jobs, he soon understood that "a European doctorate was very suspect." But in reality, the dream of becoming a scholar had changed. Dr. Ferlinghetti was also poet Ferlinghetti, novelist Ferlinghetti. While circumstances played a part in his decision to develop the creative side of his identity, the artistic impulse forged and strengthened in the loud dark winters of Paris had grown so strong that it could not be denied. It was precisely this sense of himself as a creative being that allowed Ferlinghetti to overcome the anxiety of influence, to become the artist that he is.

"Paris had a lot to do with who I am," Ferlinghetti said recently. Although it has been more than forty years since he haunted the Left Bank on a regular basis, the city endures in his own work. His most recent novel, *Love in the Days of Rage* (1988), is set in Paris during the 1968 student revolt. It evokes an earlier era, however, and through a judicious series of cut-up quotes from *Her*, also an earlier Ferlinghetti. Paris remains alive too at City Lights, which, from the early Pocket Poets edition of Prévert's *Paroles*, has consistently published French avant-garde writing in translation. Indeed, an entire generation of Americans has been able to come into contact with a variety of French and other European writing through the press's devoted publication of often lesser-known Continental literature. Of all the writers who passed through Paris during the early postwar era, few have carried forward the experience in such a determined fashion. Paris not only shaped him but gave him life as an artist.

Chapter Nine

The Legacy of Hurt:
The Odyssey of Chester Himes

UNLIKE THE majority of American writers who made their way to Paris in the early postwar era, Chester Himes was neither young nor unpublished nor idealistic. He was not in search of himself, not even enamored of Europe or expatriation, and he had no illusions that France was the utopia Richard Wright had continually made it out to be in his letters to Himes from abroad. As Himes explained it years later, "I just wanted out from the United States, that was all. I had had it."

But France was not a totally arbitrary choice either. While he did not enjoy the celebrity status accorded Wright, his reputation as a novelist there was far greater than in the United States. The year before his departure French critics had chosen his novel *Lonely Crusade* as one of the five best American books published in France in 1952. (The other writers honored were Herman Wouk, Hemingway, Fitzgerald, and Faulkner.) His first book, *If He Hollers Let Him Go*, had also been well received in France. In contrast, *Lonely Crusade* had been thoroughly and viciously attacked when it was published in the United States in 1947. One *Commentary* reviewer compared it to "the graffiti in the men's rooms." *Ebony*, in its denunciation of the book, nearly exhausted the host of negative adjectives available in the English language: "invidious, shocking, incendiary"; "virulent, malicious, full of rancor and venom"; "rabid"; "infected with a psychosis." "Hatred reeks through his pages like yellow bile," proclaimed *The Atlantic Monthly*. Even James Baldwin, writing one of the first reviews of his career for *The New Leader*, denounced the novel, complaining that the prose was "the most uninteresting and awkward . . . I have read in recent years."

It was this acrimonious reception that first turned Himes's thoughts to relocating abroad. In fact, he vowed at the time to leave the United States forever, once he got the chance, the "chance" being the money to do so. He had decided he had nothing to lose, as he felt completely outside American society anyway. "The whites rejected me, the blacks didn't want me. I felt like a man without a country." In truth, though, the alienation from American society had begun long before this negative barrage from the critics. It was in many respects an induced sense of apartness for reasons of race, which was shared by the vast majority of his black contemporaries.

But Himes's sense of separateness had been abetted by the individual acts of racism he had personally experienced as a bright, proud, self-assured young man in a country where those adjectives apply only to those for whom doors are already open. And Himes repeatedly had the door shut in his face. The steel doors had literally closed behind him when at the age of nineteen he began serving a twenty-year sentence in the Ohio State Penitentiary on a burglary charge. It was there that he began to write, selling some stories to *Esquire* and other periodicals. When the doors reopened again, in 1936, after seven and a half years, a paroled Himes felt confident that the path out of his past was through writing. But despite his formidable talent and early success, the road was not nearly as easy to follow as he had hoped. America itself, he began to feel, was a prison for black people. Alienation, for Himes as for Wright, was not a concept invented by the existentialists.

With the nearly unanimous rejection of *Lonely Crusade* by the critics, the feelings were intensified. Himes had survived prison by knowing how to gamble. He now resolved to gamble on himself by going abroad. But it took another five bitter years until the opportunity arrived. During that period, he worked at a variety of jobs—dishwasher, janitor's helper, snow shoveler, caretaker, day porter at a YMCA, bellhop. But above all, he continued to write. "No matter what I did, or where I was, or how I lived, I . . . considered myself a writer." In spite of his many jobs, he managed to produce a handful of short stories, rework an earlier, unpublished novel about his prison experiences, now entitled *Cast the First Stone*, and nearly finish another novel, *The Third Generation*.

It was Coward-McCann's acceptance of (and accompanying advance for) *Cast the First Stone* in 1951 that made Himes think he might have the means to set into motion his resolve to journey to Europe. Then, in late 1952, when World Publishing bought *The Third Generation*, he felt fully empowered and financially able to follow through on his desire. Wooed by his current French translator, Yves Malartic, and by Richard Wright, Himes decided that France was the place. "I realized that there was nothing to keep me any longer in the United States," he wrote. "Both my father and my mother were dead, my wife was gone, the only friend I had in all the publishing world was my editor, William Targ, and I knew he was going to do what he could for *The Third Generation* whether I was there or not." In reality, the reasons were a bit more complex, as Himes himself admitted:

I suppose there were many reasons for my coming to Europe, but I don't remember them clearly. . . . Race prejudice, of course. I know that was one even though I don't remember it. I am black and I was born and raised and lived in America, and the fact that race prejudice was one of my reasons for leaving it is inescapable. But I know there were many others as well. Perhaps one is that I had the money for it. Another is that I came very close to killing the white woman, Vandi Haygood, with whom I had lived; and I was both shocked and frightened.

Chester Himes arrived in Paris on April 11, 1953, with a broken toe, the result of another pre-departure altercation with his former girlfriend Vandi Haygood. This was not the dramatic incident referred to above; it was just another in a series of disputes with Haygood. On the voyage over, he had begun a romance with a middle-aged white woman from Boston, Alva Van Olden.* On debarking she was met by her husband, a dentist from Luxembourg, and set off with him for their home in that country, having vowed to return to Himes by May. But at the moment of his arrival in France, Himes had no idea what to make of this affair. He was simply hoping that his old friend Richard Wright and Yves Malartic would be on hand to meet him at the train station in Paris as they had promised. He was toting several suitcases. His toe hurt. He had no idea where to put up for the night in a strange city in a strange country. "It is no small thing to leave the United States at age forty-three—especially if you are a black man and have never been farther than Montreal," Himes remarked. But here he was, in the middle of the night in Paris, and no one was there to meet him.

After waiting at the Gare St.-Lazare for a while, Himes took a taxi to Wright's. A concierge, however, quickly appeared in front of Wright's building, barring the way. By then the taxi had departed and Himes was left on the street with his mountain of luggage. Eventually he got another taxi, went back to the station, then finally to a hotel he remembered Wright had recommended in one of his early letters, just a few blocks from his house. The next morning Himes was awakened by a furious pounding on his door. When he opened it, a frantic Richard Wright stood in the hallway. They exchanged stories of the mixup. As it turned out, Wright and Malartic had been at the station to meet him but had been on the wrong end of the platform. When Himes did not appear, Wright became quite concerned. That morning he decided to notify the police, and he stopped by the hotel to cancel the reservation he had made for Himes. It was then he learned that Himes was asleep upstairs.

* pseudonym—ED.

Wright, now relieved, reverted to the role he had originally hoped to play—that of welcoming tour guide—and insisted that a sleepy Himes accompany him to the Café Monaco for breakfast. Himes understood that Wright was as interested in showing off his status in Paris as in taking him to have something to eat. At the café, Himes remembered, "Dick greeted everyone with boisterous condescension; it was obvious he was the king thereabouts. . . . Dick expected a gathering of our soul brother compatriots, all of whom knew I was to arrive the night before, but not one of them appeared, an eccentricity which I was later to learn was the natural reaction of the envious and jealous American blacks who lived in Paris."

Wright had another reason for greeting Himes so early. He wanted to get from him copies of his new novel, *The Outsider*, which Himes had agreed to bring over from New York. When Himes informed him that the books were in his 250-pound trunk still at customs, Wright insisted on going immediately to fetch them, and in the process Himes's trunk. On arriving at the Gare St.-Lazare, however, Himes discovered that he had left his key at the hotel, and the customs official would not allow the trunk to pass unopened. Eventually Wright persuaded the *douanier* to allow the trunk to go through. But this was not the end of the difficulties. Back at the hotel they had to get the massive trunk up several flights of stairs. As it was a small hotel, there were no bellhops on hand to assist. Himes suggested they wait for some help, but Wright, increasingly determined to get his books, insisted they could lug it themselves. Finally, after an immense amount of struggle, they got the trunk up to Himes's room; in the process Wright managed to strain himself severely. Himes was not especially sympathetic, and Wright was not interested in staying around now that his objective had been accomplished. Himes opened the trunk, handed Wright his books. As soon as they were in his hands he limped down the stairs, leaving Himes the task of repositioning the trunk in the small room.

*   *   *

DESPITE THE initial lack of reception from Himes's fellow "soul brothers," he did get to know most of the black American expatriates soon thereafter. In some respects, Paris was a small town, and the resident black Americans often congregated in the same places, usually the Monaco or the Tournon. Himes also adopted these cafés as his own, and he soon met, among others, William Gardner Smith, author of the haunting war novel *Last of the Conquerors*; cartoonist Ollie Harrington, Wright's closest friend in Paris; Ish Kelley (the model for Fishbelly in Wright's *The Long Dream*); artist Walter Coleman; and the distinguished historian Dr. E. Franklin Frazier, then head of the Paris-based Mutual Security Agency.

Through Wright he also met James Baldwin. The encounter, at Deux Magots, was bizarre. "Dick sat down in lordly fashion and started right off needling Baldwin, who defended himself with such intensity that he stammered, his body trembled, and his face quivered," remembered Himes. "I sat and looked from one to another, Dick playing the fat cat and forcing Baldwin into the role of the quivering mouse." The cruel bantering continued for hours, the accusations and denunciations flying furiously. Finally, around midnight, Himes couldn't bear it anymore and got up to leave. "The last thing I remember before I left them at it," he recounted, "was Baldwin saying, 'The sons must slay their fathers.'" The remark stuck in Himes's head. It was only years later that he deciphered what Baldwin was talking about: "American blacks must always get ahead in American society by walking over each other."

While such observations of Wright's capacity for mean-spiritedness bothered Himes, it was mostly Wright with whom he socialized at first. Each morning between seven and eight, the Wrights would appear at the hotel so that they could have coffee with Himes at the Tournon. Invariably he was still asleep but would nonetheless accept the invitation. The Wrights would then disappear for the rest of the day, leaving Himes free either to go back to bed or to linger at the café. In retrospect, Himes thought that his first week in Paris had been dull. It hardly held the promise that he'd expected and that Wright touted. His fellow blacks seemed caught up in petty jealousies; the few French he'd met appeared to be interested mainly in carping about the Americans, particularly the GIs who were still stationed in fair number in France.

Himes did enjoy Wright's company but, as he said later, "it didn't take an awful lot of Dick to get on [his] nerves." Part of the problem, to be sure, was envy. Wright had money, celebrity, a status among the French and the black American expatriates nearly that of royalty. And though Himes readily admitted that this exalted position was deserved, what bothered him was the way in which Wright pandered to it. Yet his respect and genuine affection generally overcame his frustration at what he regarded as Wright's occasional lapses into condescending egocentricity.

HIMES HAD been in Paris just a week when Vandi Haygood arrived from New York. Despite the fight they'd had a few days before Himes left the States, all was, as so often in the past, now forgotten. Indeed, their relationship had nearly always been tumultuous. He had first met her during the war, when she had been acting director of the Rosenwald Foundation, while her husband, William Haygood, was in the army. The foundation had given Himes a grant to complete his novel *If He Hollers Let Him Go*. At that time the relationship was strictly business, but in the mid-forties they met up again and had a brief affair. Both were still married at the time, and living in separate cities, and they did not see each other for another five or six years. In late 1951, Haygood was living in New York, working as an executive with the Institute of International Education; like Himes, she had gotten out of her marriage. Their ardent affair, "steeped in sex and alcohol," began shortly after their reunion and, despite numerous difficulties, continued for the next eighteen months, nearly until Himes sailed for France.

In 1951, Haygood was in her late thirties. She was well educated, intelligent, thoroughly charming, physically attractive,

In response to the influx of young American writers, Paris-based English-language magazines began to flourish in the early fifties. Here a group associated with *The Paris Review* is photographed outside the Café de Tournon in 1954. Seated in the front row, from left to right, are Vilma Howard, poet; Jane Lougee, the publisher of *Merlin*; Muffy Wainhouse, the wife of Austryn Wainhouse; Jean Garrigue, poet. In the second row are Christopher Logue (*with cigarette*), poet and *Merlin* editor; Richard Seaver, then associated with *Merlin*, who subsequently became the editor of *Evergreen Review*; Evan S. Connell (*partially obscured*), novelist; Niccolo Tucci, essayist and novelist; a woman known as "Gloria the Beautiful Cloak Model"; Michel van der Plats from the Dutch publication *Het Vaderland* (*in trench coat behind the Cloak Model*); Peter Huyn, poet, translator, editor; Alfred Chester, novelist and short-story writer; and Austryn Wainhouse, novelist, translator, and *Merlin* editor. In the last row are three *Paris Review* editors—Eugene Walter, novelist, poet, librettist; George Plimpton (*with hat*); and William Pène du Bois. Next are James Broughton, poet and filmmaker; William Gardner Smith, novelist; and Harold Witt, poet.

ABOVE: George Whitman (*left*), Richard Wright, and Peter Matthiessen outside Whitman's English-language bookstore, Librairie Mistral (now Shakespeare and Company). LEFT: Whitman ardently promoted the resident expatriate writers by sponsoring readings and book signings, including (*listed here*) appearances by Richard Wright and James Baldwin. BOTTOM LEFT: *Merlin* publisher Jane Lougee with Christopher Logue. BOTTOM RIGHT: Whitman mans the desk at the Mistral, a major gathering spot for anglophone writers, travelers, and hangers-on.

Editors of the three most important Paris-based English-language literary journals of the early fifties. From left, George Plimpton of *The Paris Review*, Christopher Logue of *Merlin*, and Sindbad Vail of *Points*.

Lieutenant Lawrence Ferlinghetti, commander of a submarine chaser off the Normandy coast, days before the D Day invasion.

Sorbonne ID photograph of doctoral candidate Ferlinghetti in 1948. Along with completing his dissertation, during his stay in Paris he was writing the first of the poems that he would later publish as *Pictures of the Gone World*.

William S. Burroughs in the tiny bar at the "Beat Hotel," just after the Olympia Press publication of *Naked Lunch* in 1959.

Allen Ginsberg in his room at the hotel in the fall of 1957. Ginsberg recalled that the simultaneous residency of Burroughs, Corso, Gysin, himself, and others allowed them to "hit off each other's energy day and night."

TOP: The young Fulbright scholar and emerging poet John Ashbery with French poet Pierre Martory. BOTTOM: From left, painter Niki de Saint Phalle; her husband, poet and novelist Harry Mathews; and John Ashbery. Major literary innovators, Mathews and Ashbery explored in tandem what could be done with the American language.

TOP LEFT: Novelist James Jones, who despite years of Paris residency never shed an ounce of his Americanness. TOP RIGHT: Young Beat poet Gregory Corso at work in the warmth of the Mistral. BELOW: Artist and writer Brion Gysin at the Beat Hotel, staring into his dream machine, a revolving kaleidoscope he created for inducing drugless visions.

An embittered, impoverished, and beaten-down Chester Himes, shortly before sailing for France in 1953 (*top*), and (*bottom*) as the highly acclaimed novelist that he had become in Europe, in 1960. Himes recalled, after his initial French success, "Now I was a French writer and the United States of America could kiss my ass."

with a "knowing sensual grin." She was also addicted to Dexamyl and booze and, according to Himes, to sex. Both of them, at least in Himes's account, were fairly self-serving: "The first thing I desired now that I had money was to sleep with a white woman, and the only white woman in the city I knew at the time who was likely to sleep with me was Vandi Haygood." As for Haygood, "she always needed a man. She couldn't go to sleep without a man beside her, any man." Although sex seems to have been the base on which their relationship was founded, they appear to have had genuine affection for one another.

After more than a year of living together off and on, Himes suddenly flew into a jealous rage around Christmas 1952, when he discovered that Haygood had deceived him with an old lover. He began slapping her furiously. It was only the sight of her battered, swollen face that, in his words, brought him "back to sanity." For a brief moment Himes thought she was dead. And she nearly was. For two weeks she couldn't get out of bed; her face was blackened with bruises; she had lost her sense of equilibrium. During the interval in which she recovered, a guilt-ridden Himes took care of her, bathing her, feeding her, slowly nursing her back to health. Although they stayed together for a month or so more, and saw each other from time to time after that, it was clear their relationship was over. Himes, bewildered by his violence, afraid of it, tried to justify it on racial grounds: "The final answer of any black to a white woman with whom he lives in a white society is violence." The argument was specious, as Himes probably suspected, for the incident remained with him, and was probed in a novel he wrote a few years later, *The Primitive*.

But in the spring of 1953 in Paris, Himes was not thinking too deeply about the recent past. Even though he was fairly sure that the main reason Haygood had looked him up was that she didn't want to bother with having to "break in" a new lover, he was nonetheless pleased that she was there to rescue him from the café chitchat that was already striking him as more and more meaningless. During her one-week stay Himes took Haygood to see the Wrights, whom she'd known from her Rosenwald days, and introduced her to Malartic. But predictably, she and Himes spent most of their time in bed. It was there, on the last night of her visit, that they got into trouble, not with each other, for a change, but with the hotel management.

During an inspired lovemaking session their highly audible passion had disturbed the young woman in the room next to Himes's. She summoned the proprietress, who dutifully came upstairs and rapped at the door. A naked Himes responded to the knock, cracking the door ever so slightly. The proprietress, standing fixed and fierce, immediately went into a long harangue. But her discourse was lost on Himes, who knew no French. All at once the neighbor, who was peering over the proprietress's shoulder, said in English: "Mademoiselle was screaming so I could not sleep." At that, Haygood leaped from the bed nude and, according to Himes, "in a flaming fury . . . flung the door wide open as though she were going out [to] slap the young girl's face. Vandi was a big, strong-looking girl, and at the sight of us both standing there in the nude . . . the young French girl fled toward the stairs and even the old crone turned away with false modesty after she had taken a good long look at us."

The next morning, when Wright came around, the manager filled him in on the lurid details of his friend's escapades the night before. The upshot, in terms of logistics, was that Himes had to move to another room. But in the expatriate colony, Himes's legend spread quickly; Wright, who delighted in the episode, made sure everyone was informed.

A week elapsed between Haygood's departure and the arrival of Alva Van Olden, the woman Himes had met on the ship. Unlike Haygood, she had not come for a brief fling; she had decided to end her marriage and had left her husband and their four nearly grown daughters in Luxembourg. Also, in contrast, she was truly in love with Himes, and he thought he might be in love with her too. During the three weeks Himes had been in Paris they had written each other almost daily. As a result, he was well aware of her feelings and of the bold move she had made. At the same time, he was not quite sure what to do or how he really figured in all of this. But then, suddenly, she was in Paris.

Himes and Wright met her train at the Gare de l'Est; the reunion was somewhat strained, mainly because Wright had decided in advance that he wouldn't like her. As Himes related it, Wright "had an air of coarse jocularity that made it obvious he regarded her as a tramp, but would tolerate her because of me." Later, when they arrived in the Latin Quarter and passed Wright's house, he did not invite them in. "She felt his condescension like a slap and felt so sorry for me that she would have run away, she told me afterward. I became blindly angry, but I did not want to fall out with Dick because of her. The situation had grown tense and insupportable and it had become a question of who would give first."

The tension between Himes and Wright over Olden did not abate. If anything, it grew worse. Nonetheless, a few days later Himes and Olden accepted the Wrights' invitation to dinner. This proved to be a disaster. According to Himes, Wright's acerbic treatment of Olden had intensified. "I had never seen Dick behave so badly toward anyone but I realized that I was at fault. I had praised Alva so highly as a lady, he felt self-conscious around her and was furious with himself for feeling so. This caused a resentment that might have taken a vicious turn had it not been for me." Although Himes did not lash out at Wright during the dinner itself, he did feel that their relationship had been severely damaged, perhaps irreparably. Later that night he and Olden made a decision to take up an offer Malartic had extended to them to stay in his beach house in Arcachon for a while. A couple of days later he bid a cold farewell to Wright, who was himself soon to leave for the Gold Coast. The two did not speak or communicate with each other again for several years.

SHORTLY AFTER their arrival in the Gironde, Himes wrote to his old friend Carl Van Vechten about what had happened since his arrival in Paris:

I have left Paris after a month and come down to this pleasant little resort and fishing village on the Atlantic coast. I don't know exactly what I expected to get from Paris, but whatever it was I didn't get it. I don't think that is due entirely to the city. It seems now, looking back, that Dick Wright might have been blocking me off from meeting people or getting to know the city; he spent a great deal of time with me, but it was all quite pointless. . . .

Anyway, I never really got settled. I didn't particularly like the bistros; I've seen them all somewhere before. The good restaurants were too expensive (four to ten dollars a meal) and the inexpensive ones were bad. I found the sexuality (I'm sorry to say) dull and unimpressive. The naked women on Place Pigalle were just naked women; the titillating shows up on Montmartre were just tourist traps. Maybe the trouble is with me.

I loved the Seine, Notre Dame, the Louvre, the sidewalk cafés. . . . I saw too many chalk scribblings on the walls of the narrow streets of the Latin Quartier, "US GO HOME," and although the French whom I met swore it was the "other" Americans they hated because I wasn't "really an American" I didn't particularly like the connotation nor the exclusion. If I'm not an American, what am I? I was always overcharged. I didn't find any great welcome by the French girls. Most French girls shun Americans, Negroes included.

Himes and Olden spent two happy months in Arcachon. During this interval, away from Paris, the Wrights, and the petty café gossip, they grew quite close. Whatever Himes's initial hesitancy might have been, the idyll by the sea allowed him to plunge wholeheartedly into the relationship, allowed him truly to fall in love. He was relaxed, buoyant, exuberant, and another side of him was able to emerge during this period, that of the charming, suave, genteel, attentive gentleman. Often he buried this aspect of his character, leading with the choleric, bitter, even abusive persona that he harbored within and that frequently overtook him. But in Arcachon, loved and in love, the demons were kept at bay.

In late June, however, the restorative holiday was broken when Malartic informed them that his sister and her family were coming to Arcachon in July; Himes and Olden chose to move on. At first they considered going to Spain, then decided to head for England.

For the next seven months the two lived together in London. Although they felt the same affection and tenderness for each other as they had in France, London itself was another matter. The race problem reasserted itself constantly, albeit in subtler ways than in the United States. But as Himes knew, racism, sugarcoated or not, was still racism. With the exception of successfully fighting his landlady, who wanted to evict Himes and Olden once she became aware that he was black (and not just deeply tanned, as she had earlier thought!), Himes did not allow the race issue to preoccupy him. Instead, he devoted his energy to writing a novel with Olden.

The novel was Olden's idea: a first-person, largely auto-biographical account of life with her sadistic, philandering husband, a recent (pre-Himes) unconsummated love affair, and her subsequent nervous breakdown. Olden would write drafts of the chapters, then give them to Himes to revise, focus, and form. "Her story enthralled me, fascinated me," he noted, "and I employed all my ability and resources to shape it into a novel." Working on the book together brought them even closer: Himes became aware, through reading Olden's account of her near psychic destruction in Europe, that pain was not his alone. "Her book hurt me. . . . I didn't want to pity her; but I did."

By mid-December 1953, the book, more than 500 manuscript pages long, was finished. Himes had high hopes for it, but his British agent, Innes Rose, did not share his enthusiasm. He promptly returned the manuscript, informing Himes that it needed more work to be salable. Olden herself took it to Macmillan, but the book met the same response. By now, both were broke. London was bitterly cold and expensive, but they didn't have the funds to leave. Finally Himes phoned his editor at World, William Targ, and asked him for a $500 loan and to take an option on the novel. If Targ took the book, it was understood, the $500 would be deducted from the advance; if not, he could charge the sum against future royalties on *The Third Generation*. Targ cabled the money to Himes, but after reviewing the manuscript also turned it down.

With the money from Targ, Himes and Olden made a quick getaway to what they hoped would be warmer and cheaper climes, Majorca. Although greeted by a freak snowstorm upon their arrival, they took to the island from the start. It was cheaper, the inhabitants far more *simpáticos* than Londoners, and it did warm up quickly. They settled first in the small town of Puerto de Pollensa, about thirty-five miles from Palma. While still unhappy about the rejection of their joint novel, Himes, ever optimistic, ever the writer, set to work almost immediately on a new book. Entitled *The End of the Primitive*, it was Himes's counterpart to the story Olden had told in their combined effort; that is, the tale of his relationship with Vandi Haygood. The only difference, according to Himes, between his novel and what really happened was that the protagonist, Jesse, actually kills his white mistress, Kriss.

Once beginning *The Primitive*, as the published novel ended up being called,* Himes became almost completely absorbed in it, but in a manner different from that in the past: "I wrote slowly, savoring each word, sometimes taking an hour to fashion one sentence to my liking. . . . That was the first time in my life I enjoyed writing; before I had always written from compulsion. . . . For once I was almost doing what I wanted to with a story, without being influenced by the imagined reactions of editors, publishers, critics, readers, or anyone. By then I had reduced myself to the fundamental writer, and nothing else mattered."

The intensity of the writing is clearly reflected in what is perhaps Himes's most complex novel. Here the grotesque, often near comic exterior world of Harlem and Gramercy Park is in

---

* The published version differed from the original not only in title but also in content. Scenes were cut, language censored, the narrative significantly altered, much to Himes's distress and over his strident objections. In 1990 the original version was published in Britain by Allison & Busby as *The End of the Primitive*.

decided contrast to the sinister, violent, hallucinatory interior milieu inhabited only by Jesse and Kriss. The plot is simple, the story unfolding over six days. In the early chapters, between Tuesday and Thursday, Himes alternates his focus on the two central figures, thereby creating vivid pictures of their separate worlds. While Kriss, after popping her daily blue-gray pill, goes to work as a high-powered, enormously efficient executive, Jesse wanders the mean streets of Harlem wondering whether his latest novel has been accepted or contends with the inanities of the "pervert" Leroy, who lives in his rooming house.

On Thursday evening, Jesse arrives at Kriss's well-appointed apartment for their first rendezvous in years. They spend the evening drinking, appraising their common past, realizing in the process how estranged they are from that time, how estranged they are from each other now. But they remain together, torturing one another and themselves, popping pills, drinking excessively, making love, passing out. By Sunday night, after a weekend of debauchery, interrupted only by visits from characters from their shared past, Jesse sinks into a mad self-loathing, brought on in part by the news that his novel has been rejected because "the public is fed up with protest novels." Then, late that night, he blacks out. Awakening, he finds that Kriss is dead, a knife stuck through her heart. At first, he savagely attempts to revive her, then suddenly realizes the absurdity of his actions, as he, of course, is the murderer. "End product of the impact of Americanism on one Jesse Robinson—black man," he muses. "Your answer, son, you've been searching for it. *Black man kills white woman.* All the proof you need now. . . . Proof beyond all doubt. Jesse Robinson joins the human race."

Olden read every page of *The Primitive*, fascinated by the obsessive story. According to Himes, she kept making him tone it down, "to prevent it from becoming pornographic." But he added that "the very essence of any relationship between a black man and a white woman in the United States is sex, and generally sex of a nature which lends itself to pornography. . . . Just to put a black man into a white woman's bed is to suggest an orgy."

Although the statement may seem hyperbolic, at least by today's standards, for Himes it reflected what he had experienced first-hand, with both Haygood and Olden. "I had been made furious," he recalled, "by the hypocritical respectability of white people feigning outrage and indignation at the sight of me and Alva together, while all the time smirking and leering and revealing sick envy of our perpetual orgy that took place in their minds." In a way, this was the starting point for the fictive *Primitive*, a book that, Himes noted, would give white people "something to hate me for."

This was not, however, the end point. What began as an exploration of sex and race culminates in murder. But in Himes's construct, this too is the logical conclusion to years of hurt and rage. When Jesse kills, it is not by design. Murder is simply the outgrowth of his pent-up emotions, aggravated by a weekend of alcohol. The link between sex and violence, according to Himes, is not misogyny but misanthropy, the result of a basic devaluing of the human being, by society but also by the self. Sex comes into the equation not because it is an act of love, but because it is one of animal aggression, in which interracial sex becomes an insurrectionary act. The words of Eldridge Cleaver, commenting on his early mind-set regarding black-white rape, are especially apt here: "It delighted me that I was defying and trampling upon the white man's law, upon his system of values, and that I was defiling his women—and this point, I believe, was the most satisfying to me because I was very resentful over the historical fact of how the white man has used the black woman. I felt I was getting revenge. From the site of the act of rape, consternation spreads outwardly in concentric circles. . . . I know that if I had not been apprehended I would have slit some white throats."

The Primitive is a disturbing book, an unflinching examination of the psyche wounded from the uneasy cohabitation of violence, racism, and sexual stereotyping, legacies of the black man's ordeal in America. Or as Himes wrote in the preface to the French edition of the book: "I have attempted to present an experience: to describe the idiocy of the twentieth century."

* * *

HIMES FINISHED *The Primitive* in early July 1954. By then, nearly broke, he was hoping for a quick sale. It was not to be; World, which had published *The Third Generation*, rejected it. According to Himes's editor, it was not because he didn't like the book. On the contrary, William Targ considered it a true artistic achievement. But World was a large Bible publisher and the house feared a backlash from its substantial number of Bible buyers. For Himes, however, a rejection was a rejection, whatever the reason. In a letter to Malartic, he stated his reaction: "I think publishers all over the world are going crazy. Perhaps this is the year of the publisher's moon. I know my publishers in the U.S. are crazy; they rejected the book [Olden] and I did together and then this one, both of which stand a better chance of sales than did THE THIRD GENERATION; and in England there is a great 'clean-up' campaign going on in the publishing business. . . . I find [*The Primitive*] a much better book than I first thought. In fact it might be the best book I've yet written. I can say that I like it best of all."

By September, with no sale yet and no other resources to draw on, Himes bounced a check and returned with Olden to Arcachon, thinking they could stay in Malartic's house. Upon arrival they learned that the house had been sold during the summer. For nine days they moved into a hotel that belonged to an acquaintance; then, again destitute, Himes wrote another rubber check and they set off for Paris. Their difficulties were not at an end; not only were they short on cash, but they could not find a place to stay. To Carl Van Vechten, Himes explained: "On my arrival in Paris with an American white woman, at about 8 am, by 4 pm we had not found an inexpensive hotel room. So I sat in a cafe on rue de Seine and she walked down the street and got a small double room in the first hotel on rue de Buci (hotel Jeanne d'Arc) she came to, and when we moved in the proprietor was very angry."

Once settled in, Himes began to peddle the new book to French publishers, with Malartic's assistance. But this was to no avail, and Himes was forced to hock his typewriter and a ring belonging to Olden. Meanwhile, Targ, who believed in the book, sent a copy to New American Library, which had published the paperback edition of *The Third Generation*. After some lengthy consideration, Victor Weybright, head of NAL, responded with an offer. As Himes related it, "Weybright wrote me this long letter about how we'll pay you a thousand-dollar advance on this because we feel it's best for the author to have a small advance and have substantial accruals. . . . I'll never forget that phrase. I never got any accruals, substantial or otherwise." Himes did not feel he was in a bargaining position, however. He accepted the offer.

Despite the improvement in his fortunes, Himes's relationship with Olden had begun to collapse. The process had been gradual, starting while they were still in Majorca. "Before I had needed to make love to her in order to work on her book. But now that I had begun to work on my own book, the sex act was enough in itself. Any woman would have done. The sex act had always stimulated my thinking—not necessarily my thoughts— and of course relieved my tensions. But in that respect love was not necessary. But I still loved Alva, even though I did not need her. And although she read my manuscript page by page as it was written, she didn't share in the writing of it. And writing was my life, and the very essence of our relationship underwent a subtle change." When they arrived in Paris, the affection between them was still present, but the spark had died. On the first of December 1954, Olden sailed back to New York. The trip was made ostensibly to try to sell their novel, but both of them knew that their tender affair was over. They would meet up again, when Himes himself was back in the United States the next year; but in reality the relationship ended on that cold December day at the Gare St.-Lazare when Himes put Olden on the boat train for Le Havre. Through a flood of tears they frantically waved good-bye, both inwardly aware that this parting was not to be temporary.

With Olden gone, Himes felt distinctly at loose ends. As before, he found Paris less than a comfortable haven. Not only did he feel, as he wrote Carl Van Vechten, that the city was "profoundly hostile to American negroes," but he had also begun to believe that his French publisher, Albin Michel, was withholding money due him from one of his books issued in France. According to Himes's calculation, the house owed him some 300,000 francs (about $900) for his first novel, *If He Hollers Let Him Go*. Himes calculated this after seeing a notice in one of the books stating that it was the ten thousandth copy to be printed. The publisher, however, claimed that there had been a first edition run of 12,000 copies, but that 10,000 of them had been returned. The house did admit owing Himes some money, though: about 37,000 francs. "This incredible story sits like a hard knot in my stomach," he wrote Van Vechten, ". . . but that's the way it stands."

At Gallimard he fared better. He had originally gone to see Marcel Duhamel, who had translated *If He Hollers Let Him Go* and who was head of the firm's detective and suspense novel imprint, La Série Noire, about buying *The Primitive*. Duhamel didn't want the novel for his series, although he thought Gallimard itself might be interested. Instead, he tried to talk Himes into writing a detective novel for him. Himes, desperately short of cash, complied and turned in an outline a day or so later. Duhamel liked the idea, about a "Negro getting framed for the murder of an American whitewoman [*sic*] in Paris." But when Himes gave him the synopsis a few days later, Duhamel rejected it, suggesting instead that Himes write about Harlem. "Put plenty comedy in it," advised Duhamel, "not too much white brutality, in fact there needn't be any white people in it, just an action-packed funny story about Harlem." Himes set to work, but when Gallimard bought *The Primitive* for its Du Monde Entier imprint, he abandoned the project.

In the middle of December, by now disgusted with Paris, Himes decided to go to London for a couple of months. This turned out to be the first leg of a trip to the United States. His reason for returning so precipitately was that he felt he had to see Olden again in order to come to terms with his affair—either positively or negatively. He arrived in New York around the end of January 1955. No one, not even Olden, was there to meet him. Nearly broke, despondent, he checked into an old, run-down hotel. Olden arrived from Boston a few days later. Where before there had been affection, if not love, now there was passion but not a great deal of affection. During their separation Olden had grown more unsure of the relationship, as had Himes. Within weeks of his arrival, they came to the sad awareness that it truly was over.

By this point Himes was ready to return to France but found himself in the usual predicament: lack of funds. Typically, he threw himself into trying to raise money from writing, by sending some recent stories to *Esquire*, which had published him before. They were rejected. Finally he got a break. Berkley bought the paperback rights to *If He Hollers Let Him Go*, offering an advance of $1,000. The advance, however, did not come quickly and Himes was forced to take a series of menial jobs in order to keep alive. After repeated attempts to get Berkley to pay up, Himes took the case to legal aid. After one phone call from the lawyer, Berkley paid. It was now already December. The same day he received the check, Himes bought a ticket back to France.

While Himes wrote very little during his stay in New York, he did inadvertently manage to collect a vast amount of material about Harlem that he would later use quite profitably in his later books. At the time, though, this was not in his head: all he wanted to do was leave the United States as quickly as possible.

Arriving in Paris the day after Christmas, he felt immensely relieved to be back in France, free from a country that he equated with a "vast prison of the mind." This time, Paris seemed different and he became far more socially active than before, spending his evenings at the Tournon with his fellow "soul brothers." Although Wright was in town, Himes did not see much of him, preferring instead the more amicable cartoonist Ollie Harrington, creator of the comic strip *Bootsie*, and painter Walter Coleman. With Harrington, in fact, he became close.

Himes likened this period of his life to a "weird, grotesque, a drunken Walpurgisnacht. I got America out of my mind but in so doing I was rapidly destroying myself. The only thing that kept me from being an alcoholic was my incredible appetite. . . . I had the creative urge, but the old, used forms for the black American writer did not fit my creations. I wanted to break through the barrier that labeled me as a 'protest writer.' I knew the life of an American black needed another image than just the victim of racism." With this idea in mind he began to work on a new book, written mostly during long days spent at the heated Café au Départ. The new novel, eventually entitled *Pinktoes*, was a definite reflection of Himes's quest for a new sort of fiction, a search that led him to realize victimization was too narrow a definition to describe black people: "We were unique individuals, funny but not clowns, solemn but not serious, hurt but not suffering, sexualists but not whores in the usual sense of the word; we had a tremendous love of life, a love of sex, a love of ourselves. We were absurd."

Pinktoes is an "absurd" novel. Its central character, Mamie Mason, actually makes a brief appearance as the character Maud in *The Primitive*. But while that novel is dark and obsessive, in spite of its moments of humor, *Pinktoes* is lighter, viciously satirical, often very funny. Like *The Primitive*, though, *Pinktoes* has an autobiographical base and in many ways is a roman à clef. In a letter to writer John Williams, Himes explained the book's origin:

> I went to New York to live with Henry and Mollie Moon in their fabulous apartment at 940 St. Nicholas. It was during the time Roosevelt was running for his last term. The communists, the negroes, the negrophiles and friends were getting together to elect Roosevelt. Henry Lee [Moon] was working for the CIO Political Action Committee . . . and Mollie was giving parties sponsored and paid for by the various groups, including the Democratic National Committee. It was there I met everybody and came to know them well. There is hardly a prominent middle class negro of today I did not meet at that time—Walter White & Co., Lester Granger, Ralph Bunche—oh hell, all of them. *It was from this time and from these people I have taken the scenes and characters for my book.*

If *Pinktoes* is any indication, Himes must have felt the odd man out at these interracial gatherings, for his portrayal of this crowd in the novel (including his cousin Henry Moon) is hardly flattering. Mamie's parties, while held apparently for the purpose of promoting civil rights, are little more than bacchanals, reflecting her philosophy that the solution to the "Negro problem" is interracial sex. Himes, though never completely in control of his subject, nonetheless offers a series of eccentric, cutting vignettes, ultimately more fun than mean-spirited, in which no one—black or white—is spared from being lampooned.

Although Himes was a notoriously fast writer, about 120 pages into *Pinktoes* he became stalled and began work on another novel. "I was finding it so difficult to keep [*Pinktoes*] funny," he remarked, "that I began writing the synopsis for an epic novel about the American blacks in the Latin Quarter which was eventually published as a novel, *Une Affaire de Viol* [*A Case of Rape*]." As he noted, in this book Himes drew increasingly on his observations of Paris's black expatriate community; but it is also a "what if?" novel, in which Himes posits the question, What would have happened if Alva Van Olden had returned briefly to see him in Paris? These reflections were inspired in part by his recently learning that Olden had sold their joint novel to Beacon Press. While Himes was happy for her, the news was bittersweet, for following his advice she had submitted the novel under her name only. A lawyer, meanwhile, had gotten involved in the process and Himes was asked to sign legal papers disavowing his coauthorship. He complied, but the forced deception angered him; he decided to write the rancor out of his system by putting it into a novel.

A Case of Rape is Himes's tersest, most experimental novel, a result, no doubt, of its being more a long synopsis than the fully developed novel he had originally envisioned. Indeed, according to him, the incident around which the book is constructed was originally conceived as only one episode in "a long, Dostoievskian work, possibly consisting of several volumes." This is not to suggest that the book is incomplete or even lacking in essential material to flesh out the narrative. Rather, the austerity is beguiling, the situation completely contained, the characters well drawn.

The plot of *A Case of Rape* draws heavily on Himes's own experiences, both with Olden and with his fellow black expatriates in Paris. Told in a series of legal depositionlike statements, it is the story of Elizabeth Hancock (Olden) and Scott Hamilton (Himes), in which parallels to the real-life story abound, including an international love affair, the writing of a novel, and an ultimate separation in the United States. Up to that point, the events in Himes's novel are almost exactly those that actually happened. Then, however, Himes the novelist takes over, and the "what if?" scenario unfolds, beginning with Hancock and Hamilton's attempt to resume their relationship. This quickly falls apart. Their novel, carrying only her name, is accepted, but the publisher's attorney writes to Hancock that word has been received from someone in Paris that the book was actually ghosted by a black man. If this is not the case, she is informed, she must submit a notarized document from the suspected ghostwriter testifying that he did not have a hand in its authorship.

It is this that brings them together again. Hancock at first accuses Hamilton of informing the publisher. He vehemently denies it. In an effort to sort out the business, he asks her to accompany him to his hotel room, where his story can be corroborated by three of his closest friends, Caesar Gee, Theodore Elkins, and Sheldon Russell (modeled loosely on Ollie Harrington, William Gardner Smith, and James Baldwin). She agrees. The afternoon goes well enough, but Elkins begins to feel slighted because Hancock has not engaged him much in conversation. Out of spite, he gives her a glass of sherry tainted with cantharides (Spanish fly), which, contrary to his desires, sends her into wild, uncontrollable thrashing, followed rapidly by death. During the convulsive fit, a neighbor across the courtyard sees the men bending over Hancock in an attempt to help her and calls the police. The four men are arrested on rape and murder charges, convicted, and sentenced to life imprisonment.

After their conviction, Roger Garrison, an internationally acclaimed black writer living in Paris (read: Richard Wright), decides to champion their case and sets about to collect evidence to free them. As it turns out, he is the one who wrote to the publisher implicating Hamilton as the ghostwriter. But his motivation is not based on the fact that he is partially to blame for Hancock's death. Instead, he is on a mission to combat racism internationally, to denounce for political reasons the imprisonment of the four men, to prove that France is being taken over by racist attitudes. Perhaps because he is on such a crusade, he overlooks basic facts—such as the innocence of the accused. In the end, despite his societal and political clout, he is unsuccessful.

Although *A Case of Rape* is a short novel, slightly over a hundred pages, it is a distilled, complex work in which Himes turned his acutely critical eye to the way in which racism confounds the human psyche. The defendants are innocent, yet they are unwilling or unable to defend themselves adequately, assuming from the start, because of years of conditioning, that they will automatically be judged guilty. At the same time, Himes unflinchingly examines the psychology by which the oppressed become the oppressors. Burdened and stunted by the legacy of race hatred inflicted on them, they react by hating in turn. "It was just pure, spontaneous, unpremeditated, racially-inspired *spite* that provoked [Elkins] into giving the bottle to ... Hancock," wrote Himes. This same sort of reverse racism is what inspires Garrison as well; he is blinded to reality by his belief that the verdict was "a perfect example of the racist-political ends served by all such convictions of Negro men for raping white women." This results in his basic error: "Roger was so accustomed to condemning the dominant white group for the crimes committed by the oppressed black minorities, he completely ignored the fundamental principle of a democratic society, the assumption of innocence." The irony, of course, is that three of the defendants are completely innocent, and even Elkins did not intend for the dose to be lethal.

In the end, *A Case of Rape*, like so much of Himes's best work, must be read as a record of the destructive force of racism. At the same time, the book is not a protest novel in the sense of *Native Son*. Rather, it is a cry from the soul, an indictment of society from the inside out. Rarely did Himes write more convincingly, with such mastery over his narrative, than in *A Case of Rape*. It is a brilliant, multilayered examination of the intricacies of race, sex, and power, but what ultimately makes the novel so compelling is that it is a chronicle of doomed love. Neither Hamilton nor Hancock can live in a world fully of their own making; instead they inhabit a vicious, absurd universe, which insists on cutting up everything literally into black and white.

DURING THE period in which Himes wrote both *A Case of Rape* and *Pinktoes*, between early and late 1956, he was managing to hold on in Paris through a small advance on the French edition of *The Third Generation*. More acclimated now to living in France than he had ever been, he became a familiar figure in the Left Bank cafés. But unlike most of his fellow black American expatriates, he never felt wholly at home. In his portrayal of his alter ego Scott Hamilton in *A Case of Rape*, Himes remarked that "Scott was too old to have come to Paris. People of his age, with his background, found it hard, if not impossible, to adjust to Paris. Paris was too much like themselves, tired, jaded, blasé and cynical. People were always intolerant of their own vices when seen in another." While this is an accurate statement of Himes's own feelings toward the city, he also held another view, namely, that "he had never found anywhere that he liked." As a result, he reasoned, he might as well be in Paris.

But by the end of 1956, staying on in Paris was again proving difficult for financial reasons. Embroiled in another love affair, this time with a German woman living in Paris, he was reluctant to leave. Besides, he realized, where could he go? He concentrated on his work, thinking that somehow it would, as before, prove to be his salvation. But despite his prodigious efforts on this score, he so far had not been able to sell any of the new work. Finally, with his resources depleted, with nowhere to go and no one really to turn to, he approached Duhamel about writing the detective novel the French editor had suggested he attempt two years before. Not only was Duhamel still receptive, but he also immediately advanced Himes some money, merely with Himes's promise to deliver. The trust was not misplaced. Himes began work immediately, using as a basis a preposterous story about modern-day alchemy that Walter Coleman had told him.

According to Duhamel, "Less than fifteen days later he returned with a first draft of *Four Cornered Square* [sic], which would become *La Reine des Pommes*. There was in it enough material for three Série Noire books. I took the liberty of making some suggestions for possible cuts and perhaps for a slightly revised ending." One of the suggestions that Duhamel apparently made was that the book, which was to be a *policier*, needed police. It was this fortunate comment that resulted in the creation of two of the most outrageous fictional detectives ever: Coffin Ed Johnson and Grave Digger Jones. With this invention of the two hard-boiled Harlem detectives, Himes had the essential but heretofore missing ingredient for a sustained output, namely, continuing characters that eventually link one book to another. In fact, Coffin Ed and Grave Digger not only lend continuity from one crime novel to the next but also give Himes's books a definite flavor and, by extension, a distinct focus. At the time of their creation, however, Himes was not thinking much beyond finishing his book and collecting the rest of his advance.

It did not take him long to rework the draft. As Duhamel remembered it, "A week or so [after their previous meeting] he returned with the novel completed, along with a choice of two or three different endings, all equally astonishing and believable." Himes picked up the remainder of his $1,000 advance that day and proceeded directly to a men's clothing store. Always a sharp dresser, he laid a great deal of stock in his appearance, which he felt had been seriously undermined by his lack of funds to buy clothes. For Himes, dressing well equated to some extent with well-being. In this case it had an even more symbolic meaning: "I came out of the store," he remembered, "walking hard and feeling proud; now I was a French writer and the United States of America could kiss my ass."

With *La Reine des Pommes*, aka *The Five Cornered Square* (published in English first as *For Love of Imabelle*, then as *A Rage in Harlem*), Himes had entered a new phase in his career. For more than a decade he would write exclusively for La Série Noire, turning out nine more detective novels. All were written initially for Duhamel, most of them, like *La Reine des Pommes*, in just a few months. It was, as Himes was quick to note, an "absurd" situation. Here he was, a black American writing about Harlem for a French press and French readers, being regarded in France even as a French writer, while he couldn't even speak the language. At the same time, the circumstances were greatly to his liking. At the end of 1956 he was nearly destitute; six months later, thanks to three advances from Duhamel, he had nearly $4,000 in his pocket, two books finished, and a third well under way.

Although he continued to live off and on in the dilapidated hotel at 9 Rue Gît-le-Cœur (in the following few years better known as the "Beat Hotel"), his fortunes had definitely improved. He began to travel again and even bought a car. But financial improvement was not the only reward. In 1958, with the publication of *La Reine des Pommes*, Himes's achievement in the new genre was given an unambiguous French stamp of approval when the novel won the Grand Prix de Littérature Policière. The publication of four more novels during 1958–1959 only added to his prestige and financial security. Himes was not getting rich, but the hard times were definitely behind him.

WHILE HIMES'S switch to writing detective novels was obviously a wise "career move," it also meant relinquishing his earlier quest to become a "serious" novelist. It limited as well his scope and his themes, and forced him to concentrate on the more sordid aspects of the black experience: violence, crime, fear, poverty. To be sure, this terrain had always been fruitful for Himes, but in the crime novels he was not so free to explore a wider range of emotional substance, which he had managed to do convincingly in books such as *If He Hollers Let Him Go*, *The Third Generation*, *The*

Primitive, and *A Case of Rape*. These novels too are violent, filled with hurt, but there is also tenderness, beauty, an overriding attempt to depict the human predicament in a greater totality. The detective story, by its very nature, and particularly in the Série Noire, was based on action followed by more action; thus, the reflective quality of the earlier novels had to be largely forsaken, or subsumed under the requisite pell-mell atmosphere characteristic of the genre. This is not to dismiss the crime stories; it is simply to suggest that Himes was now forced to write under constraints imposed on him by the type of novel he was producing. What he did within the formula, however, was remarkable.

HIMES RECALLED that while working on *La Reine des Pommes* he reread Faulkner's *Sanctuary*, "to sustain [his] outrageousness and give [him] courage." The choice, not only of Faulkner but of *Sanctuary*, is illuminating, for if there is a literary parallel to the atmosphere of Himes's Harlem, it is Faulkner's Yoknapatawpha, particularly as conjured up in Faulkner's perhaps most brutal, claustrophobic, nightmarish work. In *Sanctuary*, which is also a sort of detective novel, the emphasis is not on punishing wrongdoers, as in the standard crime story, but on evoking evil itself. Frenchman's Bend, like Himes's Harlem, is a closed world, an all-encompassing trap where murder, mayhem, misogyny, and sexual aberration are the pathological norms.

While on the surface Himes's detective fiction seems to be in line with the novels of Raymond Chandler, Dashiell Hammett, or Jim Thompson, in reality he broke considerable new ground with his books, in least measure by creating black detectives pursuing black criminals. What Himes did was evoke, like Faulkner in *Sanctuary*, a completely amoral world in which justice is twisted, values erased, meaning relegated to the ash bin. Coffin Ed and Grave Digger are not really counterparts to Sam Spade or Philip Marlowe; they are not intent on restoring bourgeois order—indeed, they commit more crimes than they solve. Rather, their roles are to illuminate the increasingly absurd, disjointed fabric that Himes perceived as the Harlem nightmare.

In Himes's novels, the whole social order is parodied, the "American Dream," that is, the pursuit of wealth, a grotesque impossibility for all save the most despicable of criminals, who score their capitalist successes at the expense of their fellow black Americans. Into this world are dropped Himes's detectives, charged by the white establishment to "preserve justice and re-store order," which essentially means depriving the upstart criminal-capitalists of that American Dream. When this serves their own ends, Coffin Ed and Grave Digger are happy to comply, but just as often they subvert the very "ideals" they are supposed to uphold.

In the end, Himes's novels come much closer to conveying the dissolute landscape of the present-day inner city than do most novels. His mastery, perhaps, is that these messages, while hardly buried, never overpower the narrative. It is entirely possible to read any of Himes's crime novels as conventional thrillers. They are exquisitely plotted, often humorous, enormously fast-paced, as tight as the best of Chandler or Hammett. Only when one closely examines the underlying statements, momentarily cov-ered by the well-contrived chaos, do the intense social critique, the cynicism, the despair fully emerge, naked and undeniable.

HIMES'S IMPACT on France with this series of novels was immense. Not only did he become an extremely popular novelist, winning accolades from the likes of Jean Giono ("I give you all of Heming-way, Dos Passos and Fitzgerald for this Chester Himes"), he per-haps also indirectly began to have an effect on a younger group of writers who were attempting to explore new literary territory: the New Novelists, in particular Michel Butor and Alain Robbe-Grillet. While there is no similarity in intention—Himes was not primarily interested in literary innovation—there is a parallel fascination with using the crime story as a subtext for a multiplicity of meanings. In Butor's work, for instance, as in Himes's, the surface story slips away; nothing is quite what it seems. And one cannot help feeling that the New York of Robbe-Grillet's *Project for a Revolution in New York*, with its scenes of violence, social reversals, hollow ethics, is not in some way the logical extension of Himes's equally hallucinatory vision of Harlem. The connection is far more visceral than direct, but as both Butor and Robbe-Grillet were voracious consumers of the Série Noire novels, it is possible that somewhere in these highly cerebral constructs lurks the shadow of Chester Himes.

Despite the celebrity status that Himes was quickly winning in France, his fortunes in the United States did not immediately improve. Both *Pinktoes* and *A Case of Rape* had been turned down by several of his former publishers and would, like the crime novels, be published in the United States only after publication in France, and only after he had become a celebrated writer in Europe.* But as he wrote Carl Van Vechten in late 1957, "I am not bitter about this. . . . My present life is the happiest I have had in a very long time. I just don't like to think about the U.S. now. Maybe at some later time." He was, in fact, so discouraged by his earlier dealings with American presses that he allowed Marcel Duhamel to take full charge of selling his books (successfully) to U.S. publishers. Himes had truly become, in a curious way, a French writer. It was in Europe that he had made his reputation; it was in Europe that he would stay.

HIMES HAD long been entangled with women. For a number of years he had had a stormy, off-and-on relationship with a German woman. Then, in 1959, he met Lesley Packard, a striking Englishwoman in love with life and, shortly thereafter, with Himes. He extricated himself, with considerable difficulty, from

---

* *A Case of Rape* was not published in the United States until 1980, seventeen years after it appeared in France, when Targ Editions brought it out in a signed, limited edition of 350 copies. It was subsequently reissued in 1984 by Howard University Press. *Pinktoes* was not published in English until 1961, when Olympia Press issued it in its Traveller's Companion series. It was then republished by G. P. Putnam's Sons in 1965.

his other relationship when he realized that with Packard his quest for women, for mutuality, for love, could finally end. Despite numerous difficulties, their bond proved to be a lasting one. They married in the late seventies, and she was with him when he died, in their house in Alicante, Spain, in 1984.

FROM HIMES's return to France after his abysmal stay in New York in 1955, until his death, he visited the States only twice, and then only briefly. Yet he did not remain much longer permanently in Paris once he began to receive regular checks from Duhamel. During most of the sixties he was unusually peripatetic, rarely staying for long anywhere, preferring instead to follow his whims.

But until 1968, when he settled in Spain and largely ceased traveling, Paris was always the one place to which he returned. It was his center, his base. It had supported him, rewarded him, in a sense made him a major author in the eyes of Europeans. As Himes wrote, "It was not so much that France helped me, but that it let me live and empowered me to concentrate on my work. . . . For me, France represented the possibility of writing without having to confront the barriers imposed by race, politics, finances, or my physical appearance."

Despite Himes's reputation in Europe for more than a quarter-century, it is only now—no doubt in part because of the Hollywood films based on his detective novels—that Americans are beginning to discover in numbers one of their most gifted, most hurt, most "absurd" native sons.

Chapter Ten

Among Their Fellow Americans: Irwin Shaw and James Jones in Paris

TAXES AND McCarthy. Those were the reasons usually given for Irwin Shaw's departure for France in June 1951. Taxes, or more accurately, a desire to escape American taxation, was generally believed (at least in the press) the more valid cause, as Senator Joseph McCarthy had not yet been so thoroughly exposed as the monstrous force he would turn out to be. Of the two supposed reasons, though, only the second was actually valid at the time, for Shaw was not aware of the loophole in the tax law that allowed Americans residing abroad for seventeen out of eighteen months to take advantage of the exemption that applied to income earned outside the United States. Later Shaw did have his screen-writing income funneled through European studios, but in 1951 the possibility did not even exist for him.

McCarthy, however, was another matter. Shaw's leftist leanings had been well-known since the 1930s, when his antiwar drama *Bury the Dead* was produced in New York. Although at the time it did not cause a rumble politically, in the late forties, while working as a screenwriter in Hollywood, he came under scrutiny as the author of this and other dramas for being perhaps "anti-American." It was then that the infamous Thomas hearings were convened to purge "Communists" in Hollywood. While Shaw was not one of the "Hollywood Ten" expelled in 1948 from the motion picture industry as a result of the hearings, he was denounced by studio boss Jack Warner as a "covert Communist." Despite these attacks from within and outside the film industry, Shaw continued his career unscathed throughout the late 1940s.

But in March 1951, with the reconvening of the House Un-American Activities Committee, the situation turned even uglier. Denunciation followed denunciation. As friends and acquaintances were called up, Shaw became more worried that he too might be denounced, or worse, forced to appear and called on to name names. His concern intensified late that spring when he realized that his new novel about to be published, *The Troubled Air*, in spite of its ambiguous treatment of witch-hunting in the radio industry, could very well be perceived as an antigovernment tract. This book, he thought, might alone be sufficient cause to call into question his patriotism. In the end, though the novel was bashed for this reason among others, Shaw was not named or subpoenaed. But his fears were not unfounded: those with even less affiliation with the left had indeed been, or would be, interrogated. While arguably this was not the sole motivation for his leaving that June, it was certainly an impetus.

There was another reason for Shaw's wanting to go to Europe, which had begun as the fantasy of an eleven-year-old boy in Brooklyn who had decided to become a writer: "It may have started with the reading of Dumas or Théophile Gautier or Balzac or a book by Fitzgerald or by seeing a movie about fighter pilots in World War I, or just by sensing something in the general climate of that time that made one feel that no artist could consider himself fully prepared for his life-work without eating a croissant for breakfast in the capital of France or having a *fine* at the Dôme." At Liberation, Shaw had done just that; but the brief

5

encounter with Paris and its cafés and people had not quelled his
dream of being a writer in the City of Light. If anything, it had
strengthened his desire to return.

It was nonetheless accidental that Shaw, his wife, Marian, and
their one-year-old son, Adam, ended up settling in Paris that
summer. Indeed, when they left New York they had intended to
remain in France only for the summer. But in September, as they
were about to board the *Liberté* for the return voyage to New York,
they met an American couple who offered them their apartment
on the Rue du Boccador in Paris as a sublet for two or three
months. As Shaw remembered it, "The offer set all the old
Brooklyn literary juices going again. We had only to pay the rent,
which was seventy-five dollars a month, a sum which at that time
was well within my means. . . . Sight unseen I agreed and notified
the French Line that we were canceling our reservations on that
particular voyage."

THAT SEPTEMBER, Irwin Shaw was thirty-eight, affluent, the critically acclaimed author of *The Young Lions*, derided author of *The
Troubled Air* (both best-sellers), highly praised *New Yorker* short
story writer, with three story collections in print, playwright of
four produced plays, and successful Hollywood screenwriter. In
short, he arrived in Europe at the apex of his fame, able and
willing to afford the best. For Shaw, Paris was not the city of
cheap, seedy hotel rooms, fifty-cent meals and ten-cent bottles of
Algerian wine, not the same city where the Great Adventure was
as often as not reduced to survival itself. Instead, it was the Paris
of the George V and the Ritz; Maxim's, Alexandre, and Chez
Carrère; Dom Pérignon and Lafite-Rothschild.

The apartment at 24 Rue du Boccador, near the Champs-
Élysées in the Eighth Arrondissement, despite its low rent, was in
a beautiful building with more than a fashionable address to
recommend it. It was also the lodging place of, among others, Art
and Ann Buchwald; historian and writer Theodore White and
his wife, Nancy; Belgian novelist Félicien Marceau; and Belgian

filmmaker Raoul Lévy, later best known for discovering Brigitte Bardot. Correspondent David Schoenbrun, CBS correspondent in France at that time, recalled that "Irwin very quickly became the center of that group." According to Ann Buchwald, Shaw "was rich, famous, and the one handsome celebrity every hostess in Paris wanted to capture. The Shaws were the most affluent residents in the building. They were great hosts and the most fun to be around."

Shaw easily grew attached to the apartment and to living in Paris. "I did not have to go far for spirited company. Everybody brought everybody else's guests home," he reminisced. "And there was a lively flow of newspapermen, visiting novelists, French starlets, movie directors, photographers who had just returned from some distant catastrophe, jockeys, chess players, aspiring Ivy League writers who later turned out to be CIA agents but who didn't let it spoil their fun, and ingenious and worthwhile freeloaders who wanted to be where the drinks were."

What had begun as a temporary stay in Paris turned into a long-term affair. It was initially prolonged because the American couple from whom the Shaws sublet the apartment decided not to return. But after the Shaws had lived for some time in the French capital, it would not have mattered if they had. Shaw quickly became acclimated, even addicted, to being an American abroad. He would, in fact, remain in Europe for more than twenty-five years, and never return permanently to the United States.

Yet during this time abroad, Shaw never thought of himself as a European. "I was always an American, on an extended visit to be sure, who roamed the streets of the city fondly, dined in some of the great houses and in some that were not so great, listened to the gossip and mingled happily with the natives, working with theater people, editors, movie crews, most often in harmony and admiration. Somehow, all during the period when almost every wall was decorated with the sign, 'Americans Go Home,' it never occurred to me that they meant me."

Shaw's statement reveals a lot about his attitude toward living abroad, for unlike many of his fellow American expatriates he was secure in his identity and had little interest in penetrating beyond the surface of things European. In *Paris! Paris!*, his non-fiction account of his days in the capital, the only penetrating chapter is the one about his first encounter with Paris, on Liberation Day. It was written, not surprisingly, in 1945. The rest of the book is often a somewhat patronizing chronicle of curious French habits or customs, with substantial attention to the tourist sights. But above all it is an account of where to eat and drink in the City of Light. This does not mean that the book isn't entertaining: this charge could rarely be leveled against any of Shaw's work. But it does mean that Shaw never really experienced a Paris much outside the cafés, never really got enmeshed in the actual life of the city, never learned much at all from the French or from France. A major part of the reason, of course, is that he surrounded himself with fellow Americans, largely of his own economic class. And when he did encounter the "natives," they were generally English-speaking, cosmopolitan, members of what would later be dubbed the jet set.

THE WAY Shaw lived in Paris and later southern France and Klosters, Switzerland, was pretty well set from the beginning. During the first few years Shaw was in Europe, his attention was very much focused on socializing. There was no lack of companionship. Old friends, such as photographer Robert Capa and screenwriter Peter Viertel, were living in Paris then. Many others, mostly film people from the States, drifted in and out. Or as Shaw looking back on those days wrote: "Then there is Alexandre's, on the Avenue George V, where every midnight your American friends would congregate, as in a club, Bob Capa drawling out his Hungarian-accented English . . . John Huston in town to make *Moulin Rouge.* Carol Reed, working on his circus picture with Burt Lancaster. Gene Kelly, for *An American in Paris.* [Anatole] Tola Litvak, with his white mane of hair, the ribbon of the Legion of Honor in his buttonhole, a hero in Paris since he directed *Mayerling* . . . Art Buchwald, the next day's column finished, looking for a poker game."

Shaw's Paris was the Paris of Americans abroad, many of them celebrities. But it was not just with the famous that he associated. On the voyage over, two young Americans, Ben Bradlee and Peter Matthiessen, were also en route to France. As Bradlee had a son near the age of Shaw's son, he became friendly with the older writer. In Paris, where Bradlee was working as an assistant to the press attaché at the American embassy, they saw each other frequently, often playing tennis together. Shaw did not really get to know Matthiessen until the fall, but soon they too formed a friendship.

For Matthiessen, beginning work on his first novel, *Race Rock*, Shaw personified the successful writer. He greatly appreciated Shaw's encouragement and his friendship. But, noted Matthiessen, Shaw "was ferociously competitive with his younger friends," on the tennis court and off. Bradlee too acknowledged that Shaw liked and expected the homage shown him by younger writers. "Irwin couldn't have been much beyond his late thirties, yet he was the grand old man. But I think we both [he and Matthiessen] felt we could take it or leave it. It wasn't that constant, either. And there was such a generosity in Irwin, I don't think we let it get us too far down." Patsy Southgate (then Mrs. Matthiessen), observed that some of the occasional rivalry had to do with Shaw's perception of them as Wasps: "The irony was that while we were living in abject poverty, to Irwin we were the rich guys—the Yalies, the Harvard graduates, the upper class—and he was the poor guy from Brooklyn. Of course, he was the poor guy living in considerable wealth, everything was top of the line. He enjoyed having us around for that reason."

Through Matthiessen, Shaw met William Styron, whose first novel, *Lie Down in Darkness*, had recently been published in New York to excellent reviews and substantial sales. For Styron, meeting Shaw was momentous: "I had had this tremendous fixation on Irwin even in New York. I had a basic admiration for his stories, they made a powerful imprint on me." Styron was also awed by Shaw's Hollywood connections: "It would always give us a bang when Irwin would say, you know, 'Sam Goldwyn's in town.' And indeed, there would be Sam Goldwyn. And there would be John

Huston . . . and Gene Kelly, and Harry Kurnitz. And Darryl Zanuck!"

Yet underneath the admiration for Shaw's genuine talent and the amazement at his connections to the powerful, there was a sense on the part of the younger, emerging writers that Shaw had somehow allowed himself to become commercialized. As Patsy Southgate remarked, "That was something we were always aware of with Irwin—that he'd sold out. Beneath all this laughter and drinking, I felt a lot of sadness; I think he was highly aware of having betrayed a lot that he believed in himself, and a lot that he wanted to be true to." At the same time, she noted, "it wasn't that he'd sold out in any way that made you contemptuous of him; it was just that this was all so much more fun, and he was really turned on by that."

The assessment of Shaw by the young writers was founded not so much on his fiction or his plays as on his screenwriting, which had earned and would continue to earn him extremely hefty sums, far beyond those from his books. For them, dazzled by his financial success, it was easy, almost natural, to conclude that no one could make such money without selling out. Later, as his fiction declined in quality, the charge would have been more accurate, but at that time it was a premature judgment: Shaw was still displaying considerable artistry in his nonfilm writing. That is, when he wrote. During his first two years abroad his finished fiction output consisted of only two, albeit two very deft, stories: "In the French Style" and "The Sunny Banks of the River Lethe."

"In the French Style" was the first of Shaw's stories to focus on what became a major theme: Americans abroad. Like many of Shaw's best stories, the bittersweet tale about the end of a love affair is told mostly in quick snatches of dialogue in which the characters reveal themselves, their motivations, their histories. In this story Beddoes, a peripatetic American foreign service officer based in Paris, returns from a trip to Cairo to be told by his American girlfriend that she has decided to marry a surgeon from Seattle and return to the States with him. Her reason is simple: She is tired of always being left behind while the up-and-coming young man dashes on State Department orders to some distant part of the world, expecting her patiently to await his return. Masterfully structured, impeccably paced, economical in its language and description, it clearly revealed that Shaw was still in full command of his power as a writer.

It was a talent, though, as those around him noticed, that was not being exploited to advantage. Instead he spent most of his time during the first few years abroad exploring Europe, eating, drinking, socializing, carousing, and writing two film scripts. He was also becoming somewhat defensive about his lack of output. Thomas Guinzburg, a founding father of *The Paris Review*, along with novelist John Phillips Marquand, Jr., remembered visiting a choleric, self-pitying Shaw, who after a dinner together began to hold forth on publishing. "Irwin began to get very sulky," noted Guinzburg, "lecturing Marquand and me about the decline of standards in publishing, how difficult it was to write well and maintain standards when everyone wanted escapist literature. He himself was suffering from this, he said, being forced to write this kind of stuff, writing for the audience rather than himself. The novel he'd been working on for a year or more, he said, was a good example of that. And with that, Irwin got up from his chair, went into his bedroom, and came back with this huge manuscript. 'I'm sick of it,' he declared, and to our utter shock he heaved the manuscript into the fire."

It is impossible to know what manuscript, if indeed it even was a manuscript, Shaw tossed into the flames. It was probably not *Lucy Crown*, the next of his novels to be published, as he'd written to Donald Klopfer, his editor at Random House, just a few days before that he had written only twenty pages of that book. Nonetheless, the incident indicated that Shaw was aware of the opinions that he'd sold out. By acting so rashly, so melodramatically, he hoped to prove to the younger men that this was not the case, that he retained standards and would not be bullied into writing commercial pap.

* * *

BUT JUST as the film scripts and increasingly glib novels represented only one side of Shaw the writer, so did the dark mood that overcame him that evening represent only one aspect of Shaw the man. In fact, such an outpouring of spleen was decidedly unusual. Almost everyone who came into contact with him reported that he was exceedingly generous, with boisterous enthusiasm for life and for people. Or in Styron's words, a man of "spontaneous goodfellowship and friendliness." Styron, though, had reason to feel this way: Shaw had presided over his wedding to Rose Burgunder in Rome in May 1953, throwing the reception in the apartment he'd taken temporarily in the Italian capital while writing a film script, and making sure that all of Styron's Paris friends were on hand for the event, including most of the *Paris Review* crowd.

This was in fact the second wedding Shaw had injected himself into within a year. In 1952, he threw a nuptial celebration in Paris for Art and Ann Buchwald. She recalled the event for two reasons: one, the surprise of the party itself; and two, the come-uppance Marian Shaw delivered to a woman whom she suspected was having or wanted to have an affair with Shaw.

> I remember best one incident which had nothing to do with either Art or me, but rather with Irwin's magnetic appeal to women. As the party was getting into full swing, a glamour-ous—but uninvited—brunette made an impressive entrance on the arm of one of Irwin's pals, who should have known better. The woman was a well-known divorcée, and gossip was that she had been making a serious play for Irwin. They'd been seen together at lunch and at sidewalk cafés from time to time that autumn: her name could never have been on Marian's invitation list.
>
> But no one would have guessed the truth watching Marian's face. Her smile remained warm and welcoming as the woman approached. Only a few of us saw Marian deftly raise her right foot and with split-second timing trip the brunette at the precise moment she rushed past to greet Irwin. Afterwards, Marian acted as shocked as anyone to see the elegantly dressed intruder sprawled on the floor, gathering up the scattered con-

tents of her evening bag, smoothing her dress. Then Marian graciously ushered the woman to the door, and as far as anyone knew, out of Paris altogether.

It was not Marian's only ambush of the "other woman." Over the years the scene would repeat itself. And yet for all those Marian was able to do something about, there were far more "other women" who remained unscathed.

THE DISTRACTIONS of screenwriting, women, drink, and social life never really abated for Shaw. But he did put them to use more in his fiction, which underwent a noticeable turn after his move to France. Shaw had always been able to write about his circumstances of the moment. While in New York, he wrote about New York; when in the war, he wrote about the war. Now, as a rich American abroad, he adapted this theme as a predominant concern and source for making fiction. But where earlier his characters and preoccupations were more among the downtrodden, with the shift to writing about superficial Americans being superficial in Europe, there was a significant lack of resonance.

With the notable exception of a few stories—"Tip on a Dead Jockey," "In the French Style," and "The Inhabitants of Venus"— the work is decidedly less compelling, the European backgrounds appearing almost as stage sets for tales of fairly uninteresting Americans doing fairly uninteresting things in Europe. Compared with the upper-class Americans depicted in the work of James or Fitzgerald—or more contemporaneously in Styron's underrated, albeit occasionally clumsy, novel *Set This House on Fire*—who actually learn something as a result of being in Europe, Shaw's characters are unshaped by the experience of being abroad. Their sojourns are silly ("Love on a Dark Street"), sentimental ("Then We Were Three," "Voyage Out, Voyage Home"), or trite ("A Year to Learn the Language").

The problem was not that Shaw chose to set his work in Europe. The real flaw was that the themes he continued to explore, such as adultery, or the loss of innocence, no longer had the power of the earlier work because the characters themselves were far less worthy of attention. Adultery, for instance, so ably and understatedly treated in "The Girls in Their Summer Dresses," was now more vulgarly handled, particularly in his novels *Lucy Crown* and *Two Weeks in Another Town*, although the latter does have much to recommend it.

By removing himself to Europe, Shaw was cutting himself off not from his American material but from a stratum of American society that previously had furnished him with his plots, characters, even motivation. One suspects that had he remained in the United States the same phenomenon would have occurred, for it had to do less with locale than with life-style. As a writer who always took his inspiration from everyday life, crafting realistic fiction, he needed a wider variety of experience to draw on for his work. Europe could certainly have provided it, but when his life became more and more a hedonistic roll in the hay with bored and often boring Americans abroad, his focus narrowed and the vitality gained from the wider panorama of life, love, experience in all its forms was lost. This is why the stories—and it is almost exclusively the stories—that do have greater depth, such as "Tip on a Dead Jockey" or "The Inhabitants of Venus," seem cut from a different mold. In these works not only is Shaw the master storyteller, but the stories he tells are worth telling.

It was not success, not the film work, not money, not even Europe that caused Shaw's decline as a fiction writer; rather, it was his unwillingness or inability to encounter a world beyond the gala parties and dinners, beyond the mundane infidelities used as a substitute for adventure and experience, beyond the drinks on the terrace or yacht. But it was far easier for Shaw to blame the critics, the increased commercialization in publishing that "forced" him to write best-sellers, even fame, for depriving him of a continued presence in American letters. In the end, Shaw sold out to himself.

* * *

IN THE late summer of 1958, Shaw made a new friend in Paris. Unlike Shaw, James Jones had come to Paris with a purpose. According to Jones, his primary reason for relocating to France was to research a novel that he described as being "about Americans in Paris, Americans of *my* generation as distinct from Americans in the twenties. That in itself is fascinating: the difference in flavor between the two generations. It's a lot more complicated than that, but essentially it will have to do with jazzmen, some French and some American, and writers too. But the original idea was to build it around the life and character of Django Reinhardt, the gypsy guitarist."

There were other reasons too, not the least of which was the romance of the Lost Generation. These were the writers who had influenced him most—particularly Wolfe, Fitzgerald, and Hemingway—and in no small way he saw himself as continuing in their footsteps. In fact, Jones was always comparing himself with them, and his Paris with their Paris. Commenting on Hemingway's *A Moveable Feast*, he stated sardonically, "Hemingway's Paris doesn't exist. The book really isn't about Paris. It shocked and horrified me, the egomania of the man. He was a swashbuckler who didn't swash his buckle or buckle his swash."*

And yet for all the bravado, as Shaw noted, Jones "grappled with the ghost of Hemingway all his writing life, excoriating him, mocking him, worried about what Hemingway meant to him— Hemingway and Paris were always linked in his mind. He knew from the beginning that he wanted to go beyond Hemingway, but I think he felt to get there he had to retrace Hemingway's steps, at least part of the way."

On a more immediate level, however, Jones wanted a break

* Whether Jones was aware of Hemingway's scathing remarks about him is unknown. Among Hemingway's statements, in a letter to their publisher, Charles Scribner, Sr., were these: "[Jones] is a K.P. boy for keeps and for always. Things will catch up with him and he will probably commit suicide. . . . To me he is an enormously skillful fuck-up and his book [*From Here to Eternity*] will do great damage to our country. Probably I should re-read it again to give you a truer answer. But I do not have to eat an entire bowl of scabs to know they are scabs; nor suck a boil to know it is a boil; nor swim through a river of snot to know it is snot. I hope he kills himself as soon as it does not damage his or your sales. If you give him a literary tea you might ask him to drain a bucket of snot and then suck the pus out of a dead nigger's ear."

from New York, where he had been living for more than a year after completing his second novel, *Some Came Running*, which he had written largely in his longtime base of Marshall, Illinois. Although he claimed later that the problem was "too many parties, too many things to do, too many distractions," the real difficulty was that Jones could not adapt to the life he was expected to lead as a rising literary star with a National Book Award for *From Here to Eternity* under his belt. "He didn't talk like the rest of us," asserted writer Budd Schulberg. "His vocabulary was a string of four-letter words, and in the field of current literary gossip he was an ignoramus. . . . He didn't talk theories, ideas, social stuff the way our crowd liked to do. . . . He was a kind of literary hard-hat who talked facts, people, things, the everyday of human conflict."

These feelings of being a literary outcast were exacerbated when the critics greeted *Some Came Running* with nearly unanimous derision, a scorn he believed had something to do with his being an outsider in the New York literary establishment. At least in France, he figured, he wouldn't have to fit into any literary clique. Since he didn't know French, he was not concerned about French literary circles; and the Americans in Paris, at least those he knew about, seemed largely to be renegades of one sort or another anyway. Besides, he reasoned, he'd never been to Europe, he'd long wanted to go, and he certainly had the means to do it.

In April 1958, a thirty-six-year-old Jones and his wife of a little more than a year, Gloria, who was pregnant, sailed for England. After a month there, they set out for the Soviet Union, in what was to be a grand loop, eventually ending in Paris. But on their first stop, Copenhagen, they learned that Gloria was in imminent danger of having a miscarriage, and so they returned immediately to England. It was too late; she lost the baby and was hospitalized for several days. As a result, they stayed in England until July. They arrived in Paris in August, after a visit to the World's Fair in Brussels, and found an apartment on the Île de la Cité. Shortly afterward they met Irwin and Marian Shaw, who would quickly become their closest friends.

Although the men were in some ways opposites—Shaw sophisticated and worldly, Jones crude and a true innocent abroad—they had far more in common. Both had served in World War II and both had written best-selling war novels from their experiences, Shaw's set in Europe, Jones's in the Pacific. Both had become instant celebrities, had been for a time critically touted, then, after the publication of their second novels, thoroughly bashed, often by the same critics. Like Shaw, Jones had been involved with film and film people, although not anywhere near to the extent of Shaw's participation. Also like Shaw, Jones was fond of the good life, now that he could afford it, and he resolved that he would do just that in Paris. Writer Willie Morris, a friend of both men, noted that shortly after Jones's arrival, he and Shaw became "close as brothers."

From the beginning, Shaw played the amiable host and tour guide, taking the Joneses to his favorite restaurants, getting them invited to parties, introducing them to other American expatriates, escorting them through the fabled Paris streets that to Jones, as to so many before him, already seemed familiar through readings of Hemingway, Wolfe, and Fitzgerald. "It's very beautiful," Jones wrote his brother, "the most beautiful city I have ever seen anywhere, or expect to see." Like Shaw, he was smitten by Paris, or at least by its surface image.

Once settled, Jones plunged into "research" for his book on jazzmen by frequenting the jazz clubs, particularly the Blue Note, the Hot Club, and the Mars Club, where Reinhardt had played. He also did less atmospheric investigations, interviewing Reinhardt's widow as well as jazz greats Duke Ellington, Billie Holiday, and Lester Young, who had all known Reinhardt. By the end of the year he had completed a long series of notes for the novel, tentatively entitled *No Peace I Find*. As Jones related it, the central theme was "whether Django's type of individuality can exist today in any form." But according to Jones's biographer Frank MacShane, the projected novel was mainly an exploration of Jones's private concerns about whether the pursuit of art destroys one's capacity to love others. The theme was near his heart, for although he loved Gloria a great deal, there was a fair amount of tension in the marriage. Jones could in fact be quite brutish. Broken crockery, smashed furniture, and other evidence of domestic battles were not infrequent sights greeting visitors who arrived unexpectedly at the Joneses'.

Perhaps the questions Jones had raised for himself were finally just too overwhelming for him to deal with at that time, for despite his initial enthusiasm for the novel, he put it aside about a year after his arrival. From remarks he made then, it seems he intended one day to write the book; but for one reason or another never did. Gloria Jones claimed that he simply could not find enough material on Reinhardt to write a convincing book. To judge from the extensive notes, though, this does not seem entirely accurate.

At any rate, by the fall of 1959 he was working on a new novel, *The Thin Red Line*, on a subject that was perhaps even nearer and dearer his heart: World War II. Jones described the work in progress as "a combat novel, which, in addition to being a work which tells the truth about warfare as I saw it, would free all young men from the horseshit which has been engrained in them by my generation. I don't think that combat has ever been written about truthfully; it has always been described in terms of bravery and cowardice. I won't even accept these words as terms of human reference any more." Like his earlier books *From Here to Eternity* and *Pistol*, a novella, *The Thin Red Line* was based closely on Jones's own ordeal as a soldier in the battle for Guadalcanal. It is a powerful, complex work, and the final product, published in 1962, certainly lived up to Jones's earlier pronouncement about telling the truth about warfare.

As HARD as Jones worked—and he was a prodigious, disciplined writer—he also played hard, drank hard. He delighted in roaming through Paris, reveling in its literary associations. "When the day's stint is done," he told an interviewer, "I walk the streets with Stendhal, Proust, Rousseau and Voltaire. I stand under the arches of the Eiffel Tower and dream I'm in a pre-Zuni village at some prehistoric time. I feel lost in the primeval forest among the columns of Notre Dame. I get goosepimples just looking at the scene." George Whitman, owner of the English-language Librairie Mistral (later Shakespeare and Company), recalled that Jones would frequently drop by to browse or simply to engage in "American" conversation. "He always professed to like Paris, but I could never quite understand why," remarked Whitman. "He was the most American American, a real Army sergeant. There were, of course, a number of other ex–military men here too . . . but only Jones continued to live it out. He was given to grand gestures, potent drink, and strong cursing. He was affable—absolutely— but always underneath one felt that he wanted to be back fighting in the Pacific."

The war was much with Jones, was in fact the presence with which he lived daily as he labored over *The Thin Red Line*. "The characters get to be so real," he noted, "that the people I'm with afterwards, except for my family, I can hardly see." One way that he found conducive to unwinding was to engage others in conversation, including Shaw, with whom he lunched almost every day, often at Lipp on the Boulevard St.-Germain or at a Vietnamese restaurant on the Île St.-Louis. Over a leisurely lunch, Jones would be able to put the book aside, get fully away from his novelistic preoccupations, become the often zany, enthusiastic person he liked to show his friends. "Jim's boyish capacity for enjoying life increased the pleasure of everyone in his company," recalled Shaw. "There will never be a bitter account like *A Moveable Feast* to darken the memory." William Styron, an occasional visitor to Paris and long a friend of the Joneses, echoed Shaw's sentiments: "What I recall most about those Paris days was two people enjoying life to the utmost. . . . It was a chic life—but controlled chic. They had staked out a life of enormous zest and fun."

Jones's love of people and of a good time became well-known around Paris. The Joneses' apartment, particularly after they bought their own place on the Île St.-Louis in late 1959, was a gathering place for the American expatriate community. At one time or another just about every visiting or expatriate American writer and painter and would-be in Paris ended up at the Joneses'. These were democratic affairs: there were no guest lists, no invitations. One just came by. Among the many luminaries who attended these salons were people as different from one another as James Baldwin, Alexander Calder, Mary McCarthy, William Burroughs, Irwin and Marian Shaw, Allen Ginsberg, Peter Viertel, Gregory Corso, Art and Ann Buchwald, William and Rose Styron, Thornton Wilder, and Kenneth Tynan. "This was the place," remembered Shaw, "where the lonely could find friends, where the gregarious could converse, [where] the literary could discuss their or anybody else's work, where love affairs could be arranged and the pains of broken marriages assuaged." But as Willie Morris noted, "There was nothing very Parisian about these evenings, and sometimes people had to go look out the windows at the quai and the Seine to remind themselves where they were."

Indeed, with the exception of the French writer Romain Gary, who spoke fluent English and was married to the American actress Jean Seberg, Jones did not have much truck with the French. Shaw, not one to surround himself with the French either, remarked: "The fact that he never wholly learned French and had almost no close French friends was one of the paradoxes of his life that might be explained by his fear of losing what his instinct told him was one of his greatest assets—his profound Americanness. He loved Paris, its streets, its buildings, its cafés, its ambience, but he professed to hate the French. I don't think he ever went to a French theater or read a French novel except in translation. He absorbed Paris, all France, through his pores, not through his intellect."

Jones was markedly uninterested in the contemporary intellectual scene in France. There was his lack of language, but a more pressing reason was that he could not relate to the intellectualism of many contemporary French writers, whom he believed to be "totally emasculated by scholasticism." After reading some

Robbe-Grillet, he wrote his editor in New York that he thought the work was "completely full of shit. That the French today think the novel is a second-rate form is only to me an indication of the great lack of vitality in all French writing, except that of a few men." With the exception of Camus, whom he deeply admired (mainly from afar), he was not interested in the existentialists. And while he did meet a fair number of French writers, ranging from André Malraux to Romanian-born Tristan Tzara, he remained largely unaffected by them. He became friendly with Françoise Sagan, but again the relationship had very little to do with shared literary interests.

Jones's disinclination to be involved in the literary scene in Paris also had roots in his firm belief, forged in New York, that such immersion was detrimental to him as a writer and as a human being. He even listed freedom from the literary establishment as one of his reasons for remaining in Paris: "Living in New York, it's pretty hard not to get involved in the literary politics of the day. That's another reason I like living [in Paris]. I've got the work I want to do, and I'll go down the line doing it. I don't give a damn about the critics much, but when you're there, you get involved with invitations and non-invitations, all of which has nothing to do with the critical world as much as it has to do with jockeying for position in the Literary Establishment."

By 1959, Shaw was living more in the house he had built in Klosters, Switzerland, than in Paris, although he maintained an apartment in the French capital. As a result, the Joneses began to take their winter vacations with the Shaws in Switzerland. While Jones greatly enjoyed being with Shaw, he was not nearly the proficient or devoted skier that the older writer was. And skiing was one of Shaw's chief manias, indeed, even one of the principal reasons for his living in Klosters. Jones nonetheless put up with it, manfully submitting to the ordeal of the slopes. But he far preferred skin diving, an activity that held no interest for Shaw, as a physical sport.

Back in Paris, with Shaw absent for part of the year, Jones spent more time with new friends. Among those with whom he became quite close was James Baldwin. Although the differences between them were striking, they did share a love of jazz, a dislike of the New York literary establishment, and a kinship based on past humiliations from "the Man"—in Baldwin's case because of race; in Jones's, from the terrors of having been brutalized as an enlisted man in the Army. Most important, though, they had respect for each other as writers. They talked honestly, Jones even advising Baldwin at one point to " 'forget all that nigger shit' if he wanted to write a real novel."

William Styron remembered an evening with Jones and Baldwin in Paris in which the three of them sat up drinking in a club most of the night. Around four or five in the morning, "Jimmy Baldwin faded—a very good man with the bottle. . . . The collapse of Jimmy Baldwin should've given us pause but didn't. Dawn was coming up, a beautiful summer's morning. Jim [Jones] and I decided to carry on." Finally, around three in the afternoon, they went back to Jones's. "We went in the house and the first thing I heard was a huge crash. Gloria had hurled a big teapot at both of us which missed Jim's head by an inch and shattered against the wall. Then this scream: 'If I ever lay eyes on you again may God kill me, you drunken bum.' "

It was not the only time such an exchange took place, but by and large, the Joneses lived a fairly happy existence. With the birth of his daughter, Kaylie, in 1960, and the adoption of a son, Jamie, three years later, Jones became the doting father. One of his obsessions around the children was making sure that they did not become frenchified. On Sunday afternoons, when American westerns dubbed into French were shown on television, he and Jamie would frequently don the appropriate garb to watch. "Jim would shout things back at the TV set," remembered Willie Morris. "Don't ask for the fucking *vin rouge*—say *redeye*, you assholes." Such antics were linked to Jones's fervent belief that his identity as an American should remain unadulterated. "I'm an American, and always will be," he explained. "I happen to love that big, awkward sprawling country very much—and its big, awkward, sprawling people." When questioned as to why, then, he lived abroad, he responded: "I believe it is good for an American writer to get outside his country—outside his *continent*—and see it from a vantage point outside its pervading emotional climate."

That he remained quintessentially American for the thirteen years he lived in Paris is undeniable; whether it gave him the vantage point he thought it did is debatable. The only book of real quality that he wrote in Paris was *The Thin Red Line*, which was a novel from memory that had nothing to do with the United States proper. What Paris did give him was freedom from having always to explain himself, to justify his activity as a writer: "I think Paris is much more conducive to writing or painting than New York is. . . . The kind of predatory search for success is much less noticeable [in Paris] and has much less effect on me. If you become a successful novelist in New York, you're sort of jerked bodily from one group and planted in another, and there's very little contact between the two. . . . There is a feeling in Paris that promulgates art in any of its forms, which you don't really get in New York. When you get up here in the morning, you have the feeling that everywhere in this city there are people with the same problems and the same miseries who are getting up to create something. You're one of them. In New York, even a successful writer, if he's serious about writing, always has the feeling of being a little bit on the outside of everything."

In a sense, like so many other writers, Jones removed himself from his own terrain in order to become enfranchised, not by a literary coterie, but within himself. In short, in Paris, he didn't have to kick against the pricks; he could feel himself a respectable member of society, not some rarefied creature—the artist. For Jones, who had internalized that great American fear of art and artists, who labored under the specter of Hemingway's code of masculinity, in which the creative individual had continually to assert his "regular guy" status, found in Paris that there was no such thing as a particular way to be an artist. If he collected guns

231

and knives, it didn't diminish his standing as a writer. If he burst into tears one afternoon while writing a particularly harrowing scene in *The Thin Red Line* and answered the door (as he did) to the laundry man, who could observe the anguish in his face, the tears still wet on his cheeks, he did not feel threatened as a man. He was given some leeway in France, cut some slack as a writer, as a human being.

One cannot read either *From Here to Eternity* or *The Thin Red Line* without being aware that an inordinately sensitive man lurked behind the volatile, often violent prose. In France, the "tough guy" persona could co-exist with the shell-shocked, busted-down Private Jones who had "gone over the hill." This was not something Jones got intellectually from France; rather, as Shaw pointed out, it was absorbed "through his pores."

Although on the surface Jones's involvement with France and the French was perhaps even less than Shaw's, in the end Jones gained more from the experience, used the climate of artistic possibility in a way Shaw never did, nor apparently ever needed to do. For both writers, Paris was a playground; but for Jones, at least in the early years, the city allowed him the freedom to be himself, to continue to write from the depths of his being.

Chapter Eleven

Locus Solus et Socii:
Harry Mathews and
John Ashbery

I<small>F</small> F<small>RANCE</small> had little impact on Irwin Shaw and James Jones, the opposite would have to be said about the importance of France and French writing on Harry Mathews and John Ashbery. Whereas Shaw and Jones exemplify American writers who remained relatively insular and untouched by France or the French, Mathews and Ashbery can be seen as among the few expatriate writers who penetrated well beyond the surface culture, who engaged themselves fully in French language, literature, and life, and who transformed those lessons into unique contributions to American letters.

Indeed, of all the Americans who came to live in Paris after World War II, poet and novelist Harry Mathews is perhaps the one most identified, at least in the American mind, with France and French writing.* There are a number of reasons for this. His

---

* So much so that Mark Polizzotti, Mathews's editor, recalls that when preparing Mathews's last novel, *Cigarettes*, for production, he was asked by his colleagues at Weidenfeld & Nicolson for the name of the translator.

novels, although largely set in the United States, are not derived from a classic American tradition but reflect instead a more Continental concern with language itself. His long tenure abroad (he still lives most of the year in Paris) has also contributed greatly to the impression that he is somehow more of a European than an American writer. Add to this his membership in the Oulipo— Ouvroir de Littérature Potentielle, a group founded in 1961 by novelist Raymond Queneau, which later came to include such writers as Georges Perec and Italo Calvino—and it is not surprising that he is associated more with France than with the United States.

But Mathews does not think of himself as a French writer (even though he has written some work in French); if any label appeals to him it is that of an international writer whose literary endeavors transcend national boundaries. At the same time, Mathews does credit his long residence in Europe, in particular his discoveries of and associations with other writers and artists there, with allowing him "to overcome the necessity to write in any particular vein." His work itself bears out the statement. It is diverse and distinct, blending styles and even genres. Often difficult, loaded with conundrums and wordplay, it is also among the most delightful work produced by an American writer of the period.

HARRY MATHEWS, along with his wife Niki de Saint Phalle and their one-year-old daughter, Laura, arrived in France in July 1952, shortly after he had graduated with an A.B. in music from Harvard. His ostensible reason for making the migration was to study music for a short while at the École Normale de Musique before proceeding to Vienna, where he planned to continue his studies. But in fact his going to France had to do less with career goals than with an almost desperate desire to leave the world of his parents, "an upper-middle-class Eastern WASP environment . . . extremely hostile to the poetic and artistic enthusiasms that [he] felt were most important at that time." By escaping what he regarded as this claustrophobic American milieu, he sought to establish, as much in his own eyes as in those of his parents, his own identity, to create the notion that his family now consisted of him, his wife, and their infant daughter.

In the United States he had found this difficult to do. His parents had opposed his marriage at the age of nineteen to the eighteen-year-old Saint Phalle. Although they eventually adjusted themselves to the reality, the relationship with his parents was further entangled when Saint Phalle became pregnant in the fall of 1950. Faced with the prospect of continuing travails with his parents if he stayed in their proximity, he and Saint Phalle made the decision to leave America. The choice was facilitated when Mathews inherited $75,000 that year, thus ensuring that the "adventure" would not be undermined by financial exigencies.

From the beginning, Mathews was enthralled with France. Although he arrived speaking only rudimentary French ("I took two years in school but then I dropped it when I was thirteen or fourteen"), he immersed himself in the language and the country. "From the minute I set foot on French soil at Le Havre I started learning French. I think I actually began learning it between getting off the boat and [going through] customs. I just really wanted to be inside the language immediately. I remember being totally hypnotized by Le Havre. God knows there's nothing beautiful there, but it was another culture—but not literature and art, it was the way people stood, the way people moved, the way people related to one other in their surroundings. It was something fascinatingly different which seemed to contain some atavistic reminder of a past life. I don't know why it was so strong, but it was powerfully so." The power of place, felt so keenly on arrival, would for Mathews never recede, even after long acquaintance.

ONCE SETTLED in Paris, Mathews began attended conducting classes and began studying percussion, while the French-born, American-bred, bilingual Saint Phalle, already a successful model, pursued a career as an actress. Saint Phalle was well versed in French culture, but Mathews, unlike most other American writers who journeyed to Paris, had little awareness of the French literary tradition. "As an adolescent I didn't read French, and even in translation I hadn't read much. And those [authors who] were published in translation I didn't particularly like. I found Gide horribly unsympathetic and I hadn't read Proust yet. And so I really wasn't drawn initially to France because of French literature, with the exception perhaps of Baudelaire, although I could barely read him. It was only later, when I started reading contemporary French poetry, that I became so enthused with what the French were doing."

Mathews's artistic focus at that time was almost exclusively on music, which, however, had come as a vocation only while he was in college. Before then, he recalled, he wanted to be a writer. "By the time I was fourteen I was determined to be a poet. . . . But when I got to college, for reasons that I still don't altogether understand—although . . . I had some idea that I should preserve my enthusiasm for literature by avoiding academic lit. classes—I concentrated almost solely on music, particularly after the first year or so. As a result I wrote less and less, and by the time I had arrived [in Paris] I thought, well, that was that. I thought my days as a writer were over." At that juncture, Mathews did not think that his abandonment of writing was a renunciation or a loss, for he did not feel possessed by any great desire to write.

THE FIRST year in Paris was less than easy: "We saw very few people," noted Mathews. "We had a very intense family life and had only a couple of friends. . . . Paris was a fearful place to be in because it seemed so impenetrable. I loved it, loved it in the sense that I wanted to be a part of it, but I didn't feel a part of it at all. Especially that first year was very depressing and frustrating, very self-contained, isolated, and with a certain amount of confusion."

The "confusion" involved individual uncertainties about his

and Saint Phalle's directions in life. Even though they had made what they both regarded as a necessary break from their parents and the restrictive upper-middle-class New York milieu, they had not yet sorted out exactly what to do with their newfound freedom.

By autumn, after a stressful summer, Saint Phalle had decided to give up her career as an actress and model to embark on a career as a painter. This decision, in turn, had a profound effect on Mathews. "I watched her transformation with growing jealousy," he remembered. "And not only jealousy: with a sense that she had begun an existence that was all possibility, something like the possibility I had guessed at in my poetry-making days at school." This sense of envy and admiration continued to mount within Mathews. The more he saw the joy and engagement of Saint Phalle in making collages and painting, the more he realized that his jealousy could be overcome by again creating work himself. "Since she was so clearly thriving on art," he recalled, "I knew completely that this was the thing to do in life. And she said, quite simply, 'For heaven's sakes, why don't you try writing again?' And so I did, and I loved it."

IN THE late summer of 1954, Mathews and Saint Phalle moved to Majorca, settling in Deyá. By chance, the place they found to live was next door to the house of perhaps the island's most famous resident, English writer Robert Graves. Although Mathews acknowledges that at times Graves fully lived up to his legendary reputation for irascibility, for the most part he was helpful, entertaining, generous, but above all, intellectually fascinating. Or as Mathews noted, "I remember . . . his admirable fund of knowledge: he was the first European I knew at all well who put my exaggerated intellectual assurance in its proper place." It was Graves who introduced Mathews to ancient religion and mythology, to the history of European magic and witchcraft, and to the medieval penchant for codes, riddles, and secret societies. These themes, learned about in discussions with Graves and through his careful reading of Graves's *The White Goddess* and other works of his, would be a continual font of inspiration, and would be worked directly into Mathews's first novel, *The Conversions*, and somewhat less obviously into *Tlooth* and *The Sinking of the Odradek Stadium*.

To Deyá itself, which in those days was "tourist-free and thrillingly cheap," both Mathews and Saint Phalle took an immediate liking. But their two years there were hardly exempt from difficulties. Saint Phalle suffered from hyperthyroidism. Although her illness was as yet undiagnosed, her distress—both physiological and psychological—was clearly observable. The precariousness of her condition was further exacerbated when, during their second year on Majorca, she gave birth prematurely to a son, Philip. He too was sickly; what little strength Saint Phalle could muster was directed largely toward caring for the infant. As a result of the dire situation, neither Mathews nor Saint Phalle was able to do much sustained creative work.

But throughout this period, according to Mathews, they received considerable support—emotionally, physically, and artistically—from friends in the international community. Besides Graves, they were friendly with poet and translator Alastair Reid, whom Mathews credited with encouraging him as a poet and restraining him from becoming too self-assured and "obnoxious." They saw as well a fair amount of Anthony and Eve Bonner, friends from Paris days who had moved to Majorca at the same time. When not in proximity—the Bonners lived in Palma, some ten miles away—Mathews and Anthony Bonner carried on a continual correspondence, centered mainly on their readings of and reactions to Pound's *Cantos*. But perhaps the most important friendship Mathews made then was with a German-born American, Walter Auerbach.

Mathews met Auerbach on a visit to Barcelona. Introduced at a party given by friends they had in common, the two quickly hit it off. Auerbach, who was in his late forties, had "retired" from his career as a filmmaker and photographer, which he had pursued in Germany, Palestine, and the United States, choosing instead to support himself on an Army pension of $55 a month. Shortly after that first meeting, Mathews and Saint Phalle persuaded Auerbach to move to Majorca, where, according to Mathews, "Niki and I adopted him, and he us. We gave him a family in which he played a discreetly avuncular role. To us he brought a world of new culture: of Germany in the twenties—Brecht and Marxism, to simplify matters—and also of New York in the late forties and early fifties, distinguished by unheard-of painters such as Robert Rauschenberg and Jane Freilicher and remarkably young poets of whom the most remarked was someone named John Ashbery."

IN THE spring of 1956, shortly after Mathews and family had returned to Paris to live, Auerbach came for a visit. During his stay, Mathews recalled, "he arranged a meeting that would greatly affect my life. Walter had gotten in touch with John Ashbery, then a Fulbright scholar in Montpellier; and on a gray warm afternoon, in a café in the Jardin du Luxembourg, I first spoke with an affable, apparently diffident, conventionally suited and cravatted man in his late twenties whose first collection had just been published in the Yale Series of Younger Poets." Neither writer would remember that encounter as being momentous in any way, but within a short time the two were seeing quite a lot of each other, particularly once Ashbery was able to move to Paris definitively in the fall of 1958.

At the time of their first meeting, John Ashbery was not quite twenty-nine years old. After earning his A.B. degree in English literature at Harvard in 1949, he moved to New York, where he attended graduate school in English at Columbia. He completed his master's in 1951 (with a thesis on the English novelist Henry Green) and then worked until 1955 at both Oxford University Press and McGraw-Hill. He also continued to work on his own poetry, while immersing himself in the lively avant-garde scene of Greenwich Village. There, in the late forties and early fifties, Ashbery came to know many of the painters who were creating new and lasting directions in contemporary art: Kline, de Kooning, Johns, Pollock, Rauschenberg, Rivers, and Freilicher.

It was then that he began writing poetry in a new vein, as experimental as any of de Kooning's or Pollock's canvases, receiving support from fellow poets such as Frank O'Hara, Kenneth Koch, James Schuyler, Kenward Elmslie, and Barbara Guest. This was the work that became *Some Trees*, the book chosen by W. H. Auden (albeit a bit reluctantly) as recipient of the Yale Series of Younger Poets Award for 1956. It was also then that Ashbery decided to leave, willingly cutting himself off from the stimulus and artistic enfranchisement of New York. By the time *Some Trees* was published, to little fanfare and even fewer sales (the first edition of 850 copies took ten years to sell out), he had already been in France for nearly a year, devoting himself to mastering French and learning all he could about French poetry.

What had brought him to France in the fall of 1955 was a Fulbright grant to study in Montpellier, his major project to compile an anthology in English translation of various modern French poets, specifically, Max Jacob, Francis Ponge, Pierre Reverdy, and Pierre Jean Jouve. His reasons for applying for a Fulbright for France were simple: "I wanted mainly to get out of New York. I was in a job that was going nowhere. The Korean war had just ended, and it was the height of McCarthyism, and though I wasn't terribly political it felt to me like a very bleak period. And of course, I wanted to go to France. That, to me, seemed like enough reason. Certainly there was a lot going on in New York then, but I have never felt, and I didn't feel then at all, that I had to be in a place that had interesting movements in art or literature in order to work myself."

This period away from the distractions of New York (and for that matter Paris, at least on a regular basis) was a time of further discovery for Ashbery, a quiet interlude in which he enhanced his already considerable knowledge of what was possible in poetry, as exemplified by the experiments of the poets he was reading and translating. At the end of his first year in France, still enthused with living abroad, he managed to renew his Fulbright for another year, this time with residency in Rennes.

For Ashbery, however, the most important personal development in his life that year was meeting Pierre Martory. A few years older than Ashbery, Martory, of French Basque stock, had grown up partly in Morocco, and had served in North Africa in the Free French army during World War II. A somewhat quiet, contemplative man, Martory possessed, like Ashbery, a wry sense of humor. He was also a poet and had already published a novel; later he would distinguish himself as a journalist and dance and theater critic. When he and Ashbery met, in March 1956, he was employed as a secretary to the eminent French anthropologist Marcel Griaule. Introduced by a friend, Ashbery and Martory soon developed a close relationship. As Ashbery remembered it, he "escaped" from Rennes to Paris as much as he could that year in order to spend time with Martory and visit other friends and acquaintances he had made in Paris, chief among them Mathews.

It was with regret, therefore, that Ashbery began planning to return to the States in the late summer of 1957, when his grant finally ended. "Had I been able to stay on in France then, I would have," he explained. "But I couldn't get a further extension and had no real way of supporting myself, so I reluctantly returned to New York that fall."

Once in the United States, he enrolled in the Ph.D. program in French literature at New York University, where he also taught elementary French. He was serious about pursuing a career as a scholar, but to some extent his objective in studying for his doctorate was to get back to France. After just one year he realized this goal, returning, this time to Paris, in the summer of 1958. "I had decided to write my dissertation on Raymond Roussel and talked my parents into supporting me for a while in France in order to do the necessary research. At least I used this as the pretext for going back."

ASHBERY MOVED in with Martory and attempted to take up where he'd left off the year before. He was delighted to discover that their relationship had not suffered unduly in his absence. He also was glad to see Mathews, with whom he'd maintained contact

241

since their first meeting. Now, with Ashbery settled in Paris, the two socialized regularly, for even though Mathews and Saint Phalle had recently bought a farmhouse in Lans-en-Vercors, at the base of the Alps in southwest France, they kept their Paris apartment and were frequently in the city.

Ashbery continued to exchange ideas with Mathews about music, painting, and poetry. For Mathews, Ashbery was not only a good friend but also a mentor. But this latter role was far from the conventional concept conjured up by the term: "John has shown himself . . . utterly tolerant and encouraging: an attitude that has allowed me to evolve in my relationship to literature and the world in general in progressions that only became apparent to me after they have occurred. The spur to my development has never come from injunctions on John's part, or even advice. . . . If his witty discourse serves as a delightful, indirect medium for defining his preferences, it is above all his example as a masterly and, more impressively, as a dedicated artist that he exerts his influence on those around him."

Aside from indirectly encouraging Mathews, Ashbery shared his literary enthusiasms with him, most important, Reverdy, Michaux, and Roussel. "John was this incredibly well-read young man who through his example, and his conversation, encouraged me to get off my ass and start reading more," Mathews remembered. "He's been an absolutely unfailing stimulus, with an almost uncanny ability to suggest exactly what you need to read, exactly when you need to read it."

Just as modern French writers had initially opened new worlds for Ashbery, they now did so for Mathews, in one case actually before he'd even read them, so powerful was Ashbery's description of their work:

Soon after we met I asked John what contemporary French poets he recommended I read. He mentioned several familiar names, such as Reverdy and Michaux. A week or two later, when I showed him a new poem I'd written ("The Battle"), he commented, "Oh, I see you've been reading those poets we were talking about." But I hadn't. Somehow the words he had said about them had given me a perception of their approach to poetry, and I had at once been able to incorporate this in my writing. A simple conversation with John had let me emerge from my conservative, provincial, and precious attraction to the kind of lyric poetry then being written in America and discover the possibility of "modernism"—a world where I was allowed and in some sense obliged to invent what I wrote.

But the most important discovery for Mathews, as it had been earlier for Ashbery, was Raymond Roussel. Roussel was not then, nor is he now, a terribly well-known writer, even in France. His novels, such as *Impressions d'Afrique* (1910) and *Locus Solus* (1914), and long poems, most notably the 2,000-line *La Vue* (1902) and the book-length *Nouvelles Impressions d'Afrique* (1928), present considerable obstacles to the reader, chief among them Roussel's discarding of an exterior reality for that of a totally language-generated, almost hermetic universe. This results in the absence of a linear narrative, and in a disregard for conventional logic as well. In Roussel, associations between one idea or event and another are based not on external similarity but on a highly permutated verbal construct in which two words, nearly identical homophonically, are combined with other like phrases to yield phonetically similar sentences with entirely different meanings.* Despite the fantastic verbal inventiveness, Roussel's language has

---

* In *How I Wrote Certain of My Books*, Roussel explained his creative verbal method:

I chose two almost identical words (reminiscent of metagrams). For example, *billard* [billiard table] and *pillard* [plunderer]. To these I added similar words capable of two different meanings, thus obtaining two almost identical phrases.
　　In the case of *billard* and *pillard* the two phrases I obtained were:
　　1. *Les lettres du blanc sur les bandes du vieux billard* . . .
　　[The white letters on the cushions of the old billiard table . . .]
　　2. *Les lettres du blanc sur les bandes du vieux pillard* . . .
　　[The white man's letters on the hordes of the old plunderer . . .]
　　In the first, "lettres" was taken in the sense of lettering, "blanc" in the sense of a cube of chalk, and "bandes" as in cushions.
　　In the second, "lettres" was taken in the sense of missives, "blanc" as in white man, and "bandes" as in hordes.
　　The two phrases found, it was a case of writing a story which could begin with the first and end with the second.
　　Now it was from the resolution of this problem that I derived all my materials.

a surface appearance of order, of ordinariness; but the placid façade is only a veil beyond which the real "story" lies.

It was this intersection of the mundane and the marvelous that most attracted Ashbery and Mathews, as it had Roussel's few admirers from the preceding generations, among them Cocteau, Gide, Jean Rostand, and the surrealists, who were fervent in their support. Cocteau dubbed him "the Proust of dreams"; Éluard wrote that Roussel's imagination "carries earth and heavens on its head;" Breton noted that his thought "will have repercussions in the remotest future." What all these enigmatic statements were trying to convey was that Roussel, in a certain sense, cannot be conveyed in traditional terms. Or as Ashbery himself wrote: "With the possible exception of [Michel] Butor and Michel Leiris, none of the writers who have dealt intelligently and sympathetically with Roussel have succeeded in making clear what is so extraordinary about him: it would seem to be something that can be felt but not communicated." For Ashbery, however, what was most appealing in Roussel was the way in which he manipulated language so as to "raise the word to a new power; in Roussel's case it is about to break open, to yield true meaning at last; that is the lead which alchemy is on the verge of translating into something far more interesting than gold. The miracle does not take place, the surface of his prose remains as stern and correct as the façade of a French prefecture or the gold-lettered bindings of the Grand Larousse. But the attentive reader will have glimpsed the possibility, and his feelings about language will never be the same."

Among Roussel's most attentive readers were Ashbery and Mathews. According to Ashbery, it was poet Kenneth Koch who introduced him to Roussel. "Kenneth had been a student in France and had brought Roussel's books with him when he came back. This was before I had gone over on the Fulbright. I couldn't really read him then, but when I was in France the first time, after I knew French better, I began to read him and became quite fascinated by his work."

Roussel opened up for Ashbery the latent possibilities lurking under the most common linguistic constructions, allowing him, in Michaux's words, *"la grande permission"* to experiment with language: "Roussel, and later the surrealists who learned a lot from Roussel, set one free to do anything one wanted to do. . . . They were important primarily in helping me see what I could do with language." It was not so much what Roussel said as how he said it—more precisely, what the saying could say: "I was very attracted to [Roussel] when I first read him," remarked Ashbery, "but probably more for the effects that his processes produced almost gratuitously."

Roussel was equally important for Mathews in opening up creative possibilities. Again, as for Ashbery, Roussel functioned as a stimulus for experimentation, as an example of how Mathews could get beyond the confines of traditional narrative structure and meaning. "Reading Roussel brought me several revelations," wrote Mathews. "He demonstrated to me that psychology was a dispensable fashion, that the moral responsibilities of writing did not lie in a respect of subject matter, and that the writings of prose fiction could be as scrupulously organized as Sir Philip Sidney's double sestina. Roussel taught me that I did not have to write out of my 'experience' (the quotation marks indicate: what one thinks one has been able to avoid); that I had the universe to play with, not merely the pieties of late-capitalist society; that writing could provide me with the means of so radically outwitting myself that I could bring my hidden experiences, my unadmitted self into view."

During the first two years Ashbery spent in Paris after his return in 1958, he devoted himself primarily to his work on Roussel—a task that proved even more complex than he had envisioned. What had begun as scholarly research turned from passive archival consultation (there being very little to consult) into active literary sleuthing in pursuit of information about the life and work of his enigmatic hero. The quest had all the trappings of a Harry Mathews novel, complete with odd relatives and friends, intrigue, cul-de-sacs, and even a missing manuscript. "My method was fairly simple, really," observed Ashbery. "I just asked everybody I knew at the time whether they had known Roussel or knew anyone who did. One person led me to another."

Among those he contacted was Roussel's nephew and only heir, Michel Ney, who, according to Ashbery, really didn't know much about his uncle. But he did try to help Ashbery, motivated at least in part by the thought that perhaps his uncle would at last be financially successful. "Ney, like the rest of the relatives, regarded his uncle as the black sheep in their illustrious family," Ashbery noted. "But since an American was interested he got intrigued. I soon found out why. He asked me," noted Ashbery, "if I thought there was any chance that if Roussel were published in America he might become as popular as Françoise Sagan!"

There were also strange, Rousselian coincidences. The widow of Pierre Frondaie, who had adapted Roussel's works for the theater, and who had consistently eluded Ashbery's search, suddenly emerged as the landlady of one of his acquaintances. Others whom he knew in other contexts revealed that they had known Roussel. But the highlight of Ashbery's relentless literary detective work was the discovery of the original first chapter from Roussel's last book, left unfinished and later posthumously published, *Documents pour Servir de Canevas*. As Ashbery remembered it, he knew of the chapter's existence because he'd come across a note Roussel had sent to his printer instructing him not to print this chapter. The question was, Did the chapter still exist? For some time this became a focus of Ashbery's sleuthing. Finally, again through a lucky coincidence, he was introduced to the Romanian painter Jacques Hérold, who in the course of their meeting produced the missing proofs of the chapter.

DESPITE HIS prodigious research, Ashbery decided in the end not to write his thesis: "I realized that I just wanted to stay in Paris and that I didn't want to do a dissertation. I felt I wasn't cut out for the academic life, which would have obligated me anyway to go back to the United States to pursue it. I was enjoying myself in Paris—I very much enjoyed tracking down Roussel—but felt no need to do a dissertation because of it. Really, though, I just couldn't bear the idea of returning." This did not signal the end of Ashbery's involvement with Roussel, however. Over the years he has continued to champion Roussel, by writing several articles on him (including the introduction to the American edition of Michel Foucault's study); by overseeing the publication of the suppressed *Documents* chapter in the French journal *L'Arc*; and by translating the opening of *Impressions d'Afrique* and the whole of *Documents pour Servir de Canevas*. Roussel has been such an abiding concern that Ashbery chose him as the subject of one of his six Norton Lectures delivered at Harvard in 1989–1990.

But the greatest impact of Roussel is to be found in Ashbery's work. The Frenchman's legacy is most apparent in Ashbery's rather arcane second book, *The Tennis Court Oath*, written while he was in Paris, although Roussel's influence is discernible as early as "The Instruction Manual" in his first major collection, *Some Trees*. Yet there is a major difference between the way Ashbery imitated Roussel in this earlier poem and the use he made of him in his later poetry. In "The Instruction Manual" Ashbery picked up primarily on the capacity for conjuring that Roussel demonstrated in his long poem *La Vue*, in which an entire universe is constructed out of the poet's imaginative gazing at a seaside scene etched in his pen holder. But in *The Tennis Court Oath*, and to some extent in *Rivers and Mountains* and *The Double Dream of Spring*, Ashbery was involved with Rousselian wordplay, with the possibility of creating a poem not out of a specific situation, subject, or event, but solely out of ordinary language. In these poems, Ashbery, like Roussel, exploited the myriad meanings implicit in the combination of one word with another and in the relation between the individual word and its associative properties.

The Tennis Court Oath, written after Ashbery's return to Paris in 1958, had, not surprisingly, another concordance with Roussel. When the book was published in 1962, it met with the same reception generally accorded Roussel's works in his lifetime: derisive bewilderment. Harold Bloom, normally one of Ashbery's great supporters, is still dismayed after all these years that Ashbery is the author of this book, which he found "a great mass of egregious disjunctiveness . . . accumulated to very little effect." It is easy to understand Bloom's dismissal—the book does present considerable obstacles to the reader—and yet one cannot help thinking that the major problem for Bloom (and many others) with *The Tennis Court Oath* was that it did not lend itself to neat classification within the major American tradition in which Bloom is so fond of pigeonholing *his* authors. *The Tennis Court Oath*, to use Ashbery's phrase, exemplifies "the other tradition," not that of Whitman and Stevens, but that of Stein and Roussel, in which the point of both departure and arrival is language itself.

Ashbery has noted, in connection with *The Tennis Court Oath*, that "it was a process of taking language apart to see what could be done with it. . . . I was interested mainly in exploring language and its possibilities, as well as, of course, its limitations." Among the possibilities experimented with most fully in this book is the collage poem, or poem constructed out of found materials rearranged in an often startling, highly evocative manner so that the end product is far more resonant than any of the individual constituent elements by themselves. Following a practice that was the hallmark of the surrealists, Ashbery juxtaposed incongruous elements to create a meaning beyond that contained in the original source. The effect is one that stretches the imagination, for while the found meaning is not erased entirely, it is subordinated to the conjunctive message in place in the new formation. In many of the poems in this collection, Ashbery deliberately paired phrases purloined from American magazines and pulp novels with lines that mimic "poetic" verse, thus counterpointing mundane observations with vivid enigmatic introspective.

Ashbery's reliance on the collage form is linked to a notion, derived largely from Roussel, that words themselves can be the subject of a poem. By using language to generate more language rather than to relate or describe an observable scene or event (or a specific idea or state of mind), Ashbery was clearly working in a manner very different from that of his American predecessors, and even contemporaries.

And yet for all of the Rousselian-surrealist process, the poems in *The Tennis Court Oath* are not really surrealistic, as has often been asserted by Ashbery's American critics. Despite his appropriation of surrealist techniques, his mission is different. Where the surrealists were concerned with wonder, with the marvelous, with stretching perception, Ashbery is concerned mainly with calling attention to the words themselves rather than what they evoke. In this, he is truly following Roussel's lead, for Ashbery's work here turns on puns and associative linguistic properties—delivered as often as not in a deadpan fashion—to create unusual combinations. But ultimately these new conjunctions are not "about" anything other than themselves. Even the perfectly wrought sestina "Faust" is far more a display of Rousselian word transformation than a poem with a definite subject.

As with much exploration, Ashbery's excursions into the frontiers of language, meaning, and poetic practice were inspired equally by the personal adventure inherent in the process as by the idea that the quest would yield a load of riches that could be appreciated publicly. The lessons learned here, while often dazzling, are warm-up exercises for the distinctive style that will later come to mark Ashbery's work, where "found" lines are seamlessly integrated into the more coherently elaborated poetic structure, where old context fuses with new context to open up a plethora of meanings and discoveries. This is not to say that *The Tennis Court Oath* does not stand on its own, or that it should be read only as a footnote in Ashbery's poetic development, for it is a unique book which forces the reader into a new regard for what poetry can achieve.

Ashbery did not originally conceive of *The Tennis Court Oath* as a publishable collection: "I wasn't at all sure that I'd have an audience, and wasn't really thinking too much about that at the time. . . . In fact, I wasn't expecting that I'd publish another book

of poems. A lot of *The Tennis Court Oath* was pure experimentation which I didn't feel was destined for publication."

But as fate would have it, in 1961 he was unexpectedly presented the opportunity to publish another book. Poet John Hollander, who had admired *Some Trees*, invited Ashbery to submit a
manuscript to Wesleyan University Press, where he had temporarily taken over the editorship from Richard Wilbur. Ashbery
knew that his style, particularly in this book, would not have
meshed at all with Wilbur's tastes, so he had very little time to
assemble a manuscript for publication. He gambled and sent
Hollander the various experimental poems he'd been working on
for the last few years. Hollander, to Ashbery's surprise, accepted
the poems and put the book into production before Wilbur's
return.

BETWEEN 1958 and 1961, when Ashbery devoted himself to
exploring language, his true literary comrade-in-arms on the
European side of the Atlantic was Harry Mathews. "It was
wonderful to have a fellow American interested in the same sort
of writing," Ashbery explained. "Harry probably encouraged
me as much as I did him. I guess it was mostly that Harry
validated my experimentation. I realized that I wasn't the only
freak in Paris."

Mathews, for his part, had also changed artistic directions as a
result of having been introduced to Roussel. So powerful was
Roussel's model, in fact, that after reading the French writer's
work, he decided to discard a novel he'd begun many years
earlier, after his return from Majorca, and to try to translate
what he had learned from Roussel into a new type of fiction.
"Roussel was the man who allowed me to write fiction," Mathews
stated without equivocation. "I was dying to write prose, but I
couldn't figure out how, starting from Cheever or Faulkner or
even Proust, for that matter, what there was for me to do.
Roussel was something else. It was a whole new place to move on
from. It was a way of combining storytelling with organizing

prose the way you would a poem. The arbitrariness of Roussel's approach, with these spectacular [and] at the same time terribly banal but utterly original results, for me just authorized things I'd never contemplated doing before. And so I gave up the whole notion of what looked to me like the American idea of fiction at the time, and started *The Conversions*."

While Mathews did reject the American fiction model of thirty years ago, he was not without precedent in France. In many ways, *The Conversions* was completely in line with much French fiction of the time, with its penchant for inventing rather than recording reality, and its concern for language as the generative fictional unit. Aside from Roussel, there are discernible echoes of Queneau's novels *Le Chiendent* (1933) and *Saint-Glinglin* (1948), with their convolutions of plot, surprising coincidences, accidental turns of fortune, and in *Saint-Glinglin*, mythology and ritual. Robert Pinget's "picaresque" religious/ mythological quest novels *Le Renard et la Boussole* (1953) and *Graal Flibuste* (1956) also come to mind, as does Robbe-Grillet's 1953 novel *Les Gommes* (*The Erasers*).

In all of these books the posited search is for some sort of temporal-spatial reality which the author, often through his narrator/protagonist, continually subverts, knowing from the outset that his goal is highly elusive, perhaps even nonexistent. Divagation follows textual disruption; chronologies are bent; linguistic codes are cracked only to reveal other, often indecipherable ones; the narrative frequently winds back on itself, exposing the arbitrariness of the plot. While these elements are now present in American writing—in the work of Robert Coover, John Barth, Thomas Pynchon, and Joseph McElroy for example—when Mathews wrote *The Conversions* this was not yet perceived as a viable fictional form in English.

On the most basic level, *The Conversions* is a quest novel in which the hero/narrator embarks on an epic journey in an attempt to solve three riddles. The ostensible reason for the quest is that the protagonist can gain a fortune if he can come up with the correct answers. In the course of his travels and travails to solve the mysteries, the narrator leads his readers on a perilous, often hilarious excursion through the mythology and ancient rites of pre-Christianized Europe, transmitted to Mathews originally via Graves, in which one maze opens into another, each populated by bizarre yet compelling characters. As the tale progresses, it becomes increasingly evident that the "leads" pursued by the hero continually turn in and back on themselves, the effect being that of a journey through a Klein bottle.

At the end, the third riddle is still not solved; this is a source of anxiety for most readers, as by this point Mathews has succeeded in making them co-conspirators in his hero's quest for untangling the solution. And yet upon further reflection, what becomes apparent is that solving the riddle is ultimately not the point, for while this may seem the narrator's mission, it is not Mathews's. Indeed, for him the novel is about opening up language not about closing it—the inevitable result of pinning down the elusive meaning of the third riddle.

Mathews is working in prose in a manner parallel to that of Ashbery in poetry: *The Conversions*, for all its commentaries (and pseudo-commentaries) on religion, symbols, cults, codes, art, even horse racing, is not really "about" any of these things. And just as Ashbery looked to Roussel for the inventive possibilities inherent in ordinary discourse without mimicking his actual subject or style, so too did Mathews. In *The Conversions* his debt to Roussel is evidenced most directly in the often preposterous narrative fabulation told in such a matter-of-fact way. Or as Mathews noted, "I brought my Rousselian enthusiasm for freely and puzzlingly inventing new things to write about, as well as an ear entranced by Roussel's frighteningly, provocatively, movingly neutral voice."

Perhaps the best summing up of Mathews's contribution to advancing fiction are the words of French writer Georges Perec: "For the first time since Raymond Roussel, Harry Mathews has provided us with a novelistic configuration whose imperious requirements, contiguous with the written text itself, secrete symbols, allegories, points of contact and discontinuity, true and false scientific discoveries, lexical, verbal, and syntactic deformations, myths and obscurities, none of them having, ultimately, reference to anything beyond themselves. Everything that happens . . . [is] nothing more than the ghostly, frail delineations of the legendary wrestling match in which from the beginning of time we have been engaged with the world of words, signs, meanings, and dreams, and which we call fiction."

IT IS not surprising, given their shared interests in the transformation of literary form, that Ashbery and Mathews would have been prime readers of each other's work. Although they were experimenting with language in a way derived largely from avant-garde and contemporary French literature, both were writing work in American English destined for American readers. As a result, they relied on each other to detect false notes, not just in phrasing but in the authenticity of statement, avoiding preciosity or poetic language.

Ashbery, who at least initially associated primarily with the French, remarked that after a few years abroad he started to feel somewhat out of touch with common American speech: "I began to experience what I can describe only as withdrawal symptoms from the American language. For that reason I began to read a lot of American magazines and pick up American books along the quay. That brought the language back to me, allowed me to stay in touch with how Americans sounded." Not infrequently when writing *The Tennis Court Oath*, Ashbery would pilfer phrases from these sources for use in his collage poems. "Europe," for example, is created almost entirely out of found words.

There was also the cinema, of which Ashbery was a devotee. He reveled particularly in the undubbed screenings of American B films, including gangster and schlock horror movies, as well as forties musical comedies. Again, as with the books and magazines, he attentively attuned himself to the nuances of dialogue, occasionally making a mental note of a particular line for later poetic use.

Mathews, on the other hand, has claimed that he never experienced a sense of loss of the American language, despite living largely a francophone existence. Indeed, he has said that his long residency abroad has sharpened his sense of the American language. In this context, he recalled what French poet André du Bouchet once told him: "You have [a] great privilege [in] living in a country where your language is not spoken, because it obliges you to be conscious of your own language in a way that you never would be if you were living at home." Mathews agreed: "I think it's especially true for an American writer. In America we still have the feeling that our language is like the sky and the trees and the streets . . . that it's there and it's natural and it covers everything. You don't have to think about it very much and you don't have to be particularly conscious or self-conscious about it."

Mathews observed that his immersion in French, rather than estrange him from English, has contributed to a greater awareness of what can be accomplished in his own language. "Because the French are so conscious of their language, so enormously aware of the role it plays as perhaps the single element which is most determining of behavior, thought, and everything else, that is beneficial. This adds to the sense of responsibility in the use of one's own language [and leads] to an appreciation of the jubilation that Americans can have in their language. I wouldn't want to give up the rapport that Americans have with their language, that ability just to run with it, not hold a magnifying glass up to it in order to take it apart. And yet this French language consciousness has definitely affected the way I write." This important notion is borne out in Mathews's work, which while having a quintessential American feel is marked by extraordinarily careful attention to the way in which language is manipulated in order to create original effects.

BETWEEN 1956, when Ashbery and Mathews first met, and 1960, a number of significant developments took place in each of their lives. Mathews had become sure of himself as a novelist, writing a good deal of *The Conversions* between 1959 and 1960. In turn he had sustained Saint Phalle through long periods of illness, as well as an operation on her thyroid gland. He had also witnessed— without envy—the burgeoning of her career as an artist, while continuing to see her as an example of a creative person.

Ashbery, during this period, had completed most of his initial work on Roussel and had abandoned the idea of turning his research into a doctoral dissertation. His experiments with language that would eventually be selected for *The Tennis Court Oath* were well under way. With Mathews he had become close friends; his relationship with Martory had grown deeper and stronger.

Ashbery had also embarked on what would be an eventual career—that of art critic—but at the time he didn't think of it that way. It was just an opportunity to be slightly more independent financially. He remembered how the job came about: "I had written some pieces for *ArtNews* when I had gone back to the States in 1957 and then did an article for them on Jean Hélion sometime after I returned to Paris. Then, in the spring of 1960, I met the woman who wrote the [*International*] *Herald Tribune* art column, who was leaving the paper. Since I had some experience and interest, she chose me to replace her. I was never really on the staff of the paper, though. Everything was free-lance, but regular free-lance: one column a week. They paid $15 an article. Well, you could have a nice dinner or two on that."

Ashbery continued to contribute reviews on art and artists to *ArtNews* (which paid $75 an article) and during 1960–1961 wrote a regular "Paris Letter" for *Art International.* He augmented his income by writing gallery catalogues (occasionally in French) and served as a translator for his friend Frank O'Hara, who as assistant curator of painting at the Museum of Modern Art in New York had brought a traveling exhibition to Paris in 1959. Ashbery noted in retrospect that while he genuinely enjoyed reviewing shows, "I liked it mostly because it allowed me to live in Paris."

For his readers, there was more to it than that: Ashbery's criticism has been not only consistently informative and elegant, but entertaining as well. His incisive eye most often managed to penetrate the essence of what an artist was actually trying to do, thereby aiding potential viewers in seeing the work—all this without his ever feeling the need to pontificate or rarely even theorize. As he wrote in one of his columns, "The greatness of art can only be discussed, not explained." He also brought to his criticism and reviews his poet's sense of the language, and the ability to see the interconnection between the two arts. Throughout his articles he liberally sprinkled quotations from poets and writers, particularly Stevens, Auden, Eliot, Stein, and of course Roussel, as a natural way of describing the often ineffable quality of certain works, or to make a parallel to a similar poetic image.

Although the editor of Ashbery's recently published selection of art criticism, *Reported Sightings*, has said that Ashbery's writing of art criticism had an impact on his poetry, the reverse seems more accurate. It is the poet who wrote the reviews, not the reviewer who wrote the poetry. His 1964 review of a Parmigianino show for instance, is about seeing with a poet's eye what is special about the artist: "It is hard to remain unmoved by his craftsmanship at the service of a sense of the mystery behind physical appearances." About a decade later Ashbery explored the concept far more fully in his poetic masterpiece "Self-Portrait in a Convex Mirror." While it is arguable that the origin of the poem is in the review, it seems far more likely that had Ashbery not brought his own poetic insight to bear on Parmigianino's self-portrait, there would have been no poem.

Ashbery does readily acknowledge one major benefit to his poetry that comes from writing about art: "I don't think that the way I was writing had very much effect on my poetry, but the fact of having to sit down and do it for a deadline without really having much time to think about what I was going to say certainly made me less intimidated by the idea of sitting down and writing a poem, and in that way I'm certain it was helpful."

AMONG THE earlier pieces Ashbery contributed to the *International Herald Tribune* was a review of a show by Niki de Saint

Phalle. Ashbery wrote that "for Niki, who is married to the American writer Harry Mathews, painting is a communal affair. . . . First of all, it is up to her husband to lug home the heavy bags of plaster. Their two young children, Philip and Laura, help fill the bags with paint and grudgingly contribute an occasional toy or piece of clothing for the picture." The mention of Saint Phalle's work being a "communal affair" is somewhat curious in this July 1961 article, for while perhaps not yet a fait accompli, by the close of 1960 her marriage with Mathews had all but officially ended.

Although Mathews acknowledged that Saint Phalle was right to get out of the relationship "once she saw that the life had gone out of it," he also remembered how difficult it was for him to accept the separation. "Our marriage had given us a context in which to finish growing up, and now that we were potential adults, new contexts for new kinds of growth were in order. At the time, I was far too attached to our marriage to see this. Marriage had become the sheltering family without which I secretly believed I could not survive. Niki's departure left me in a state of recurrent gloom whose surface symptoms would require almost two years to be cured and whose less obvious, more pernicious effect—a paralysing reluctance to risk loving or being loved—would stay with me for well over a decade."

Immediately after the breakup, Mathews, suddenly a single father, moved back to Paris permanently from Lans-en-Vercors (previously he had spent only one week a month in the city). During this period he relied on Ashbery a great deal: "I just came to count on John tremendously. We'd spend five evenings a week together. . . . John was absolutely wonderful. He'd talk with me. He'd drink with me. He'd drag me to those horrible films he was so fond of. He introduced me to others, most important, [to poets] Denis Roche and Marcelin Pleynet."

Ashbery engaged Mathews in another scheme as well: the founding of a literary magazine, *Locus Solus*. Although their later accounts differed slightly, both Ashbery and Mathews agreed that the journal was basically a result of friendships: Mathews's with Ashbery; Ashbery's with New York poets, particularly Koch,

Schuyler, and O'Hara. According to Mathews, these poets felt a "great deal of confidence in what they were doing but had, to say the least, insufficient publishing outlets." Unlike most maverick publishing enterprises, however, the then unnamed review did not have early funding problems, for in 1959, Mathews had inherited $20,000 from his grandfather. "I used half of it to pay off a loan on the house in Lans," he recalled. "And I thought I'd use $5,000 for fun and the other $5,000 to do this magazine that John had suggested. And then Kenneth [Koch] came over in the summer [of 1960] and was very enthusiastic as well. I remember he said to me, 'You see, Harry, what we really want to do is start a magazine so we can publish our own work and that of our friends.' I felt somewhat left out initially. I'd published very little at the time and I think Kenneth probably looked at me and thought this is someone whose money should be taken and [who should be] otherwise ignored. After he read some things [of mine], though, he changed his opinion and has been extremely supportive ever since."

From conception to reality did not take long. By the fall of 1960, with work contributed by Ashbery, Koch, Mathews, O'Hara, Schuyler, and others, and with the title *Locus Solus* chosen to honor their hero Raymond Roussel, the first issue of the journal was ready to be printed. For this, Ashbery and Mathews took the inaugural material to a printer Walter Auerbach had found for them in Majorca. (Subsequent issues were printed in Geneva.) At the beginning of the new year *Locus Solus*, edited by Mathews and Ashbery in France and Koch and Schuyler in New York, made its debut.

It was not, to those outside a small circle, an immediate publishing event. But looking back at the four issues of the magazine that struggled into print between January 1961 and the journal's demise in the fall of 1962, one sees that it should have been. It truly provided a vehicle for new, original, often outstanding voices on the contemporary scene. Major work by writers who would shortly thereafter become recognized as defining new tendencies in American writing graces every issue, and among these writers are, of course, the founders. Mathews's career as a published writer, in fact, was really launched by the appearance in the review of several chapters of *The Conversions*. In addition, the associations he made brought him out of the lack of connection he was feeling with the American literary scene and allowed him, even from his outpost in Paris, to become a member of a thriving literary community. Or as Mathews noted, "What really drove *Locus Solus* and lasted long after it was a great writing and personal friendship."

As a partial consequence of that friendship, *The Conversions* was aided into print. "Kenneth [Koch] was responsible for getting the novel published," stated Mathews. "Once he read the manuscript he became very enthusiastic. As a result, he pushed the manuscript on Jason Epstein at Random House [and Epstein] took it." With its publication in 1962, Mathews was suddenly on a small corner of the literary map. His position has grown tremendously since then, although even now he is still better known in Europe.

ASHBERY STAYED on in Paris until 1966, when he returned to New York, in part to take a position as an executive editor for *ArtNews*. One of the last articles he wrote before leaving for the United States was entitled "American Sanctuary in Paris." Although its focus was on American painters in Paris, much of Ashbery's commentary rang true for himself as well, especially in observations such as this: "The feeling of being a stranger even in moments of greatest rapport with one's adopted home is the opposite of the American 'acceptance world' which so often ends up stifling an artist's originality through the efficacious means of over-encouragement. If indifference and even hostility are not exactly beneficial for an artist, too much success is usually worse, for it corrupts subtly. What is especially moving in the work of Americans abroad is a general resolution in the face of apathy and apartheid to determine their individuality, to create something independent of fashion."

For Ashbery, Paris functioned very much like this for him, in that it allowed him *"la grande permission"* to work out his own aesthetic directions without being unduly swayed by convention, anticonvention, or, as he has called it, "fashion." By the time Ashbery left Paris he had developed a distinctive voice, a uniqueness, a poetic conviction that he has continued to draw on and expand over the many years since. Within a decade of his return to the United States, these fundamental lessons, learned and acted upon, in his words, in "the calm and the isolation of exile," would establish him as one of the premier poets writing in the English language. As he noted about "this perilous experiment" of his fellow American artists in Paris: "When it succeeds, [it] can result in an exciting art that is independent of environment, as art must be in order to survive when the environment has been removed."

Chapter Twelve

At the Beat Hotel

I N   T H E   summer of 1957, in Venice, Gregory Corso gave his friend Allen Ginsberg the address of a cheap hotel in Paris. The hotel, on Rue Gît-le-Cœur, didn't have a name, Corso informed him, but it wouldn't be difficult for Ginsberg to locate. It was on a little street in the Left Bank, around the corner from the Place St.-Michel. The proprietress was a woman named Madame Rachou. Several months later, in October, when Ginsberg and his companion, poet Peter Orlovsky, arrived in Paris, they promptly made their way to the small, seedy hotel and talked the rather formidable-appearing Madame Rachou into giving them a room.

They were by no means the first artists to take up residence at the hotel. Indeed, the place was something of a mecca in those years for the less than prosperous international artistic set. Chester Himes, for one, had lived there between 1956 and 1957; now staying at the hotel was the usual odd assortment of prostitutes, junkies, jazz musicians, hustlers, painters, and writers. Soon after the arrival of Ginsberg and Orlovsky, other illustrious residents would include Corso, William Burroughs, and Brion Gysin; hence the appellation "Beat Hotel."

"Beat-up Hotel" would probably have been a better sobriquet. Of the thirteen categories assigned French hotels, the Rachou establishment, with its forty-two rooms, was at the bottom. The paint peeled from gray walls, the windows were perpetually glazed with a brownish sheen inside and out, the room furnishings were minimal—a sagging bed, a table, a single wooden chair, a small, often stained cold-water sink. Cooking was done over a gas ring or alcohol stove (generally provided by the residents). Because of the ancient wiring, only a single forty-watt bulb was allowed for illumination in each room; if another appliance such as a tape recorder or radio was used, the light had to be turned out. On each stair landing was a Turkish toilet, with torn newspaper hanging from a hook for use as toilet paper. On the ground floor was a bath, where for an additional charge, and at advance request, water would be heated.

Despite its drawbacks in terms of appointments and amenities, the hotel had two major advantages: its price—120 francs ($30) a month—and the tolerant attitude of the aged Madame Rachou. (Himes remembered a Monsieur Rachou as well, but by the time Ginsberg arrived, Madame alone presided over the premises.) A small woman with white hair rinsed shockingly blue, she was unfazed by any of the antics of her diverse clientele, as long as such behavior was confined to quarters. And yet, according to William Burroughs, "Madame Rachou was very mysterious and arbitrary about who she would let into the hotel. 'She has her orders,' Brion [Gysin] always said. And if her orders said NO, you didn't get in and that was that."

She also protected her guests, as much as she could, from arbitrary police searches and unwanted visitors. The police, in fact, rarely bothered any of the residents without cause, as Madame took pains to maintain good relations with them, always inviting them in for a coffee or a meal in the curtained dining room. This room, screened from an adjacent zinc-countered bar that doubled as the front desk, allowed the various residents to pass through the entrance unnoticed by the visiting *gendarmes*.

* * *

GINSBERG IMMEDIATELY took to the hotel, impressed more by its prime location and cheap price than by its tawdriness.

> The room was probably fifteen by twenty [feet], more than ample for the two of us. We had a two-burner gas stove and an adequate supply of pots and pans so we could cook, which cut costs a lot. We'd shop at the great open-air markets near the Rue de Buci. . . . We'd pick up fresh fish, fresh vegetables, wine, a baguette, and we were set. And it was cheap, which was a major advantage. I remember we ate a lot of mussels in Paris that fall and winter because they were the cheapest item you could buy, much less expensive than meat. And of course, all of Paris was available to us. We'd take long walks, go to the museums, just enjoy the bewildering beauty of Paris.

That October in which he took up residence in the city, Ginsberg was thirty-one years old. He was more infamous than famous, as a result of the newsmaking *Howl* trial, which had just ended in his favor the same month in San Francisco; but his outward appearance—clean-shaven, short-haired, studiously bespectacled—was opposite the image of the perverted, sex- and drug-crazed young poet out to overturn American values portrayed by the prosecution at the trial (and gleefully picked up in the American press). Both impressions were correct. *Howl* was and is a subversive poem, an incantatory exhortation of feeling, of empathy, and a denunciation of the American nightmare. But it is also a poem of homage to Ginsberg's masters: Christopher Smart, Walt Whitman, William Carlos Williams, Federico García Lorca, Guillaume Apollinaire. As such, it is a poem of learning, not a learned poem, for its young author was acutely aware that he was only at the beginning of his quest for knowledge in all its forms. Paris was another stop on this mission of discovery.

While France and French literature had long inspired him, as with much of his learning, his exposure to them was largely outside of the academy. "I wasn't that well educated about French writing," noted Ginsberg, "but in the mid-forties I'd had the good fortune to stumble on *VVV* and *View* [avant-garde literary magazines] and [Robert] Motherwell's *The Dada Painters and Poets* and *The European Caravan*, and Carl Solomon, and his enthusiasm for Artaud. From Burroughs, I learned about Camus, and I'd read Gide at school. And then in the late forties came Céline's works, Artaud, Roger Shattuck's Apollinaire translations, and [there were] Cocteau's films *Orpheus* and *The Blood of a Poet*. It was rather unsystematic, but that was really the beginning of my acquaintance with modernism in France."

Unsystematic though his preparation may have been, Ginsberg was already imbued with the modernist French tradition when he arrived in Paris. "I'd walk the Left Bank streets, thinking that Apollinaire or Rimbaud or Baudelaire had walked down these same streets," he remembered. "It was both spooky and thrilling." At the same time, he hardly spent his days in a cloud of nostalgia for a past he never knew, for he lived fully in the present, taking in every aspect of Paris that he could. It was just that for Ginsberg the past was part of the present. "You can't escape the past in Paris, and yet what's so wonderful about it is that the past and present intermingle so intangibly that it doesn't seem a burden."

This dual sense of life in Paris is reflected in many of Ginsberg's poems written there. In "Europe! Europe!" for instance, the immediate situation is transfused with a past literary association:

> in February it rains
> as once for Baudelaire
> one hundred years ago
> planes roar in the air
> cars race thru streets

The evocation of the past, however, was most pronounced when Ginsberg actively sought to draw on his literary antecedents in order to get closer to his own experience in what for him was often a city filled with ghosts. Enthralled by a recording of Apollinaire reading "Le Pont Mirabeau," Ginsberg visited Père Lachaise cemetery "to look for the remains" of the poet. His poem "At Apollinaire's Grave" recounts the visit, while also paying homage to its subject through an attempt to imitate his style, particularly that of Apollinaire's long poem *Zone*.

"At Apollinaire's Grave" is one of Ginsberg's finest from the period, and in it he free-associates, interweaving anecdotes about Apollinaire, including a description of the voice just heard on the recording, with his present experience at graveside, which in actuality is a meditation on death. Ginsberg noted that "the point of the Apollinaire poem was to show my literary antecedents with the hope that others would go out and read them. Unfortunately [the poem] was largely ignored at the time. Everybody said, 'Oh, Ginsberg is imitating [Kenneth] Patchen and Carl Sandburg.' There was no notion at all of the European tradition. The montage, free association, nonpunctuated *Zone* style that I used in that poem was largely missed."

But Ginsberg's most important excursion into the past that fall was not literary. Rather, it was a poem of mourning, of wailing, of personal history, of coming to terms with the death of his mother the year before: a personal Kaddish. It began, as he wrote Jack Kerouac, on a gray November day: "I sat weeping in Cafe Select, once haunted by Gide and Picasso and the well dressed [Max] Jacob, last week writing first lines of great formal elegy for my mother—

> Farewell
> with long black shoe
> Farewell
> smoking corsets & ribs of steel
> Farewell
> communist party & broken stocking
> with your eyes of shock
> with your eyes of lobotomy
> with your eyes of stroke
> with your eyes of divorce
> with your eyes of alone
> with your eyes

It would take Ginsberg another year to finish *Kaddish*, with this becoming part of the fourth section in the final version. But the beginning was in Paris, where death consciousness—of past poets, of Père Lachaise—was fused with his own personal loss. "I write best when I weep," he remarked in the same letter. "I wrote a lot of that weeping anyway and got idea for huge expandable form of such a poem, will finish later and make a big elegy, perhaps less repetitious in parts, but I gotta get a rhythm up to cry."

NOT ALL of Ginsberg's time in Paris was so poetic, apparently. According to Joan Dillon, daughter of the U.S. ambassador to France, Douglas Dillon, Ginsberg and Orlovsky paid a memorable visit to the headquarters of *The Paris Review*, located in the Right Bank on the Rue Vernet. In her version—an account both Ginsberg and Orlovsky term "a total fabrication"—she recalled that the two poets arrived at the office while she was working alone: "Suddenly a couple of *horrors* pushed through the door speaking a language incomprehensible to me. I recognized at once that my intruders were Allen Ginsberg and Peter Orlovsky. They were doped to the hilt. They had an idea that we had original correspondence with Ezra Pound. . . . I told them this was not true and asked them to leave. They tried to get at my files. . . . I defended the files physically, behaving abominably, as I had no wish to clean up the mess they were sure to make." The standoff lasted for a while, but the incident apparently ended when a young English advertising executive "rescued" Dillon by escorting Ginsberg and Orlovsky from the office.

Another Ginsberg mission that fall was the promotion of William Burroughs's work. It was hardly a new role for him. From almost the beginning of their association, Ginsberg had taken it upon himself to attempt to market Burroughs's work (as well as that of Jack Kerouac). It was Ginsberg who had convinced his friend Carl Solomon, who was working in the early 1950s as an editor at Ace Books in New York, to publish Burroughs's first novel, *Junky*. Now, in his continuing role of literary promoter,

Ginsberg paid a visit to Maurice Girodias to try to interest him in publishing *Naked Lunch*. According to Ginsberg, he decided to approach Girodias mainly because "*Naked Lunch* seemed a natural for him, not from the point of view of being a porn novel—which it isn't anyway—but because he'd published Durrell, Miller, Nabokov, Genet, Beckett." The problem was that the manuscript Ginsberg took to Girodias was, by his own admission, "a mess physically, [with] tattered pages pasted together, marginal additions, etcetera." Girodias declined even to look at the manuscript until it was put in a more readable form. This was a more awesome task than simply retyping, however, for as Ginsberg recalled, "it was just fragment after fragment strung together."

Creating some sort of narrative structure had always been a problem with the novel, since Burroughs had never paid attention to linear order during its composition. "What you have to realize," Ginsberg observed, "is that *Naked Lunch* was written over years and years, without any regard for how it fit together. I knew what the book was about because I'd been in on it from the beginning. Bill invented the first routines back in the late forties, and then when he was living with me in the early fifties got really involved with it. And the rest of the routines, like Benway and the 'talking asshole' were developed in letters to me between 1953 and 1956 in which he'd amplify them in overlay after overlay. The whole process was one of cumulative accretions."

To turn these "accretions" into a novel was a formidable challenge. The first attempt had been made in the spring of 1957, when Kerouac, and then Ginsberg, Orlovsky, and poet Alan Ansen visited Burroughs in Tangier. According to Ginsberg, "Our purpose in Tangier was to finally get this book together. Jack was the first typist; then I took over. Then Alan Ansen arrived and he took over. But the big question—the overhanging question—was how to edit it. Bill had tried to figure it out, Jack had tried, Alan had tried, I'd tried, but it just wouldn't come together in anything resembling a linear order. This was the manuscript I took to Girodias—just this series of different fragments which even to us didn't make sense as a coherent piece of work. What we didn't realize at the time was that it could in fact be a novel and be a montage, a composite. But nobody was writing like that then, and though we knew Bill had a work of genius, we mistrusted—and this included Bill even—our own sense of what we knew *Naked Lunch* to be."

Ginsberg conveyed Girodias's rejection to Burroughs in Tangier but noted that there was some hope: Girodias had asked to see the book in a more edited form. Burroughs, meanwhile, was growing tired of Tangier and decided to go to Paris to see if he could prepare *Naked Lunch* for publication. Ginsberg booked him a room at his hotel and awaited his arrival, scheduled for January 16, 1958, with more than a little apprehension. It was not editing *Naked Lunch* that was causing his anxiety; rather, it was the uncertainty about their personal relations. The matter was complex, and dated back to 1953, when Ginsberg, while avowing his love for Burroughs, had decided he no longer wanted to be involved with him sexually.

After 1953 the two corresponded regularly, but they did not see each other again until Ginsberg showed up in Tangier in April 1957. The situation there had been strained. Burroughs took an instant dislike to Orlovsky; Ginsberg tried to resolve the problem by taking Burroughs to bed with himself and Orlovsky, but according to Ginsberg, "this idea wasn't any good and didn't improve things a bit."

In the months since Ginsberg's departure from Tangier, he and Burroughs had exchanged numerous letters in which Burroughs consistently maintained that he had changed his position, that he had come to an understanding within himself about his relationship with Ginsberg. Despite Burroughs's words, Ginsberg was uncertain. In his mind, the problem was compounded by Orlovsky's planned departure for New York the day after Burroughs's arrival: Ginsberg was not sure what this meant for either relationship.

His fears, as it turned out, were for the most part unfounded. Burroughs had changed considerably, though one suspects that Orlovsky's departure helped matters. Ginsberg thought him calmer, more congenial than he'd seen him in a long time. Nearly coincidental with Burroughs's arrival was the reappearance in Paris of Gregory Corso. He had been in the city off and on that fall, even sharing the room with Ginsberg and Orlovsky, but he now became a full-fledged resident with his own room at the Beat Hotel. Outrageous, gifted, funny, Corso was a welcome addition for both Ginsberg and Burroughs, and probably contributed to lightening up the situation.

Corso's exuberance, in fact, was a decided contrast to Burroughs's introspection, and even to Ginsberg's more serious bent. For Corso, inordinately gregarious, in love with life, Paris was a vast playground, which he insisted his old friends share. "Gregory had this incredible ability to get around and make connections," recalled Ginsberg. "I don't know how he met anybody. He just met them. He was totally indiscriminate as to who people were. They could be down-and-out junkies or princesses, it didn't matter to him, as long as they were authentically that. But he had no tolerance for bullshitters and could detect [them] in seconds." Burroughs remembered once going out to dinner with Corso at a restaurant around the corner from the hotel. They ordered wild boar, but when it came, "Gregory took one sniff and refused to taste it. I chided him overbearingly for being provincial, and took a mouthful myself—and came near to spitting it right out on the plate, with the words of Samuel Johnson when he spat out some over-hot food, 'A fool would have swallowed that.' It had a horrible, rank musky taste." Obviously Corso's "bullshit detector" extended also to food. But above all, as Burroughs noted, "there was a special quality about him, a radiant, childlike charm."

It was this charm that could dissipate a foul mood, that could lead his fellow writers into various madcap adventures, among them meeting John Huston. According to Ginsberg, he and Corso were out for a walk one day when they saw the film director. While Ginsberg remained at a respectful distance, Corso went up to Huston and immediately began talking with him, inviting him to join them at a nearby café. Huston accepted, and over leisurely drinks Ginsberg and Corso began to talk with him about making

Naked Lunch into a movie. Intrigued, Huston invited them "and this Mr. Burroughs" that evening to a cast party (he had just finished shooting *The Roots of Heaven* with Errol Flynn) on a boat in the Seine. Ginsberg decided also to bring along a young actor friend who was staying at the hotel. "I should have known better," Ginsberg remembered. "The kid got drunk quickly and started a fistfight with Errol Flynn, which got him kicked off the boat. I felt so bad for him that I walked him off. Gregory and Bill stayed on and talked to Huston and [Darryl] Zanuck, but it was really a shame because they all got this idea that these [were] the beatniks—irresponsible, aggressive kids who start fights with their superiors—and so they felt no need to take us seriously any longer."

Another Corso connection was Jean-Jacques Lebel, whose father had been a member of the surrealist circle in the 1930s. The younger Lebel was now himself close friends with the surviving members of the group. Knowing the great interest and admiration of Corso, Ginsberg, and Burroughs for the surrealists, he invited them to a party in honor of Man Ray and Marcel Duchamp. Stunned at being in the presence of his great masters, Ginsberg, according to some accounts, proceeded to get drunk. Burroughs, who thought Duchamp "very urbane, suave, witty, very much the French intellectual," was stunned himself when he noticed Ginsberg crawling on all fours after Duchamp, clawing at his pantleg, calling him "Cher Maître." "Duchamp was unfazed by Allen's demonstration," recalled Burroughs. "He just looked down at him and said, 'But I'm only human.' " Ginsberg, however, persisted, insisting that he bestow a kiss on Burroughs as a symbolic gesture of "passing the mantle." Duchamp complied.

Lebel, for his own part, took a great interest in the Beats and was one of the early proponents of their work in France. Later, when running the American Center in Paris, he arranged readings for them. At that time, however, the only public readings any of them gave in Paris were at the Librairie Mistral. "Ginsberg read from *Howl*," recollected the bookstore's proprietor, George Whitman. "There was a great crowd outside the store, just mesmerized. Even if they couldn't understand the words, they understood the power of the language. Corso read here too, several times, again always to enthusiasm." But the most amazing event, Whitman said, came when Burroughs gave perhaps the first public reading of parts of *Naked Lunch*. "Nobody was quite sure what to make of it, whether to laugh or be sick. It was something quite remarkable, quite different."

Ginsberg and Corso were invited in 1958 to give readings at Oxford. The first, at Jesus College, went well; the second, at New College, took an unexpected turn during Corso's rendition of his new poem "Bomb," a satiric attack on the proliferation of nuclear weapons. The students attending completely misunderstood Corso's poem. Thinking that Corso was celebrating the atomic bomb, one outraged listener took off his shoe and flung it at the poet. Corso responded like the old street fighter he'd earlier been, shouting obscenities at the crowd, inviting them to engage in one-on-one fisticuffs with him. Ginsberg too excoriated them. The potential melee ended peacefully, and the poets were quickly escorted from the room. At a party later that night, the two of them convulsed in laughter, their ire vanishing as they realized how absurd the event had been.

While on that trip, Ginsberg and Corso also managed to have audiences with W. H. Auden and Edith Sitwell. Auden initially was cool. The year before, they had become embroiled in an argument over revolution in poetry when Ginsberg had visited him in Ischia, and he was now understandably wary of "the ragtag rabble-rousers." He did, however, warm to them, inviting them to walk with him around campus. Sitwell was very cordial, inviting them to tea at her club.

BACK IN Paris, Ginsberg continued his quest of the French writers he admired. Of all the writers in France, the one he and Burroughs most wanted to meet was Louis-Ferdinand Céline. He had influenced them both and had long been a major literary hero; and although both were well aware of his anti-Semitism and

procollaborationist activities during the war, they were nonetheless entranced by his writing. In particular, they admired his
ability to sustain a "tone of delirium" throughout an entire novel,
in which every encounter, event, and idea is described not objec-
tively, but in terms of the emotions it evokes. They also had a
fondness for Céline's use of spoken language—as opposed to
literary language—to create his narratives.

They were somewhat skeptical, though, that he would see
them, for he was known as a difficult, bitter, almost reclusive
character. Finally Ginsberg decided the best way to meet him was
to arrange a formal introduction through his publisher. Michel
Mohrt, Céline's editor at Gallimard, who later became a great
supporter of the Beats, was surprised at the request, but gave
them a letter of introduction. And on a sun-filled day in July
1958, Burroughs and Ginsberg took a bus to Meudon, a suburb
of Paris, to pay homage to the master.

"He was still practicing medicine," remarked Burroughs, "and
lived in a run-down suburban atmosphere, plastered villas with
the stucco flaking off. His house was set back from the street, had
a fence around it with rusting bedsprings in the yard and five big
dogs that barked incessantly, which he kept, he said, to protect
him from the Jews. He told us he'd had arguments with everyone
in the neighborhood, [and he] complained about his medical
practice, including the pharmacists who wouldn't fill his prescrip-
tions. But he put up with us for the afternoon, introduced us to
his wife, who was a dancer, showed us around his house, told us a
few stories."

Ginsberg's account of the visit is somewhat more detailed: "He
and Burroughs had a very long talk about how you never know a
country unless you see it through its jails. This led him to tell us a
whole string of anecdotes, some of which I recognized from his
books. . . . We asked him what modern French writers he liked,
and he told us only C. F. Ramuz, Paul Morand, and Henri Bar-
busse. The others—Beckett, Sartre, Michaux, Camus, the big
names—he just dismissed. I gave him a copy of *Howl* and *On the
Road* and Bill gave him *Junky*, but I doubt if he ever read them.

And it didn't really matter. We weren't looking for his approval. I was there simply to pay homage. Bill too, but I was more naive about it. When we left I said, 'We have come on behalf of American literature to salute you as the greatest living writer in France.' His wife corrected us: 'In the universe!' "

They met another great literary hero that summer: Henri Michaux. Aside from their considerable interest in his poetry, they felt a decided link with Michaux because of his use of hallucinogens. According to Ginsberg, Michaux came around to the hotel in response to a postcard Ginsberg had sent him inviting him to visit. When he arrived, Ginsberg was naked, in the process of taking a sponge bath. The poet quickly excused himself but agreed to return in the evening. That night, Ginsberg, Burroughs, Corso, and Michaux sat up discussing their various mescaline experiences. The next evening Michaux came again, and at some point one of his hosts committed the faux pas of urinating in the sink. This apparently had the effect of convincing Michaux to exit the gathering. Although he and Ginsberg later had amicable relations, the French writer never returned to the hotel. "Michaux, for all of his interest in mescaline and related hallucinatory intoxicants, was really quite straight-laced, very proper, courteous, refined like many Frenchmen of his class," observed Burroughs. It was this side of his personality that took offense when one of them used the sink as a toilet. The American response was perhaps best represented by Corso's comment on the incident: "So fucking European even to detect such an action."

GINSBERG, BURROUGHS, and Corso hardly spent all their energies socializing with the great French writers whom they took to be their masters. The ongoing revision of *Naked Lunch* was a continual preoccupation. While the same difficulties were present, some progress was made in terms of becoming more confident that the nonlinear narrative might be a viable form itself. In this regard, Burroughs had received a boost when portions of the novel, given previously by Ginsberg to Robert Creeley, had appeared in the magazine Creeley edited, *Black Mountain Review*, in the fall of 1957. This was the first publication of any of the manuscript and represented a validation, at least in the eyes of Burroughs and Ginsberg, of the publishability of the book. Ginsberg now tried to get more of Burroughs in print, feeling that ultimately this would lead to interest on the part of publishers in bringing out the work as a whole.

He sent a piece to *Encounter* in London, as well as a section to Irving Rosenthal, who was planning an "experimental issue" of *The Chicago Review*, a literary magazine at the University of Chicago. Stephen Spender, then editing *Encounter*, responded promptly and simply: "This would be a matter of interest only for a psychiatrist." Ginsberg was so angered by the response that he sent back a letter in which he posed the prescient question: "What are you, the CIA?" With *The Chicago Review*, however, Burroughs fared better. Rosenthal immediately accepted the excerpt for the autumn issue and asked for more, which Burroughs happily sent. At long last, he felt, his work was being taken seriously.

By July 1958, Ginsberg had been abroad for eighteen months and was beginning to feel it was time to return home. He was not so much homesick for the United States; rather, he was acutely missing Orlovsky, as he testified in his poem "Message," written in May of that year:

> It's too long that I have been alone
> it's too long that I've sat up in bed
> without anyone to touch on the knee, man
> or woman I don't care what anymore, I
> want love I was born for I want you with me now
> . . . .
> The leaves are green on all the trees in Paris now
> I will be home in two months and look you in the eyes

274

He tried to persuade Corso and Burroughs to return with him, but neither was interested. Both told Ginsberg that in effect, they had no one to return to there. But since Ginsberg did, he departed Paris in July, leaving Burroughs and Corso behind at the Beat Hotel. Upon arriving in America he discovered that partly as a result of the controversy surrounding *Howl* he had become a celebrity. The book was in its fifth printing; articles on Ginsberg and the "Beatniks," most of them quite sensationalized, were featured in all the glossies. From the relative anonymity of Paris, where he was the one seeking out the masters, he was now the one being sought out. Never again, even in Europe, would Ginsberg be able to enjoy life outside the spotlight. Although he was pleased with the celebrity, those nine months at the Beat Hotel now began to seem more precious than ever. Soon after returning to the States, Ginsberg wrote Burroughs: "There's no end in sight to fame and I really see what you mean by the hideousness of all that. I'm such a myth in the Village, every time I go into a bar people rush up and talk to some idealized image they have of me. . . . I hardly exist and talk as simple Allen anymore."

NOT TOO long after Ginsberg left, Burroughs ran into an acquaintance he'd known in Tangier: Brion Gysin. In Morocco, despite the attempts to bring them closer together on the part of writer Paul Bowles, who knew and respected them both, they had not really connected. "Brion . . . didn't approve of my way of life or my association with the Spanish, since he was tied up with the Arabs," remarked Burroughs. "Or he thought I was incompatible with this Arab-oriented life he'd set up." But then, on a summer night in 1958, as Gysin recorded it, "I ran into grey-green Burroughs in the Place St Michel. 'Wanna score?' For the first time in all the years I'd known him, I really scored with him."

Gysin had been in Paris about the same amount of time as Burroughs, having left Morocco, where he had lived since 1950, after a set of circumstances forced him out of the restaurant business, in which he'd been engaged for several years: "I fell out of business, not over money but [because of] magic," Gysin recalled. The magic consisted of an amulet he found concealed in a ventilator at the restaurant, presumably placed by his "partners," Moroccan musicians of the Ahl Serif hill tribe; suspicious of Gysin's own investigation into magic, they retaliated with magic of their own. The charm, consisting of pebbles, seeds, mirror shards, pubic hair, newt's eyes, menstrual blood, and other, undefinable ingredients, also contained a message written in rusty ink: "May Massa Brahim [Brion] leave this house as the smoke leaves this fire, never to return." A few days after its discovery, thanks to a disastrous deal made with some American Scientologists, Gysin lost the restaurant.

Although at loose ends in Paris after that debacle, Gysin was no stranger to France. In the 1930s he had studied at the Sorbonne and exhibited paintings with the surrealists. He had returned after the war with a Fulbright grant, garnered on the basis of two scholarly books on slavery. But then he'd put aside his promising career as a scholar to pursue painting and music and magic in Morocco. Brilliant, talented, intense, a fabulous storyteller, like Burroughs, he was an uncompromising artist, dedicated to exploring the outer bounds of the avant-garde.

By the end of 1958, Gysin had moved into the Beat Hotel. By the early spring of 1959, he had become as involved with trying to figure out what to do with *Naked Lunch* as had Ginsberg, Kerouac, and Ansen previously. Gysin described Burroughs's seemingly unending quest to put the book together: "*Naked Lunch* manuscript of every age and condition floated around the hermetically sealed room as Burroughs, thrashing about in an ectoplasmic cloud of smoke, ranted through the gargantuan roles of Doc Benway, A. J., Clem & Jody and hundreds of others he never had time to ram through the typewriter. 'Am I an octopus?' he used to whine as he shuffled through shoals of typescript with all tentacles waving in the undersea atmosphere. It looked, in those days, as though *Naked Lunch*, named so long before its birth by Kerouac, might never see the light of day outside room 15."

But things had already begun to change with regard to its ultimate publication. In late October 1958, *The Chicago Review* had appeared with nine pages from *Naked Lunch*. It created an immediate stir, but not in quite the way Burroughs had hoped. "Filthy Writing on the Midway" was the headline in a column in the October 25 edition of the Chicago *Daily News*. Citing Burroughs's work, the columnist, Jack Mabley, urged the University of Chicago to "take a long, hard look at what is being circulated under its sponsorship." The university responded to Mabley's exhortation. They queried Rosenthal, then a graduate student, about the contents of the next issue. When he responded that the upcoming winter number was devoted entirely to three writers—Kerouac, Edward Dahlberg, and Burroughs—he was told that the university would not approve the publication. Rosenthal protested and tried to drum up support, but none was to be found. Finally, after learning that the university had interceded with the printer to suppress the issue, Rosenthal resigned to start his own magazine.

Big Table, the reincarnation of the winter issue of *The Chicago Review* (with additional contributions by Corso), hit the stands in March 1959. Within days it was seized by postal authorities as obscene. Burroughs fell into despair thinking that publication was now all but impossible. What he had not counted on was that the attention caused by the banning would bring Maurice Girodias, ever ready to champion a "suppressed work," to take an interest in the book. In June he sent Burroughs a note through his assistant, Sinclair Beiles—a fellow Beat Hotel resident and a great admirer of Burroughs's work—saying that he'd like to look at the novel again. A few weeks later Girodias gave Burroughs a contract and an $800 advance. He also informed him that he had just ten days to prepare the manuscript for the printer.

Together, Burroughs, Gysin, and Beiles, working nearly nonstop, assembled the novel in time. Gysin described the frenetic process: "The raw material of *Naked Lunch* overwhelmed us. Showers of fading snapshots fell through the air: Old Bull's Texas farm, the Upper Reaches of the Amazon ... Tangier and the Mayan Codices ... shots of boys from every time and place. Burroughs was more intent on Scotch-taping his photos together into one great continuum on the wall, where scenes faded and slipped into one another, than occupied with editing the monster manuscript. . . . What to do with all this? Stick it on the wall along with the photographs and see what it looks like. . . . Stick it all together, end to end, and send it back like a big roll of music for a pianola. It's just material, after all. There is nothing sacred about words. 'Word falling. Photo falling. Breakthrough in grey room.' "*

Burroughs described the completion of the novel somewhat more prosaically: "The final form of *Naked Lunch* and the juxtaposition of sections were determined by the order in which material went—at random—to the printer." In essence, the problem of how to edit *Naked Lunch*, struggled over for more than a year, solved itself with the realization that there was no need to order the sections into a linear narrative.

And yet for all the legendary randomness, there is, as Ginsberg pointed out, "a psychic structure" to the novel: "The opening sentence in the book, 'I can feel the heat closing in, feel them out there making their moves'—Bill's vision of the cosmic police—is dispersed at the end, when Burroughs fights back and shoots the two narcs and realizes what has happened: 'I had been occluded from space-time like an eel's ass occludes when he stops eating on the way to Sargasso. . . .' In other words, the heat were phantoms. And so the book is stitched together at the end when these phantom police representatives are dissolved by Burroughs's consciousness. As a result, what you have is this incredible psychic structure—a mapping, really, of the junkie vision—which embraces all the routines, all those fabulous scenes."

The first of the 10,000 copies of the first printing of *The Naked Lunch*, as the original Olympia Press edition was entitled, rolled

* Many of the sections not included in the final assemblage of *Naked Lunch* were published in Burroughs's *Interzone* (Viking, 1989).

off the presses at the end of July, just three weeks after the printer had received the typescript. The book was an immediate sensation. Within months of its publication Grove Press bought the American rights for $3,000 (all of which eventually went to Girodias). Mondadori bought the book for Italy; Calder for England; Limes for Germany; Gallimard for France.

Burroughs's major concern at the time, however, was not with *Naked Lunch*; rather, his energy was directed toward defending himself in the French courts on drug charges. The French case rested not on possession, but on suspicion that Burroughs was involved in a scheme to smuggle hashish from Morocco into France. The evidence was a letter that Burroughs had written to an English friend in Tangier, a petty gangster named Paul Lund, in which he had suggested, half in jest, that they go into business together smuggling hashish in camel saddles. In April 1959, Lund had been arrested in Tangier for drug possession, and in an attempt to reduce his sentence, he had implicated Burroughs, who in fact had had nothing to do with the reason for Lund's arrest. But the Moroccan police had turned the information over to French authorities, who arrested Burroughs in June and detained him for a day. A preliminary trial was scheduled for late September. Through Girodias, Burroughs obtained an English-speaking lawyer who advised him simply to explain that the scheme had never been implemented.

On September 25, Burroughs appeared before the examining magistrate, who recommended that the case go to trial. At the hearing in October his lawyer pleaded that not only was Burroughs innocent, but he was an established man of letters. It is unclear which defense carried the more weight; the French court gave Burroughs a suspended sentence and a fine of $80.

Drug use, of course, is synonymous with the name William Burroughs. *Junky*, his first book, published in 1953, was a straightforward, slightly fictionalized recounting of his addiction; *Naked Lunch*, a visionary account. In 1956, after fifteen years of being addicted to opiates, Burroughs kicked the habit through an experimental treatment pioneered by an English doctor, John Dent. Dent's cure involved the use of a morphine derivative, apomorphine, injected along with decreasing doses of morphine, over a two-week period. At the end of the treatment, Burroughs miraculously had no physical dependency. But in the fall of 1958, after meeting a rich French addict named Jacques Stern, he became readdicted. He went to London to take the cure, but this time it was not as long-lasting. By the following spring Burroughs was again using morphine. With the possibility of prison looming because of the French drug charges, however, and with the realization that *Naked Lunch*, while a chronicle of drug visions, was not in fact written while he was on opiates, Burroughs decided that summer to kick the habit once again. Using apomorphine he had obtained on his 1958 visit to London, he managed to cure himself of his addiction.

While drug experiences have continually fueled Burroughs's writing, he has been adamant about the inefficaciousness of hard drugs for writing:

> I have written a good deal under the influence of cannabis; many sections of *Naked Lunch* were so written. . . . I have attempted to write after taking mescaline, but was deterred by nausea and lack of physical coordination. On the other hand, after the drug had worn off I was able to describe the psychic areas revealed to me by the drug. Amphetamine and cocaine are quite worthless for writing and nothing of value remains. I have never been able to write a line under the influence of alcohol. Under morphine one can edit, type, and organize material effectively but since the drug acts to decrease awareness the creative factor is dimmed. *Junkie* [*sic*] is the only one of my books written under the influence of opiates. The other books could never have been written if I had been addicted to morphine at the time.

BURROUGHS'S FRIENDSHIP with Brion Gysin grew increasingly intense during 1959, so intense, in fact, that they often alienated others. A great repository of esoteric knowledge, which he delighted in expounding, Gysin intrigued Burroughs in a way that few ever had. To their amazement, some even thought that Burroughs, usually the one to cast spells on others, had become mesmerized by Gysin and was now under *his* spell. In retrospect it seems to have been less a matter of spells than a meeting of minds. Burroughs's biographer Ted Morgan writes: "Their minds converged on such matters as the evil nature of women and the importance of the magical universe. Brion conversing at his best was a stellar performance made up in equal parts of free association, baroque descriptions, bits and pieces of arcane information, puns, japes and drollery, snatches of French and Spanish phrases, and much imaginative embellishment. Listening to Brion talk was like watching a man covered with elaborate Japanese tattoos. You might wonder what the point of it all was, but it was hard to take your eyes away."

According to Burroughs, "[Gysin] was the only man I have ever respected. I have admired many others, esteemed and valued others, but respected only him. His presence was regal without a trace of pretension." This respect was frequently incomprehensible to others who felt, as did Ginsberg and Corso, that Gysin "exaggerated some of Bill's worst tendencies—his suspiciousness, his antifemale stand, his penchant for seeing people as agents."

With Gysin, as Corso put it, "Burroughs got into some very heavy psychic things." Indeed, Burroughs was considerably impressed with Gysin's parallel interests in power and psychic control, magic and superstition. It was these concerns that led them, during the spring of 1959, to experiment with altered states of consciousness. Using a stainless-steel dowsing ball on the end of a keychain, they practiced the medieval technique of scrying, in which scenes of a paranormal nature could be perceived through prolonged staring at the ball. They also took up mirror gazing—sitting for prolonged periods, unblinking, in front of a mirror until the image began to distort—which enabled them to see different aspects of themselves, or according to Gysin, different incarnations.

For Burroughs, exploration of psychic phenomenon went hand in hand with writing. "What do writers do except have psychic experiences?" he asked rhetorically. He saw himself acting as a "map maker, an explorer of psychic areas" in his writing. These experiments, the way Burroughs perceived them, had to do not so much with the occult as with preparing the mental ground for creating art. In Gysin he had a fellow adventurer, who likewise saw "no point in exploring areas that have already been thoroughly surveyed."

But the real convergence of minds came one October day in 1959 when Gysin, working in Burroughs's room, sliced through a pile of newspapers while cutting a mount for a drawing. "I picked up the raw words," Gysin wrote later, "and began to piece together texts. . . . At the time I thought them hilariously funny and hysterically meaningful." When Burroughs returned, Gysin showed him the "cut-ups." Burroughs was as immediately hooked on the possibilities of this form as he had been years earlier on morphine. "The cut-up method brings to writers the collage, which has been used by painters for fifty years," noted Burroughs.

In actuality, Gysin's "discovery" had been around even longer than collage. Lewis Carroll defined the technique at the end of the nineteenth century in a piece of doggerel: "For first you write a sentence, / And then you chop it small; / Then mix the bits, and sort them out / Just as they chance to fall: / The order of the phrases makes / No difference at all." Later, at the beginning of this century, the Dadaists experimented with similar techniques, as perhaps best exemplified by Tzara's suggestion of making texts out of newspaper clippings or out of words drawn randomly from a hat, and by Duchamp's *Rendez-vous du dimanche 6 février 1916* . . . , in which four "nonsense" texts written on postcards are framed together. In the twenties and thirties the surrealists were enamored of similar forms of chance operations, including automatic writing and the composite-text or composite-image game, *cadavre exquis.**

The aim, for both Gysin and his predecessors, was to go be-

---

* In the early 1960s, Tzara, in fact, challenged Gysin to explain why he and Burroughs were reinventing what the Dadaists had done forty years before. Gysin replied: "Because you didn't do it well, because the real significance of the problem was not explored. The Dadaist methods are valuable in that the economic and social structures in place are still the same. Our method cuts at the interior of the system in order to confound the very function of media."

yond the conscious mental censor that attempted to impose a rational order on verbal expression. Or as Burroughs commented: "Cutting and rearranging a page of written words introduces a new dimension into writing enabling the writer to turn images in cinematic variation. Images shift sense under the scissors smell images to sound sight to sound sound to kinesthetic. This is where Rimbaud was going with his color of vowels. And his 'systematic derangement of the senses.'" A major reason for Burroughs's enthusiasm was that he felt he'd been applying the principle for years: "The cut-up method was used in (on?) *Naked Lunch* without the author's full awareness of the method he was using."

More experiments followed. By the late fall Burroughs and Gysin had recruited Corso and Beiles. Corso, although reluctant, joined them because of his strong admiration for Burroughs. Beiles, meanwhile, found a publisher for their cut-up poems, a young doctor named Jean Fanchette, who had just started a literary magazine, *Two Cities*, run out of George Whitman's Librairie Mistral. Another backer in the venture was Gait Frogé, proprietress of The English Bookshop on the Rue de Seine. The title, *Minutes to Go*, was given to the work at the last minute, the result of Beiles's admonition to "get this going. There are only minutes to go."

The book was published in March 1960 by Two Cities Editions, with an afterword by Corso expressing his doubts about the project.* Nonetheless, he did participate enthusiastically with the others at a book signing and party at Frogé's bookstore, for which Girodias supplied the champagne. Notwithstanding the throng at the party, the book didn't sell well. Burroughs was not perplexed, feeling that the lack of sales had more to do with the general conservativeness of the population, stuck in their Aristotelian logic, "one of the great shackles of Western civilization." His next three books—*The Soft Machine, The Ticket That Exploded,* and *Nova Express*—all made use of cut-ups and a later technique, fold-ins.

---

* Despite Corso's apparent disdain, he and Burroughs did contribute some cut-ups of Rimbaud poems to a special 1962 "collaborative issue" of *Locus Solus*.

If Corso was a less than reliable ally in the creation of cut-ups, two other young men Burroughs met during the late summer of 1959, the American poet Harold Norse and the English mathematician Ian Sommerville, soon became enthusiasts. Norse, who had arrived in Paris that summer from Italy, looked Burroughs up at the hotel. According to Norse, the first meeting was anything but propitious, with Burroughs maintaining complete indifference. Later, however, they became more friendly, and Norse would create a series of cut-up poems and win the endorsement of both Burroughs and Gysin.

But Norse's greatest service to Burroughs was undoubtedly mentioning to him that he should meet Ian Sommerville, who was living at the Librairie Mistral, where he helped out around the store in exchange for a free bed. In his early twenties, Sommerville was then a student at Cambridge and a mathematical prodigy. One day Burroughs decided he might as well take Norse's advice and went to the Mistral. Sommerville was on a ladder putting away books. One of them fell on Burroughs standing underneath. This provided an opening, and soon the two were involved in a deep conversation. Within a few weeks Sommerville had become Burroughs's lover, staying with him at the hotel, helping him kick his regained morphine habit. Their relationship would last until Sommerville's untimely death in 1976.

The contrast between the two men was extreme. At forty-five, more than twice Sommerville's age, Burroughs was worldly wise and worldly weary. Sommerville was energetic, extremely orderly, naive, scientific, impressionable. But he shared the Burroughs–Gysin predilection for experimenting with language and quickly expanded from the scissors-and-paste method to tape recording. Later, he would extend the technique by creating computer permutations of a given text. After his return to Cambridge in the fall, he continued to correspond with Burroughs and Gysin, all the while working, with a scientific-mathematical rigor, on refinements to the various experiments the three had discussed in Paris.

One of the most exciting of these enhancements was that of stimulating alpha brain waves through the use of flickering light.

In December 1958, Gysin had accidentally discovered the effect of shimmering light on the brain: "Had a transcendental storm of color visions today in the bus going to Marseilles. We ran through a long avenue of trees and I closed my eyes against the setting sun. An overwhelming flood of intensely bright patterns in supernatural colors exploded behind my eyelids: a multi-dimensional kaleidoscope whirling out through space." When Gysin, who did not know what had happened to him, related the experience to Burroughs, he told Gysin about the experiments reported in a book he had recently read, *The Living Brain* by William Grey Walter.

Sommerville also read the book and became intrigued by the possibility of creating a device to replicate Gysin's accidental experience. In February he wrote Burroughs and Gysin that he had succeeded in making "a simple flicker machine; a slotted cylinder which turns on a gramophone at 78 rpm with a light bulb inside. You look at it with your eyes shut and the flicker plays over your eyelids. Visions start with a kaleidoscope of colors on a plane in front of the eyes and gradually become more complex and beautiful, breaking like surf on a shore until whole patterns of color are pounding to get in." Soon Gysin had constructed his own Dream Machine at the Beat Hotel and he and Burroughs became avid devotees.

For Gysin, the visionary invention lead to a total change in his style of painting; for Burroughs, it opened up, in the same way as hallucinogenic drugs had, the world of interior vision, in which the most extraordinary images were revealed to him. In Burroughs's words: "Anything that can be done chemically can be done in other ways, with sufficient knowledge of the mechanisms involved. . . . The consciousness-expanding experience can be induced by flicker—that is, rhythmic light flashing in the retina at the rate of from ten to twenty-five flashes per second."

IN APRIL 1960, Burroughs was given a message by Madame Rachou to call the American embassy. He was not particularly

285

surprised to discover that the number he'd been told to dial was that of the narcotics bureau. "Voices" had been telling him for a while that it was time to leave Paris. When Burroughs went to the embassy he was told that because of his arrest and conviction on drug charges the year before, it would be wise for him to go back to the United States before the government felt the need to confiscate his passport. The narcotics officer also suggested that the French were making moves to deport him. Burroughs had his French lawyer check into the matter. No plans were afoot on the part of the French government to deport him, the lawyer told him, but the Americans could do whatever they wanted. Burroughs did not need further warning. At the end of April he packed up his bags and moved to England, where he could be nearer to Sommerville and away from the American authorities in France, who were sure to be planning some sort of drug bust of their own. Corso and Gysin stayed on for a while, but with both Burroughs and Ginsberg no longer in residence, the Beat Hotel was no longer as Beat as it had been.

The time Ginsberg and Burroughs had spent at the hotel had been important for both, however, perhaps more so for Burroughs, whose life and career were forever altered by his days in Paris. In Tangier, the locals had dubbed him *"el hombre invisible."* The description was apt, as Burroughs himself noted: "I lived in one room in the Native Quarter of Tangier. I had not taken a bath in a year nor changed my clothes or removed them except to stick a needle every hour in the fibrous grey wooden flesh of terminal addiction. I never cleaned or dusted the room. Empty ampule boxes and garbage piled to the ceiling. Light and water long since turned off for non-payment. I did absolutely nothing. I could look at the end of my shoe for eight hours. I was only roused to action when the hourglass of junk ran out." The real change, of course, had come while he was still in Tangier, when he had managed to get off opiates; but in Paris, his new "health" was supported in a way it had not been in the relative isolation of Morocco. In France, he shook off his invisibility, became *"el escritor visible."*

Ginsberg and Gysin played major roles in Burroughs's becoming the writer he is, through their belief in his work and in him, and through their practical editorial efforts on his behalf. Maurice Girodias too, for all his wheeling and dealing, has to be given credit for putting *Naked Lunch* on the literary map. Corso, Sommerville, Beiles, Norse, and others contributed as well to Burroughs's sense of the possibility of it all. And from Burroughs, they learned not just about the esoteric side of things but about pushing their own work beyond "safe" limits. What was so special about the Beat Hotel was that it was a veritable community of artists. "Things were happening in every room," commented Burroughs. "People were writing, painting, talking, and planning." Harold Norse, who lived at the hotel from 1960 until it was sold in 1963, wrote: "In that hotel levels of consciousness and horror (and humor) were reached that few men even dream could exist."

Besides providing these writers with a point of artistic convergence, Paris supported and enfranchised them and their work, allowed them to create in an atmosphere that was conducive to experimentation. And though the Beat legacy never made its way very strongly into French writing, Ginsberg and Burroughs have long been regarded as major writers in France. Indeed, years before Burroughs was recognized in his own country, he was enshrined in France, published in translation by Gallimard, certainly one of the most prestigious imprints in France at that time. Paris also brought them closer to their French literary forebears, permitted them, particularly in the case of Ginsberg, to begin working in new directions inspired by his discoveries there.

But most important, as Ginsberg observed, "our coming together at the hotel allowed us to spark each other. That was its contribution: getting us all under the same roof at the same time so we could hit off each other's energy day and night." Synchronicity, chance, fate—whatever one chose to call it, the interval at the little hotel at 9 Rue Gît-leCœur played a key role in the formation of the writers who lived there at the end of the fifties and who created, together and separately, an impressive chapter in contemporary American literature.

The Continual Pilgrimage

IN "THE New Spirit," the first section of *Three Poems*, John Ashbery wrote:

> And what about what was there before?
>
> This is shaped in the new merging, like ancestral smiles, common memories, remembering just how the light stood on the water that time. But it is also something new. Outside, can't you hear it, the traffic, the trees, everything getting nearer. To end up with, inside each other, moving upward like penance. For the continual pilgrimage has not stopped. It is only that you are both moving at the same rate of speed and cannot apprehend the motion.

Not by any means a Parisian poem or a Parisian context, but not any the less accurate for it. The continual pilgrimage of American writers to Paris, begun the century before by Henry James and sustained by so many others between the wars, did not stop. It was, for the pilgrims in this book—most of them young, as yet untested—a foray into a familiar unknown, because Paris had a legendary reality (regardless of whether they pursued the French or Lost Generation traditions). And yet the Paris that existed for this group was soon made into their own Paris, the literary past merging with the lived present of cramped, unheated hotel rooms, and of Parisian traffic, trees, and the sun going down over the Seine.

This accounts perhaps for the unique achievements of this generation. While fully aware of the past and of the giants who had written in Paris, they set about creating their own books, in tune with the currents of their own time. Although it is impossible to argue that these works would not or could not have been written on American soil, the fact that Paris was artistically electric cannot be discounted either.

Few cities have had such a profound influence on the arts for so long. A major reason, quickly discovered by nearly all transplanted writers who took up residence in the capital, was that there they felt enfranchised, and respected as artists. In a sense, Paris allowed its resident American writers to have a true artistic home. Or as Gertrude Stein put it, "After all everybody, that is everybody who writes is living inside themselves in order to tell what is inside themselves. That is why writers have to have two countries, the one where they belong and the one where they live really. The second one is romantic, it is separate from themselves, it is not real but it is really there."

In short, Paris empowered, granted permission to be an artist in a way the United States never had. In the accounts of almost all of the writers profiled in this book, Paris was equated with artistic freedom, with the ability to experiment, to succeed, even to fail without feeling oneself to be a social deviant. This does not explain every reason why this diverse group thrived in Paris, but it is a continuing theme reiterated by so many who sought the city.

In some cases, it was also an underlying reason for initially leaving the United States. In America, they felt, one was more often measured by how financially successful one was, not by what one actually did. Status accrued to those who made money, and the writer, generally not so able to generate an enviable income, was rarely accorded a position of importance in the eyes of the general public. It was hard to imagine an American landlord giving a writer a rent reduction because he had seen a piece of his in a literary magazine. But this happened in Paris, as William Styron wistfully recalled.

No amount of support or atmosphere, of course, can give a writer talent. For all those who succeeded in creating significant work, hundreds of others did not. But talent needs nurturing; and in France, as Stein wrote, "If you are a writer you have privileges, if you are a painter you have privileges, and it is pleasant having those privileges."

Notes

Unless noted otherwise, translations into English are by the author.

INTRODUCTION: "WHAT IT DOESN'T TAKE AWAY"

4 "WHAT IT DOESN'T TAKE AWAY": Gertrude Stein, *Paris France* (London: Peter Owen, 1971), p. 19.

4 "SUSPICION HE ENCOUNTERS HERE": James Baldwin, "The Discovery of What It Means to Be an American in Europe," in *The Price of the Ticket: Collected Non-Fiction 1948–1985* (New York: St. Martin's/Marek, 1985), p. 174.

4 "OUTSIDE OF EVERYTHING": James Jones quoted in John Bainbridge, *Another Way of Living: A Gallery of Americans Who Choose to Live in Europe* (New York: Holt, Rinehart & Winston, 1968), p. 220.

4 "MUCH LESS WELL ACCEPTED": William Styron quoted in *Conversations with William Styron*, ed. James L. W. West III (Jackson: University Press of Mississippi, 1985), p. 26.

4 "SEEMS A LITTLE UNREAL": Richard Wright quoted in Michel Fabre, *The World of Richard Wright* (Jackson: University Press of Mississippi, 1985), p. 147.

5 "WISH TO STICK AROUND": William Styron, "*The Paris Review*," in *This Quiet Dust and Other Writings* (New York: Random House, 1982), p. 297.

6 "WHAT YOU CAN DO WITH LANGUAGE": John Ashbery, conversation with author, May 1, 1991.

8 "LIVING AWAY FROM AMERICA": George Whitman, conversation with author, July 15, 1990.

CHAPTER ONE: THE LIBERATION OF SYLVIA BEACH, AND OTHER TALES OF AUGUST 1944

11 "LOVE BEST IN ALL THE WORLD": Ernest Hemingway, *By-Line Ernest Hemingway*, ed. William White (New York: Charles Scribner's Sons, 1967), p. 383.

12 "CHICKENSHIT AS TO FIGHTING": Ernest Hemingway, *Selected Letters: 1917–1961*, ed. Carlos Baker (New York: Charles Scribner's Sons, 1969), p. 564.

12 GERMAN-HELD COMPLEX: David Bruce quoted in Carlos Baker, *Ernest Hemingway: A Life Story* (New York: Charles Scribner's Sons, 1969), pp. 415–16.

13 MUST SURELY BE NEAR AN END: "Paris Is Free Again," *Life*, Sept. 11, 1944, p. 25.

13 "NICKED ONE OF ITS SIDES": David Bruce quoted in Baker, *Ernest Hemingway*, p. 416.

14 THE HOTEL'S NEW GUESTS: Baker, *Ernest Hemingway*, p. 417; Jeffrey Meyers, *Hemingway: A Biography* (New York: Harper & Row, 1985), p. 389.

14 "BARRICADES IN OUR PATH": Irwin Shaw, *Paris! Paris!* (New York: Harcourt Brace Jovanovich, 1977), p. 13.

15 AT 9:40 THAT MORNING: Richard Whelan, *Robert Capa: A Biography* (New York: Harper & Row, 1985), p. 223; Shaw, *Paris! Paris!*, pp. 22–25; Michael Shnayerson, *Irwin Shaw: A Biography* (New York: G. P. Putnam's Sons, 1989), pp. 142–43.

15 "GRATITUDE WAS BEGINNING IN EUROPE": Shaw, *Paris! Paris!*, p. 26.

15 WAS NOT REGISTERED EITHER: Mary Welsh Hemingway, *How It Was* (New York: Alfred A. Knopf, 1976), pp. 108–9.

15 STOOD IN THE HALL OUTSIDE ROOM 31: Ibid., p. 109.

16 THE RITZ THAT AFTERNOON: Ibid., pp. 109–10.

16 "ANSWER TO DE BEERS DIAMONDS": Shnayerson, *Irwin Shaw*, pp. 133–34; Mary Welsh Hemingway, *How It Was*, p. 94.

16 DENUNCIATIONS INTO THE CONVERSATION: Mary Welsh Hemingway, *How It Was*, p. 261.

17 BOOK FROM HER IN 1921: Sylvia Beach, *Shakespeare and Company* (New York: Harcourt, Brace, 1959), p. 77.

17 ENDURE BEFORE BEING RELEASED: Ibid., p. 216.

18 "IN THE WINDOWS CHEERED": Ibid., pp. 219–20.

18 "IN THE RUE DE L'ODÉON": Ibid., pp. 219–20; Baker, *Ernest Hemingway*, p. 418.

18 "IT IS ALL A DREAM": Ernest Hemingway, *Selected Letters*, pp. 564–65.

18 "BEEN BY THE CHAMPAGNE": Mary Welsh Hemingway, *How It Was*, p. 110.

18 "*VIVENT LES AMÉRICAINS*": Ibid., pp. 111–12.

19 "WORK FOR ANY ORGANIZATION": Lawrence Lee and Barry Gifford, *Saroyan: A Biography* (New York: Harper & Row, 1984), pp. 114–15; Shnayerson, *Irwin Shaw*, pp. 96–97, 130–31; Mary Welsh Hemingway, *How It Was*, pp. 90–91.

19 IN THE MID-THIRTIES: William Saroyan, *Letters from 74 Rue Taitbout* (New York and Cleveland: World, 1969), p. 37.

19 AGAINST SAROYAN IN PRINT: William Saroyan, *The Daring Young Man on the Flying Trapeze* (New York: Random House, 1934), p. 34; Ernest Hemingway, "Notes on Life and Letters," *Esquire*, 3, (Jan. 1935), pp. 48–56.

19 SAROYAN, FUMING, WALKED AWAY: Shnayerson, *Irwin Shaw*, p. 144; Baker, *Ernest Hemingway*, p. 442.

20 HEMINGWAY'S BARBAROUSNESS: Baker, *Ernest Hemingway*, p. 442.

20 ONLY REWARDING MINUTES OF THE ENTIRE WAR: Ian Hamilton, *In Search of J. D. Salinger* (New York: Random House, 1988), p. 86; Baker, *Ernest Hemingway*, p. 646.

21 CLAIMED TO HAVE BESTED MALRAUX: Leicester Hemingway, *My Brother, Ernest Hemingway* (Cleveland and New York: World, 1962), p. 262; Ernest Hemingway, *Selected Letters*, p. 803.

21 "HE WILL GO BY HIMSELF": Ernest Hemingway, *Selected Letters*, pp. 803–4.

22 "I HAVE READ IN TEN YEARS": Ibid., p. 420.

22 "OLD STUFF UNFAKED IN IT": Ibid., p. 467.

22 "THEY DID NOT PUNISH ME FOR IT": Pablo Picasso quoted in Mary Welsh Hemingway, *How It Was*, p. 117.

22 "THE THING MAY BE SPURIOUS": Ernest Hemingway quoted ibid.

23 "NEED TO CIRCULATE SOUVENIRS": Pablo Picasso quoted in James Lord, *Où Étaient les Tableaux . . . : Mémoire sur Gertrude Stein et Alice Toklas*, trans. Pierre Leyris (Paris: Mazarine, 1982), p. 34.

23 HOUSE ON THE RUE CHRISTINE: Mary Welsh Hemingway, *How It Was*, p. 117; James Mellow, *Charmed Circle: Gertrude Stein and Company* (New York: Praeger, 1974), pp. 454–55.

23 "THE TRUTH FROM BOTH OF US": Ernest Hemingway, *Selected Letters*, p. 650.

24 ENGAGED IN MOP-UP OPERATIONS: Baker, *Ernest Hemingway*, p. 419.

24 AT LEAST TO HIS WAY OF THINKING: Ibid., p. 420.

24 "NEVER FELT HAPPIER": Ernest Hemingway, *Selected Letters*, p. 570.

24 TERSE, TAUT NARRATIVE: Ernest Hemingway, *The Complete Short Stories of Ernest Hemingway* (New York: Charles Scribner's Sons, 1987), pp. 579–89.

24 WAS INSTANTLY ACQUITTED: Denis Brian, *The True Gen* (New York: Grove, 1988), pp. 323–31.

25 NOTORIOUSLY OFF-KEY RENDITIONS: Mary Welsh Hemingway, *How It Was*, pp. 127–28.

26 "GET THIS FINISHED WITH ME": Martha Gellhorn quoted in Bernice Kert, *The Hemingway Women* (New York: W. W. Norton, 1983), p. 411.

26 SHE REALLY HAD LITTLE OPTION: Meyers, *Hemingway*, p. 412.

26 "STAY THE DISTANCE WITH YOU": Mary Welsh Hemingway, *How It Was*, p. 129.

26 "NEEDING TO CHECK [HER] NAVIGATION": Ibid., p. 129.

27 THREW HIM OUT OF THE ROOM: Ibid., pp. 130–31.

27 SHE GIVE HIM A BATH: Ibid., pp. 132–33.

27 DOWN WITH PNEUMONIA: Baker, *Ernest Hemingway*, pp. 432–38.

28 NEXT TO THE BED: Simone de Beauvoir, *Force of Circumstances*, vol. 1: *After the War*, trans. Richard Howard (G. P. Putnam's Sons, 1965; repr. Harper & Row, 1977), p. 16.

28 AS HE IN FACT STATED FREQUENTLY: Malcolm Cowley, *The Faulkner–Cowley File: Letters and Memories 1944–1962* (New York: Viking, 1966), p. 29; Ernest Hemingway, *Selected Letters*, p. 769.

28 "HEALTHY AS HELL, SEE?": Leicester Hemingway, *My Brother, Ernest Hemingway*, pp. 261–62; Beauvoir, *Force of Circumstance*, vol. 1, p. 16.

28 HE WAS NOT ABLE: Brian, *The True Gen*, p. 168.

28 FORGIVING AS THE HOTEL STAFF: Mary Welsh Hemingway, *How It Was*, p. 147.

29 "THE GROUND IN IT": Ernest Hemingway, *Selected Letters*, p. 574.

29 "VERY FINE, GOOD, GROWNUP NOVEL": Ibid., p. 568.

CHAPTER TWO: "LIVING LARGELY ON VEGETABLES AND MOSTLY WITHOUT MEAT"

31 DECEMBER 15, 1944: Janet Flanner, *Paris Journal: 1944–1965* (New York: Atheneum, 1965), p. 3.

31 "EVERYTHING'S BEGINNING": Beauvoir, *Force of Circumstance*, vol. 1, p. 3.

31 FILL AN ENTIRE NEWS RACK: Herbert Lottman, *The Left Bank* (Boston: Houghton Mifflin, 1982), p. 219.

32 CROWDED CAFÉ TABLES: [Mary Welsh Hemingway], "Paris: The City of Light Comes out of the Darkness Again," *Life*, Oct. 2, 1944, p. 93.

32 "*ILS SONT FOUTUS*": Beauvoir, *Force of Circumstance*, vol. 1, p. 3.

32 KICKING OFF THE NEW SEASON: Mary Welsh Hemingway, *How It Was*, p. 118.

32 "EXPLAIN, EXPLAIN": [Mary Welsh Hemingway], "Paris: The City of Light Comes out of the Darkness Again," p. 95. See also Beauvoir, *Force of Circumstance*, vol. 1, p. 11.

32 "WAS OVER LONG BEFORE THE WAR ITSELF": James Lord, conversation with author, June 18, 1990.

33 PRECARIOUS, IF NOT IMPOSSIBLE: Flanner, *Paris Journal*, p. 6; "Paris Is Free Again," *Life*, Sept. 11, 1944, p. 39.

33 OTHER PROVISIONS THE NEXT: Flanner, *Paris Journal*, p. 6.

33 FREQUENT POWER OUTAGES: Charles Wertenbaker, "The Streets and the People," *Life*, Sept. 11, 1944, p. 39.

34 "THE TRAITORS PERISH": Paul Éluard, "Les Vendeurs d'Indulgence," in *Oeuvres Complètes*, ed. Lucien Scheler (Paris: Gallimard, 1968), vol. 1, pp. 1273–74.

34 "THEY SHOWED ME": Janet Flanner quoted in Brenda Wineapple, *Genêt: A Biography of Janet Flanner* (New York: Ticknor & Fields, 1989), p. 187.

34 "IMMOBILE FOR SO LONG": Vercors, "A Plea for France," *Life*, Nov. 6, 1944, p. 55.

35 "LEG SHOW IN THE WORLD": "Paris: The City of Light Comes out of the Darkness Again," p. 90.

35 "GRABBED OUT OF THE GUTTER": Wertenbaker, "The Streets and the People," p. 38.

36 "RATION POINTS AS WELL": Virgil Thomson, *Virgil Thomson* (New York: Alfred A. Knopf, 1966), p. 364.

36 "IT WAS DIFFERENT": Lord, conversation with author, June 18, 1990.

36 "FREEDOM INCARNATE": Beauvoir, *Force of Circumstance*, vol. 1, p. 4.

36 "SIMPLY BEING AMERICANS": Lord, conversation with author, June 18, 1990.

37 "TO CHECK FOR LICE": John Phillips quoted in "The *Paris Review* Sketchbook," *The Paris Review*, 79 (1981), p. 343.

37 "COFFEE AND TINS OF SPAM": Beauvoir, *Force of Circumstance*, vol. 1, p. 16.

37 "MOSTLY WITHOUT HEAT": Flanner, *Paris Journal*, p. 4.

38 "AVAILABLE FOR MERELY CIGARETTES": Thomson, *Virgil Thomson*, pp. 366–67.

38 "YOU WILL HAVE TO FIGHT AGAIN": Gertrude Stein, "Off We All Went to See Germany," *Life*, Aug. 6, 1945, p. 54.

38 THE REALITY THAT FOLLOWED: Flanner, *Paris Journal*, p. 6.

38 APPROVAL FROM THE PATRONS: Ibid., p. 22.

39 "WE USUALLY DO IN PEACE": Ibid., p. 21.

39 "COVERED IN CRIMES AND SHAME": Vercors, "A Plea for France," p. 62.

39 "NAZIS TRIED TO DO": Ibid., p. 55.

41 THE NON-COMMUNIST LEFT: See Lottman, *The Left Bank*, pp. 219–47.

41 THE AWARD "DERISORY": Flanner, *Paris Journal*, p. 17.

42 "OF THE ENTIRE COUNTRY": Quoted ibid., p. 19.

43 "THE PAST SIX MONTHS": Ibid., p. 20.

44 "STENCH OF ILLNESS AND DIRT": Ibid., pp. 25–26.

44 "LIKE CIGARETTE PAPER": Marguerite Duras, *The War: A Memoir*, trans. Barbara Bray (New York: Pantheon, 1986), pp. 57–58.

CHAPTER THREE: "COURAGE TO BE COURAGEOUS": THE LAST WORKS AND DAYS OF GERTRUDE STEIN

46 "AMERICA TODAY SO HAPPY": Gertrude Stein quoted in Eric

Sevareid, *Not So Wild a Dream* (New York: Alfred A. Knopf, 1969), p. 461.

47 "THAT WAS ALL RIGHT": Gertrude Stein, *Selected Writings of Gertrude Stein*, ed. Carl Van Vechten (New York: Random House, 1962), pp. 622–23.

47 " 'HERE WE STAY' ": Ibid., p. 624.

48 "THE STATE OF MIND": Gertrude Stein, *Mrs. Reynolds and Earlier Novelettes* (New Haven: Yale University Press, 1952), p. 267.

48 "COURAGE TO BE COURAGEOUS": Ibid., p. 1.

48 "LIVING AN ORDINARY LIFE": Ibid., p. 267.

49 "DEFEAT OF THE GERMANS": Gertrude Stein, *Wars I Have Seen* (New York: Random House, 1945), p. 87.

50 "ALL IS CONSIDERABLE": Ibid.

50 "CHARGES OF COLLABORATION": W. G. Rogers, *When This You See Remember Me: Gertrude Stein in Person* (New York: Rinehart, 1948), p. 215.

50 "IN HAVING SO MANY": Stein, *Wars I Have Seen*, p. 82.

50 CIRCUMSTANCES THAN BY IDEOLOGY: See Robert O. Paxton, *Vichy France: Old Guard and New Order, 1940–44* (New York: Alfred A. Knopf, 1972).

50 "YES IS FOR A VERY YOUNG MAN": Gertrude Stein to Francis Rose, undated [1946], Gertrude Stein Collection, Beinecke Rare Book and Manuscript Library, Yale University Library.

51 "RISE FROM THE ASHES": Gertrude Stein, *Last Operas and Plays*, ed. Carl Van Vechten (New York: Rinehart, 1949), p. 15.

51 "NEIGHBORS ARE NEIGHBORS": Ibid., p. xv.

52 "TAKE SIDES IN PRISON": Ibid., p. 4.

52 "QUITE COMPLETELY FUNNY": Stein, *Wars I Have Seen*, p. 50.

52 "WAS ITS UNREALITY": Ibid., p. 51.

52 CLAIMED THIS TO BE THE CASE: Bernard Faÿ to François Monahan, July 22, 1955, Stein Collection, Yale.

53 "SHOULD I TELL THEM?": Sevareid, *Not So Wild a Dream*, p. 459.

53 "ANYBODY TO KNOW IT": Stein, *Wars I Have Seen*, p. 55.

53 "KEEP ALIVE ANTI-SEMITISM": Gertrude Stein to Robert Graves, Feb. 4, 1946, Stein Collection, Yale.

55 "HERSELF AS A CHRISTIAN": Virgil Thomson, "A Portrait of Gertrude Stein," in *A Virgil Thomson Reader* (New York: E. P. Dutton, 1984), pp. 77–78.

55 "A WORD WITH AMERICA": Stein, *Wars I Have Seen*, p. 245.

56 "MOST FAMOUS LITERARY EXPATRIATE": "The Liberation of Gertrude Stein," *Life*, Oct. 2, 1944, p. 83.

57 CONFISCATE PERSONAL POSSESSIONS: Katherine Dudley to Gertrude Stein, November 14, 1944, in *The Flowers of Friendship: Letters Written to Gertrude Stein*, ed. Donald Gallup (New York: Alfred A. Knopf, 1953), p. 370.

57 OMINOUSLY AGAINST A WALL: Alice B. Toklas, *What Is Remembered* (New York: Holt, Rinehart & Winston, 1963; repr. San Francisco: North Point, 1985), p. 168.

57 "THE DRAWINGS, WERE SAFE": Ibid.

57 WOULDN'T FIT IN THEIR APARTMENT: Ibid.

57 LOVED ONE ANOTHER: Ernest Hemingway, *Selected Letters*, p. 650.

57 "JUST THAT WAY": Gertrude Stein to Bobsy Goodspeed, May 8, 1945, Stein Collection, Yale.

58 "PAINTER DID NOT EXIST": Gertrude Stein (in French), *Riba-Rovira* (Paris: Galerie Roquépine, 1945), n.p.

58 "INTERESTING YOUNG PAINTER": Gertrude Stein to Francis Rose, Oct. 1, 1945, Stein Collection, Yale.

58 "NO DOUBT ABOUT THAT": Gertrude Stein to Francis Rose, undated [1946], Stein Collection, Yale.

59 "THE LIFE OF THE CITY": Gertrude Stein to Bobsy Goodspeed, July 11, 1945, Stein Collection, Yale.

59 "GET AND BE THANKFUL": Ibid.

59 "TOOTHPASTE WE NEED THEM": Gertrude Stein to Bobsy Goodspeed, May 8, 1945, Stein Collection, Yale.

59 "TO SPARE ON ROUTINE": Mellow, *Charmed Circle*, pp. 458–59.

59 "SEE IT ALL": Gertrude Stein to Rosellen Stein, Jan. 6, 1945, Stein Collection, Yale.

60 "OBSERVED THEIR LANGUAGE": Thomson, *Virgil Thomson*, p. 365.

60 CONCERNS OF THE TIME: Donald Sutherland, *Gertrude Stein: A Biography of Her Work* (New Haven: Yale University Press, 1951), p. 168.

60 "AS GI AS POSSIBLE": Ibid., pp. 166–67.

61 "FEEL ALL ALIKE": Gertrude Stein, *Brewsie and Willie* (New York: Random House, 1946), p. 55.

61 "AS EASY AS YOU CAN": Ibid., pp. 113–14.

62 "WHERE IS AMERICA": Ibid., p. 63.

62 "FACE OF THE EARTH": Ibid., p. 114.

62 "WHO NEED PIN-UPS": Ibid., p. 89.

62 "SENATORIAL ORATORS QUOTED": Thomson, *Virgil Thomson*, p. 365.

63 "NOW BE MOVING RAPIDLY": Ibid., p. 366.

63 REQUIRED READING LIST: Ibid.

63 "THERE ARE ONLY LAWS": Stein, *Last Operas and Plays*, p. 77.

64 "THEY ARE GULLIBLE": Ibid., p. 60.

64 "MEN ARE AFRAID": Ibid., p. 80.

64 "MARRIED TO ANY ONE": Ibid., p. 75.

65 THOMSON THINKS NOT: Thomson, *Virgil Thomson*, p. 366.

65 "IN MY LONG LIFE": Stein, *Last Operas and Plays*, pp. 87–88.

65 "TO WHAT WAS DONE": Ibid.

65 CONSULT A SPECIALIST: Toklas, *What Is Remembered*, p. 171.

66 "AND NOT KEEP IT": Ibid., p. 173.

66 "I NEVER SAW HER AGAIN": Ibid.

66 "DENTISTRY WAS PRACTICAL": Stein, *Paris France*, pp. 18–19.

CHAPTER FOUR: THE CHOSEN EXILE OF RICHARD WRIGHT

67 "RELIEVED": Richard Wright, "I Choose Exile," unpublished essay, Richard Wright Collection, Yale, p. 7.

67 "GENIUSES OF THIS ERA": Gertrude Stein to Richard Wright, May 1945, Stein Collection, Yale.

68 JUST A FEW DAYS: Wright, "I Choose Exile," pp. 6–7.

68 DECISION TO GO TO FRANCE: Ibid., p. 4.

68 "HONOR BOUND TO SEE FRANCE": Richard Wright to Gertrude Stein, May 27, 1945, Stein Collection, Yale.

69 "I WILL, BY GOD": Richard Wright, unpublished journal entry, Jan. 28, 1945, quoted in Fabre, *The World of Richard Wright*, p. 145–46.

69 "HYSTERICAL DEMOCRACY": Wright, "I Choose Exile," quoted in Fabre, *The World of Richard Wright*, p. 147.

69 AT STEIN'S FOR LUNCH: Constance Webb, *Richard Wright* (New York: G. P. Putnam's Sons, 1968), pp. 245–46.

69 " 'HURL AT OUR WINDOWS' ": Wright, "I Choose Exile," quoted in Fabre, *The World of Richard Wright*, p. 179.

70 "WITH GENTLE MANNERS": Richard Wright to Edward Aswell, May 15, 1946, quoted in Fabre, *The World of Richard Wright*, p. 147.

70 "PROBLEM MORE VIVID": Richard Wright to Mr. Scanton, [1946], quoted in Fabre, *The World of Richard Wright*, p. 151.

70 "KNOW ITS FREEDOM": Richard Wright, "À Paris les G.I. Noirs Ont Appris à Connaître et à Aimer la Liberté," *Samedi-Soir*, May 25, 1946, p. 2; original (English) version, Wright Collection, Yale, p. 7.

70 "BUT ONE'S SELF": Ibid. (English version), p. 8.

71 "NIGHT BEFORE CHRISTMAS": Webb, *Richard Wright*, p. 248.

71 "HIT YOU HARD": Fabre, *The World of Richard Wright*, p. 253.

72 "KNOTHOLE IN THE FENCE": Richard Wright, *Native Son* (New York: Harper & Brothers, 1940; repr. New York: Harper & Row, 1969), p. 23.

72 "LIKE OTHERS ACTED": Ibid., pp. 101–2.

72 "MURDER AND FLIGHT": Ibid., pp. 224–25.

73 "WITH NO EXCUSES": Jean-Paul Sartre, "Existentialism Is a Humanism," in *Existentialism*, trans. Bernard Frechtman (New York: Philosophical Library, 1947), p. 26.

73 "MOMENT TO INVENT MAN": Ibid., pp. 26–27.

73 "HE KILLS!": Wright, *Native Son*, pp. 366–67.

73 " 'TO KILL FOR 'EM' ": Ibid., pp. 391–92.

73 "FOR WHIPPED FOLKS": Ibid., p. 330.

73 "THEY PLAY IT": Ibid., p. 331.

74 EIGHT MONTHS IN EUROPE: Raphaël Tardon, "Le Problème Blanc aux U.S.A.," *Action*, Oct. 25, 1946, p. 2.

74 "IDENTITY CARDS, RATIONS, ETC.": Richard Wright to Paul Reynolds, quoted in Michel Fabre, *The Unfinished Quest of Richard Wright*, trans. Isabel Barzun (New York: William Morrow, 1973), p. 315.

74 "EVEN IN THEIR SUFFERING": Wright quoted in Fabre, *The World of Richard Wright*, p. 150.

74 "BEGGARS AND CHEATS": Ibid.

75 FOOD OR FUEL: Michel Fabre, conversation with author, June 21, 1990.

75 "INTO THE MODERN WORLD": "Niam N'goura or *Présence Africaine*'s Raison d'Être," *Présence Africaine*, 1 (Nov.–Dec. 1947), p. 185.

76   THE REVIEW AFLOAT: Fabre, conversation with author, June 21, 1990.

77   "FOR BEING FRENCH": Richard Wright, *Black Power: A Record of Reactions in a Land of Pathos* (New York: Harper & Brothers, 1954), p. 236.

78   HAPPY AND CONVENIENT UNION: Fabre, conversation with author, June 21, 1990.

78   "SEES WHAT IS TRUE": Wright quoted in Webb, *Richard Wright*, p. 279.

78   "HE AGREED": Wright quoted in Fabre, *The World of Richard Wright*, p. 162.

78   "ARE NOT PRIMARILY": Wright quoted in Fabre, *The Unfinished Quest of Richard Wright*, p. 321.

78   AS SOME HAVE ARGUED: Arna Bontemps, "Three Portraits of the Negro," *Saturday Review*, March 28, 1953, p. 15.

79   "TO SEE OURSELVES": Richard Wright, "Introduction to *The Respectful Prostitute*," *Twice a Year*, 1948, p. 15.

79   "SATISFACTION OF THEIR DEMANDS": Jean-Paul Sartre quoted in Annie Cohen-Solal, *Sartre: A Life*, ed. Norman MacAfee, trans. Anna Cancogni (New York: Pantheon, 1987), p. 302.

80   FRINGE POLITICAL VIEWS: Fabre, conversation with author, June 21, 1990.

80   "PRAISED THE ATOMIC BOMB": Jean-Paul Sartre, *On A Raison de Se Révolter* (Paris: Gallimard, 1974), p. 29.

82   "BY INTERNATIONAL POLICY": Fabre, *The Unfinished Quest of Richard Wright*, p. 337.

82   LEFT FOR ARGENTINA: Ibid., p. 338.

82   "PRETEND IT IS": Richard Wright to Paul Reynolds, August 6, 1951, quoted ibid., p. 349.

84   "TRADITIONS AND CUSTOMS?": Richard Wright, "American Negroes in France," *Crisis*, June–July 1951, pp. 381–82.

84   "ENGLISH MELODRAMAS": James Baldwin, "Alas, Poor Richard," in *The Price of the Ticket*, p. 283.

85   "CANNOT BE TRANSCENDED": James Baldwin, "Everybody's Protest Novel," in *The Price of the Ticket*, p. 33.

85   "IN ORDER TO BE DESTROYED": Baldwin, "Alas, Poor Richard," p. 277.

86   "ITS OWN IMPLICATIONS": James Baldwin, "Many Thousands Gone," in *The Price of the Ticket*, p. 76.

86 "IN SOCIAL TERMS": Ibid.

87 "MINORITY GROUPS TO IT": William Gardner Smith, "Black Boy in France," *Ebony* 8 (July 1953), p. 40.

88 "TWO LITTLE GODS": Richard Wright, *The Outsider* (New York: Harper & Brothers, 1953; repr. New York: Harper & Row Perennial Library, 1965), p. 230.

88 "CHARACTER AND DESTINY": Richard Wright to Paul Reynolds, May 1, 1952, quoted in Fabre, *The Unfinished Quest of Richard Wright*, p. 366.

88 "ROLL IN THE HAY": Bontemps, "Three Portraits of the Negro," p. 15.

89 "POPULAR CONCLUSIONS": Richard Wright to Paul Reynolds, June 28, 1952, quoted in Fabre, *The Unfinished Quest of Richard Wright*, p. 367.

90 AMOUNTS TO 228 PAGES: Addison Gayle, Jr., *Richard Wright: Ordeal of a Native Son* (Garden City, NY: Doubleday, 1980), p. xi.

90 "I'LL NEVER TESTIFY": Chester Himes, *The Quality of Hurt: The Autobiography of Chester Himes*, vol. 1 (Garden City, NY: Doubleday, 1972), pp. 198–99.

90 " 'BIG WONDERFUL COUNTRY' ": Ralph Ellison quoted in "Native Doesn't Live Here Anymore," *Time*, March 31, 1953, p. 92.

91 "LAID IN THIS COUNTRY": Paul Reynolds to Richard Wright, April 6, 1953, quoted in Fabre, *The Unfinished Quest of Richard Wright*, p. 388.

91 "OF AMERICAN LIFE": Wright, "I Choose Exile," quoted in Fabre, *The World of Richard Wright*, p. 151.

92 "GREAT VALUE TO YOU": Paul Reynolds to Richard Wright, April 6, 1953, quoted in Fabre, *The Unfinished Quest of Richard Wright*, p. 388.

92 "COLOR DID NOT HELP ME": Wright, *Black Power*, p. 137.

94 "WHERE YOU ARE GOING": Paul Reynolds to Richard Wright, Jan. 24, 1956, quoted in Fabre, *The Unfinished Quest of Richard Wright*, p. 432.

94 EVEN MORE CAUTIOUS: Fabre, conversation with author, June 21, 1990.

95 "RAISED THE ROOF": Baldwin, "Alas, Poor Richard." p. 285.

95 JEALOUSY AND RIVALRY: Herbert Gentry, conversation with author, Dec. 4, 1990.

96   *A CASE OF RAPE*: Chester Himes, *My Life of Absurdity: The Autobiography of Chester Himes*, vol. 2 (Garden City, NY: Doubleday, 1976), p. 216.

96   "HE HAD DROPPED IT": Ibid.

96   "GUTTER LIKE YOU": Ibid.

97   "GREW UP IN MISSISSIPPI": "Tract in Black and White," *Time*, Oct. 27, 1958, pp. 95–96.

98   WRIGHT WAS NOT WELL: William Targ, conversation with author, Jan. 12, 1990.

98   PRODUCED A HEART ATTACK: Ibid.

98   "ENTIRE UNITED STATES!": Wright, "I Choose Exile," quoted in Fabre, *The World of Richard Wright*, p. 146.

CHAPTER FIVE: JAMES BALDWIN: EQUAL IN PARIS

99   "INTENDED TO COME BACK": James Baldwin quoted in Fern Marja Eckman, *The Furious Passage of James Baldwin* (Philadelphia: M. Evans/Lippincott, 1966), p. 113.

99   "THE FRENCH LANGUAGE": James Baldwin, "Equal in Paris," in *The Price of the Ticket*, p. 114.

100   "YOUNGER AND HAPPIER": Baldwin, "Alas, Poor Richard," p. 277.

100   "DISAGREE WITH HIM": Ibid., p. 279.

101   "ALAS! MY FATHER": Ibid., p. 274.

101   "REJOICE IN IT": Ibid., p. 279.

101   "FATHER AND SPIRITUAL SON": Ibid.

101   SPIRITUAL PATRICIDE: Sigmund Freud, *Totem and Taboo*, in *The Basic Writings of Sigmund Freud*, ed. and trans. A. A. Brill (New York: Random House, 1938), pp. 915–16.

102   "THE REIGNING DEITY": Himes, *The Quality of Hurt*, p. 201.

102   "*BLACK MAN* STARVING": Baldwin quoted in Eckman, *The Furious Passage of James Baldwin*, p. 118.

103   "CADGED HIS DRINKS": Otto Friedrich quoted in William J. Weatherby, *James Baldwin: Artist on Fire: A Portrait* (New York: Donald I. Fine, 1989), p. 80.

103   "SEA OF ACQUAINTANCES": Baldwin, "Equal in Paris," p. 115.

103   "GREAT ADVENTURE OR ME": Ibid.

103   "HAVE ME SHIPPED HOME": Baldwin quoted in Weatherby, *James Baldwin*, p. 71.

104 "PATRON" NOW AND THEN: Ned Rorem, conversation with author, Sept. 26, 1989; Weatherby, *James Baldwin*, pp. 71, 80.

104 "TWO HAPPENED SIMULTANEOUSLY": Friedrich quoted in Weatherby, *James Baldwin*, pp. 80–81.

104 "TORE UP PAPER": James Baldwin quoted in "The Art of Fiction LXXVII: James Baldwin," *The Paris Review*, 91 (1984), p. 50.

104 IT WAS AN EXISTENCE: Rorem, conversation with author, Sept. 26, 1989; Baldwin, "Equal in Paris," p. 115; Weatherby, *James Baldwin*, p. 80.

105 "SINISTER IN APPEARANCE": Gidske Anderson quoted in Michel Fabre, *La Rive Noire: De Harlem à la Seine* (Paris: Lieu Commun, 1985), p. 202.

105 RETURNED TO PARIS: Fabre, *La Rive Noire*, pp. 202–3; James Campbell, *Talking at the Gates: A Life of James Baldwin* (New York: Viking, 1991), p. 56.

106 "SEX, THEY WANTED": James Baldwin, "Here Be Dragons," in *The Price of the Ticket*, p. 685.

106 HIS OWN IDENTITY: Fabre, *La Rive Noire*, pp. 203–4.

106 AGAINST THEM WERE DISMISSED: Baldwin, "Equal in Paris," pp. 113–26.

106 "I WAS, BUT *WHO*": Ibid., p. 118.

106 "ANY TEXAS GI": James Baldwin, "The Discovery of What It Means to Be an American in Europe," in *The Price of the Ticket*, p. 172.

107 "ONE FROM ANOTHER": James Baldwin, "Encounter on the Seine: Black Meets Brown," in *The Price of the Ticket*, p. 36.

107 "HIS OWN VALUE": Baldwin, "The Discovery of What It Means to Be an American in Europe," p. 174.

108 "THE FIRST TIME": Ibid.

108 VERSION OF *GIOVANNI'S ROOM*: Weatherby, *James Baldwin*, p. 80.

108 ANY SORT OF RECONCILIATION: Ibid.

109 NOVEL, *CRYING HOLY*: Ibid., p. 79.

109 "FIND SOMEONE ELSE": James Baldwin quoted in David Leeming, "An Interview with James Baldwin on Henry James," *Henry James Review*, Fall 1986, p. 48.

109 "MEANT TO ME THEN": Ibid.

110 "WOULD HAVE GONE UNDER": Baldwin quoted in "The Art of Fiction LXXVII: James Baldwin," p. 50.

110 " 'I MAY DO IT' ": Ibid., p. 55.

110 "ALLOWED ME TO WRITE": Baldwin quoted in Leeming, "An Interview with James Baldwin on Henry James," p. 48.

111 "ON JOHN'S BIRTHDAY": Baldwin quoted in "The Art of Fiction LXXVII: James Baldwin," p. 58.

112 "A LIVING WONDER": James Baldwin, "Silence in the Village," in *The Price of the Ticket*, p. 81.

112 WILLIAM MORRIS AGENCY: Eckman, *The Furious Passage of James Baldwin*, p. 125.

113 IDENTITY IS BALDWIN'S OWN: For autobiographical details see James Baldwin, "The Fire Next Time" and "No Name in the Street," in *The Price of the Ticket*.

113 "ALL OBSERVATION, ALL VISION": Henry James, "The Art of Fiction," in *The Art of Criticism: Henry James on the Theory and Practice of Fiction*, ed. William Veeder and Susan Griffin (Chicago: University of Chicago Press, 1986), p. 177.

114 "INTENTIONS OF MY NOVEL": Baldwin quoted in Weatherby, *James Baldwin*, p. 97.

115 PAID ON ACCEPTANCE: Weatherby, *James Baldwin*, ibid.

115 "A KIND OF LIMBO": Baldwin quoted in Eckman, *The Furious Passage of James Baldwin*, p. 124.

115 " 'USUALLY DIRTY—MIND' ": James Baldwin, "This Morning, This Evening, So Soon," in *Going to Meet the Man* (New York: Dial, 1965), p. 152.

116 TWO OTHER ARTISTS: Eckman, *The Furious Passage of James Baldwin*, p. 128.

116 FIND A BENEFACTOR: Ibid.

117 "WITH AMERICAN PASSPORTS": Baldwin, "Alas, Poor Richard," p. 271.

117 ARAB PEANUT VENDOR: Baldwin, "No Name in the Street," pp. 461–62.

117 "DELIVERED TOO LATE": Ibid., p. 463.

117 "*VOUS POUVEZ PARTIR, MONSIEUR*": Fabre, *La Rive Noire*, p. 208.

118 ASSAULT HIM SEXUALLY: Baldwin quoted in "The Art of Fiction LXXVII: James Baldwin," p. 59.

118 DID EXACTLY THAT: Barry Miles, *Ginsberg: A Biography* (New York: Simon & Schuster, 1989), pp. 50–53.

118 DETAIL AND EMOTIONAL INTENSITY: Fabre, *La Rive Noire*, p. 212.

119 "BELIEVED, ABOVE SUSPICION": Baldwin, *Giovanni's Room* (New York: Dial, 1956; repr. New York: Dell, 1964), pp. 32–33.

119 "SUM OF ME SIGHED *YES*": Ibid., pp. 86–87.

119 "MAY NOT OFFER A PLACE": James, "The Art of Fiction," p. 178.

120 IN THEIR BED: Rorem, conversation with author, Sept. 26, 1989.

120 "MUCH TIME IN FLIGHT": Baldwin, *Giovanni's Room*, p. 31.

121 "HAPPINESS WAS ALL WE HAD": Ibid., p. 218.

121 "NO ROOM FOR IT": Baldwin quoted in "The Art of Fiction LXXVII: James Baldwin," p. 59.

121 "I HAD TO FACE": Ibid.

122 "HOW AWFUL *AMERICA* WAS": Baldwin quoted in Eckman, *The Furious Passage of James Baldwin*, p. 134.

123 BLACK AMERICAN COMPATRIOTS: Fabre, *La Rive Noire*, pp. 212–13.

124 "HOME AND PAID MINE": Baldwin, "No Name in the Street," p. 475.

124 "COMING AFTER US": Baldwin, "The Fire Next Time," p. 373.

CHAPTER SIX: THE REBIRTH OF PARIS ENGLISH-LANGUAGE PUBLISHING: LITTLE MAGAZINES, LITERATURE, AND D.B.'S

126 CONTRIBUTED TO THEIR DEMISE: See Hugh Ford, *Published in Paris: American and British Writers, Printers and Publishers in Paris, 1920–1939* (New York: Macmillan, 1975).

126 "'FAME' OR 'NOTORIETY'": Sindbad Vail, in *Points*, no. 18 (1953–54), p. 2.

126 "TURN TO LITERATURE?": Ibid.

127 "WRITERS AND IDEAS": Ibid.

127 "HUNDRED THAT GAVE OUT": Ibid., p. 5.

128 LET *ZERO* DO THE WORK: Ibid., p. 6.

128 ACTUALLY ABLE TO SELL: Ibid., p. 7.

129 "BEATS OFFICIALLY EXISTED": George Whitman, conversation with author, July 16, 1990.

129 "FATHER WAS A BANKER": Ibid.

130 "PRINT DRESS AND A CAMEO": Eugene Walter quoted in "The *Paris Review* Sketchbook," *The Paris Review*, no. 79 (1981), p. 321.

130 "OSTENTATIOUS ABOUT IT": Whitman, conversation with author, July 16, 1990.

130 "WRITING MORE EXPRESSIVE": Alexander Trocchi, in *Merlin*, Sept. 1952, p. 2.

130 "WRITERS ON THE OTHER": Alexander Trocchi, in *Merlin*, March 1955, p. 2.

130 IN THE FRENCH MAGAZINE: George Plimpton quoted in "The *Paris Review* Sketchbook," p. 334–35.

130 PERSONALLY DISCOVERED HIM: Whitman, conversation with author, July 16, 1990.

131 "ASSOCIATED HIM WITH JOYCE": Richard Seaver, "*Watt*," in *The Olympia Reader*, ed. Maurice Girodias (New York: Grove, 1965), p. 222.

131 "TWO STUNNING WORKS": Ibid.

131 "VIRTUALLY INTACT": Ibid.

131 BINDER, AND DISAPPEARED: Ibid., p. 223.

131 "HAD FINISHED IT": Ibid.

132 "HAVE TO BE REJECTED": Ibid.

132 "TOTAL ABSURDITY": Ibid.

132 "SOMETHING BY BECKETT": Ibid.

132 " 'YOUR CASE IS CLOSED' ": Ibid., p. 224.

132 "BY PUBLISHING BOOKS": Ibid.

132 MINUIT FOR *MOLLOY*: Jérôme Lindon, "First Meeting with Samuel Beckett," in *Beckett at 60: A Festschrift*, ed. John Calder (London: Calder & Boyars, 1967), p. 18; Seaver, "*Watt*," p. 224.

134 "NEAR-COMPLETE BUMHOOD": Maurice Girodias, introduction to *The Olympia Reader*, p. 11.

134 "ECONOMIC ANNIHILATION": Ibid.

134 "LACK OF CAPITAL": Ibid., pp. 11–12.

134 "ELOQUENT, SUAVE, COMPELLING": Seaver, "*Watt*," p. 225.

135 "ONLY INTERESTED IN PORNO": Maurice Girodias quoted in Deirdre Bair, *Samuel Beckett* (New York: Harcourt Brace Jovanovich, 1978), p. 433.

135 OLYMPIA ENTERPRISE—PORNOGRAPHY: Bair, *Samuel Beckett*, pp. 433–43.

136 EDITION TO SELL OUT: Ibid., p. 433.

136 "REDOING OF THE ORIGINAL": Richard Seaver quoted in Bair, *Samuel Beckett*, p. 438.

136 "IN THE NEW LANGUAGE": Patrick Bowles, translator's note to Friedrich Dürrenmatt, *The Visit* (New York: Grove, 1962), p. 6.

137   ROSSET WAITED: Bair, *Samuel Beckett*, p. 438.

137   "AGONIZED OVER IT": Richard Seaver quoted ibid.

138   "HOW TO ANSWER THAT": George Plimpton quoted in "The *Paris Review* Sketchbook," p. 358.

139   "BRAND OF EROTIC WRITING": Girodias, introduction to *The Olympia Reader*, p. 18.

139   NO LONGER AVAILABLE: Plimpton quoted in "The *Paris Review* Sketchbook," p. 336.

139   "WERE QUITE ENOUGH": Ibid.

139   "REVEAL ATTRACTIVE TALENTS": Girodias, introduction to *The Olympia Reader*, p. 23.

140   "BLUE-EYED, CURVACEOUS CANDY": Ibid., p. 21.

140   "FITTED THE DESCRIPTIONS": Ibid., p. 19.

141   SIGNED UP THE BOOK IMMEDIATELY: Maurice Girodias, "A Sad, Ungraceful History of *Lolita*," in *The Olympia Reader*, p. 535.

141   "FROM YOUR LIST": Responses to *Lolita* quoted in Ted Morgan, *Literary Outlaw: The Life and Times of William Burroughs* (New York: Henry Holt, 1988), p. 278.

141   "BOOKS OF THE YEAR": Graham Greene quoted in Girodias, "A Sad, Ungraceful History of *Lolita*," p. 538.

142    $300,000 ON THE DEAL: Morgan, *Literary Outlaw*, p. 279.

142   A CONSIDERABLE INVESTMENT: Ibid., p. 280.

143   "REPREHENSIBLE OR FORBIDDEN": Girodias, introduction to *The Olympia Reader*, p. 20.

143   "A FEW MENTAL COBWEBS": Ibid., p. 19.

CHAPTER SEVEN: *THE PARIS REVIEW*

145   "MADE HIM IMPOSSIBLE": Peter Matthiessen quoted in "The *Paris Review* Sketchbook," p. 309.

145   "IN THE TWENTIES": James Lord, conversation with author, June 23, 1990.

146   "STORY ALL OVER AGAIN": Matthiessen quoted in "The *Paris Review* Sketchbook," p. 309.

146   "RUINED HIS WHOLE LIFE": Peter Matthiessen quoted in Shnayerson, *Irwin Shaw*, pp. 210–11.

147   "*EN AMÉRIQUE!* INDEED": William Styron, "*The Paris Review*," in *This Quiet Dust and Other Writings*, p. 296.

147 RUE DE PERCEVAL IN MONTPARNASSE: William Styron, "Peter Matthiessen," in *This Quiet Dust and Other Writings*, p. 249.

147 "PLIMPTON'S ABSINTHE": Styron, "*The Paris Review*," p. 297.

148 "STOCK PAGES, DID WE?": John Train quoted in "The *Paris Review* Sketchbook," p. 313.

148 AROUND $1,000: "Big Little Magazine," *Time*, Aug. 11, 1958, p. 91.

148 "OUR FRENCH COUNTERPARTS": Train quoted in "The *Paris Review* Sketchbook," p. 311.

148 "LITERARY AND ARTISTIC SCENE": Ibid., p. 312.

149 FRENCH *ENGAGÉ* REVIEWS: George Plimpton quoted in "The *Paris Review* Sketchbook," pp. 334–35.

149 "NO REPUTATION AT ALL": George Plimpton, "Enterprise in the Service of Art," in *The Little Magazine in America: A Modern Documentary History*, ed. Elliot Anderson and Mary Kinzie (Yonkers, NY: Pushcart, 1978), p. 527.

149 PLIMPTON'S MOTTO: Ibid.

149 "FEELING AND STRENGTH": Train quoted in "The *Paris Review* Sketchbook," p. 313.

150 "BACK OF THE BOOK": William Styron, "Letter to an Editor," *The Paris Review*, 1, no. 1 (Spring 1953), p. 11.

150 "BECOME A CRITIC": Ibid., p. 13.

151 ARM GAVE OUT: "The *Paris Review* Sketchbook," p. 310.

152 "EUROPE LOOKED LIKE": Evan Connell, Jr., conversation with author, July 18, 1989.

152 "MAINSTREAM AVANT-GARDE": George Whitman, conversation with author, July 14, 1990.

153 "IN FLYING SQUADS": Plimpton, "Enterprise in the Service of Art," p. 527.

153 RETURNED TO ENGLAND: "Big Little Magazine," p. 91.

153 "DEPARTMENT OF WORLD LETTERS": Reviews quoted in *The Paris Review*, 1, no. 2 (Summer 1953), p. 135.

153 "IN A LONG TIME": "Advance-Guard Advance," *Newsweek*, March 30, 1953, p. 94.

154 MAGAZINE AND ITS EDITORS: Plimpton quoted in "The *Paris Review* Sketchbook," p. 317.

154 "AN OFFICIAL FUNCTION": Ibid., p. 318.

154 "ANYTHING ABOUT IT": Ibid.

154 "TURNED UP SOONER OR LATER": Eugene Walter quoted in "The *Paris Review* Sketchbook," pp. 320–21.

155 "RAUNCHY, BEAT-UP CAFÉ?": Ibid., p. 324.

155 "WENT ON BETWEEN WRITERS": Connell, conversation with author, July 18, 1989.

156 "FRIENDS OF THE *PARIS REVIEW*": John Phillips quoted in "The *Paris Review* Sketchbook," p. 345.

156 "THAT TEXAS COOL": Ibid., p. 346.

157 "APOLOGIZE TO ALL CONCERNED": Peter Matthiessen, "Erratum," *The Paris Review*, 1, no. 2, p. 7.

157 ABANDONED THE IDEA: Plimpton quoted in "The *Paris Review* Sketchbook," pp. 380–81.

159 "GET WHAT WAS OWED": Connell, conversation with author, July 18, 1989.

159 CONTINUED FOR MUCH LONGER: Plimpton quoted in "The *Paris Review* Sketchbook," pp. 350–51.

160 AROUND PARIS TO DO IT: Ibid., pp. 374–75.

160 "FOR PRACTICAL REASONS": Blair Fuller quoted in "The *Paris Review* Sketchbook," p. 362.

161 "SO LONG AS THEY'RE GOOD": Styron, "Letter to an Editor," p. 12.

CHAPTER EIGHT: "IN PARIS IN A LOUD DARK WINTER"

162 "BLASTED TREES": Lawrence Ferlinghetti, poem 1 in *A Coney Island of the Mind* (New York: New Directions, 1958), p. 9.

163 BY AN IMPORTANT POET: Lawrence Ferlinghetti, conversation with author, Feb. 18, 1991.

164 M.A. IN 1947: Ibid.

164 "MY GOING OVER": Ibid.

165 "I WASN'T INTERESTED IN": Lawrence Ferlinghetti quoted in Barry Silesky, *Ferlinghetti: The Artist in His Time* (New York: Warner, 1990), p. 27.

165 9 PLACE VOLTAIRE: Ferlinghetti, conversation with author, Feb. 18, 1991.

165 "YOUNG DAUGHTERS AS WELL": Ibid.

166 "FRENCH ROMANTIC POETRY": Lawrence Ferlinghetti quoted in Neeli Cherkovski, *Ferlinghetti: A Biography* (Garden City, NY: Doubleday, 1979), p. 52.

166 "A *MANIFESTO* SURREALIST": Ferlinghetti, conversation with author, Feb. 18, 1991.

166 "BEGINNING OF LITERATURE": Ferlinghetti quoted in Silesky, *Ferlinghetti*, p. 29.

167 "OF *LOOK HOMEWARD, ANGEL*": Ferlinghetti, conversation with author, Feb. 18, 1991.

167 "WRITE ALL MORNING": Ibid.

167 "OVER 10,000 WORDS": Ferlinghetti quoted in Cherkovski, *Ferlinghetti*, p. 52.

167 "IN ABOUT A YEAR": Ibid.

167 "JUST WATCH PARIS": Ferlinghetti, conversation with author, Feb. 18, 1991.

167 "TO SUPPORT FAMILIES": Ibid.

168 "LOTS OF BICYCLES": Ibid.

168 "JUST SIT AND READ": George Whitman, conversation with author, July 13, 1990.

168 "A CAN OF STERNO": Ferlinghetti, conversation with author, Feb. 18, 1991.

169 SHAKESPEARE AND COMPANY: Lawrence Ferlinghetti quoted in John Foy and Kyle Jarrard, "Interview with Lawrence Ferlinghetti," *Paris Magazine*, Summer 1989, p. 23.

169 TO SIMON & SCHUSTER: Ferlinghetti, conversation with author, Feb. 18, 1991.

169 "ONLY A FEW PAGES": Ferlinghetti quoted in Silesky, *Ferlinghetti*, p. 31.

169 "WITH IVORY PAPER": Lawrence Ferlinghetti, *Her* (New York: New Directions, 1960), p. 116.

169 "LETTERING ON A LINTEL": Ibid.

170 HAS DESCRIBED THEM: Ferlinghetti, conversation with author, Feb. 18, 1991.

170 "DO NOT HOLD IT UP": Ferlinghetti quoted in Silesky, *Ferlinghetti*, pp. 30–31.

171 "SUMMER OF SAUTERELLES": Lawrence Ferlinghetti, poem 4 in *Pictures of the Gone World* (San Francisco: City Lights, 1955), n.p.

171 "HAVE LONG TO LIVE": Ferlinghetti quoted in Silesky, *Ferlinghetti*, p. 32.

172 "QUOTES FROM THE NOVEL": Ferlinghetti, conversation with author, Feb. 18, 1991.

172 "APPROPRIATION OF *NIGHTWOOD*": Ibid.

173 "TEMPORARILY LIVING THERE": Ibid.

173 "OTHER PARISIANS THEN": Ibid.

174 "POTBELLIED STOVES": Ibid.

174 "LONGER THAN THIS SPRING": Ferlinghetti quoted in Cherkovski, *Ferlinghetti*, p. 58.

175 "HE GOES WALKING ON": Ferlinghetti, *Her*, p. 95.

175 "HAUNT ANOTHER GENERATION": Ibid., p. 65.

176 " 'CALL YOUR OWN' ": Ibid., pp. 66–67.

177 *"THE COLOSSUS OF MAROUSSI"*: Lawrence Ferlinghetti, "Adieu à Charlot (Second Populist Manifesto)," in *Endless Life: Selected Poems* (New York: New Directions, 1981), p. 202.

177 "IN THOSE MAGAZINES": Ferlinghetti, conversation with author, Feb. 18, 1991.

178 *"C'EST PAS / SYMBOLIQUE!"*: Ferlinghetti, poem 24 in *Pictures of the Gone World*, n.p.

179 "AND NUMBER 13 IN *PICTURES*": Ferlinghetti, conversation with author, Feb. 18, 1991.

179 MONTHS OF TRUE LEISURE: Ibid.

179 "IN FOURTEEN LANGUAGES": Selden Kirby-Smith quoted in Silesky, *Ferlinghetti*, p. 38.

180 "WASN'T BROUGHT UP": Ferlinghetti, conversation with author, Feb. 18, 1991.

180 *AVEC MENTION* (WITH DISTINCTION): Ibid.

181 "LIFE OF THE PROFESSOR": Ibid.

181 "WAS VERY SUSPECT": Ibid.

181 "WITH WHO I AM": Ibid.

CHAPTER NINE: THE LEGACY OF HURT: THE ODYSSEY OF CHESTER HIMES

182 "I HAD HAD IT": Himes, *The Quality of Hurt*, p. 141.

183 "IN THE MEN'S ROOMS": Milton Klonsky, "The Writing on the Wall," *Commentary*, Feb. 1948, p. 190.

183 "INFECTED WITH A PSYCHOSIS": "Time to Count Our Blessings," *Ebony*, Nov. 1947, p. 44.

183 "LIKE YELLOW BILE": Stoyan Christowe, "Lonely Crusade," *The Atlantic Monthly*, Oct. 1947, p. 138.

183 "READ IN RECENT YEARS": James Baldwin, "History as Nightmare," *The New Leader*, October 25, 1947, p. 11.
183 "WITHOUT A COUNTRY": Himes, *The Quality of Hurt*, p. 103.
184 "MYSELF A WRITER": Ibid., p. 117.
184 "I WAS THERE OR NOT": Ibid., p. 139.
184 "SHOCKED AND FRIGHTENED": Ibid., pp. 3–4.
185 "FARTHER THAN MONTREAL": Ibid., p. 144.
186 "WHO LIVED IN PARIS": Ibid., p. 179.
186 IN THE SMALL ROOM: William Targ, conversation with author, March 28, 1991.
187 "THE QUIVERING MOUSE": Himes, *The Quality of Hurt*, p. 200.
187 " 'SLAY THEIR FATHERS' ": Ibid., p. 201.
187 "WALKING OVER EACH OTHER": Ibid.
188 "GET ON [HIS] NERVES": Ibid., p. 196.
188 "SEX AND ALCOHOL": Ibid., p. 136.
189 TO HIMES, TO SEX: Ibid., p. 119.
189 "VANDI HAYGOOD": Ibid., p. 135.
189 "BESIDE HER, ANY MAN": Ibid., p. 136.
189 "BACK TO SANITY": Ibid.
189 "SOCIETY IS VIOLENCE": Ibid., p. 137.
189 MORE AND MORE MEANINGLESS: Ibid., p. 190.
190 "LOOK AT US": Ibid., p. 195.
191 "BECAUSE OF ME": Ibid., p. 217.
191 "WHO WOULD GIVE FIRST": Ibid.
191 "HAD IT NOT BEEN FOR ME": Ibid., p. 220.
192 "AMERICANS, NEGROES INCLUDED": Chester Himes to Carl Van Vechten, May 13, 1953, Carl Van Vechten Collection, Yale.
193 "INTO A NOVEL": Himes, *The Quality of Hurt*, p. 264.
193 "BUT I DID": Ibid., p. 265.
194 WHITE MISTRESS, KRISS: Ibid., p. 136.
194 "NOTHING ELSE MATTERED": Ibid., p. 302.
195 "WITH PROTEST NOVELS": Chester Himes, *The Primitive* (New York: New American Library, 1955), p. 93.
195 "THE HUMAN RACE": Ibid., p. 158.
195 "BECOMING PORNOGRAPHIC": Himes, *The Quality of Hurt*, p. 285.
195 "SUGGEST AN ORGY": Ibid.
196 "PLACE IN THEIR MINDS": Ibid.
196 "TO HATE ME FOR": Ibid., p. 301.

196 "SOME WHITE THROATS": Eldridge Cleaver, *Soul on Ice* (New York: Dell, 1968), p. 14.

196 "THE TWENTIETH CENTURY": Chester Himes, preface to *Fin d'un Primitif* [*The Primitive*], trans. Yves Malartic (Paris: Gallimard, 1956), p. 8.

197 BIBLE BUYERS: Targ, conversation with author, March 28, 1991.

197 "BEST OF ALL": Chester Himes to Yves Malartic, July 20, 1954, quoted in *The Quality of Hurt*, pp. 310–11.

197 "WAS VERY ANGRY": Chester Himes to Carl Van Vechten, Dec. 16, 1954, Van Vechten Collection, Yale.

198 *THE THIRD GENERATION*: Targ, conversation with author, March 28, 1991.

198 "SUBSTANTIAL OR OTHERWISE": Chester Himes quoted in John Williams, "My Man Himes: An Interview with Chester Himes," in *Amistad 1*, ed. John Williams and Charles F. Harris (New York: Vintage, 1970), p. 32.

198 "A SUBTLE CHANGE": Himes, *The Quality of Hurt*, p. 300.

198 "TO AMERICAN NEGROES": Chester Himes to Carl Van Vechten, Dec. 16, 1954, Van Vechten Collection, Yale.

199 ABOUT 37,000 FRANCS: Ibid.

199 "THE WAY IT STANDS": Ibid.

199 "WHITEWOMAN IN PARIS": Ibid.

199 "STORY ABOUT HARLEM": Ibid.

200 "PRISON OF THE MIND": Himes, *My Life of Absurdity*, p. 11.

201 "VICTIM OF RACISM": Ibid., p. 36.

201 "WE WERE ABSURD": Ibid.

201 "*CHARACTERS FOR MY BOOK*": Chester Himes to John Williams, Oct. 31, 1962, Chester Himes Collection, Yale.

202 "*UNE AFFAIRE DE VIOL*": Himes, *My Life of Absurdity*, p. 38.

202 "SEVERAL VOLUMES": Michel Fabre, "A Case of Rape," *Black World*, March 1972, p. 40.

204 "BOTTLE TO ... HANCOCK": Chester Himes, *A Case of Rape* (New York: Targ, 1980), p. 98.

204 "RAPING WHITE WOMEN": Ibid., p. 27.

204 "ASSUMPTION OF INNOCENCE": Ibid., p. 98.

205 "SEEN IN ANOTHER": Ibid., p. 55.

205 "ANYWHERE THAT HE LIKED": Ibid., p. 54.

206 "SLIGHTLY REVISED ENDING": Marcel Duhamel, preface to

Chester Himes, *L'Aveugle au Pistolet* [*Blind Man with a Pistol*], trans. Henri Robillot (Paris: Gallimard, 1970), p. 16.

206   "ASTONISHING AND BELIEVABLE": Ibid.

206   "KISS MY ASS": Himes, *My Life of Absurdity*, p. 113.

208   "GIVE [HIM] COURAGE": Ibid., p. 106.

209   "FOR THIS CHESTER HIMES": Jean Giono quoted ibid., p. 181.

210   "SOME LATER TIME": Chester Himes to Carl Van Vechten, undated, quoted in Himes, *My Life of Absurdity*, p. 171.

211   "MY PHYSICAL APPEARANCE": Chester Himes quoted (in French) in Fabre, *La Rive Noire*, p. 238.

CHAPTER TEN: AMONG THEIR FELLOW AMERICANS: IRWIN SHAW AND JAMES JONES IN PARIS

213   "*FINE* AT THE DÔME": Shaw, *Paris! Paris!*, p. 3.

214   "THAT PARTICULAR VOYAGE": Ibid., p. 5.

215   "CENTER OF THAT GROUP": David Schoenbrun quoted in Shnayerson, *Irwin Shaw*, p. 204.

215   "FUN TO BE AROUND": Ann Buchwald and Art Buchwald, *Seems Like Yesterday* (New York: G. P. Putnam's Sons, 1980), p. 43.

215   "WHERE THE DRINKS WERE": Shaw, *Paris! Paris!*, p. 7.

215   "THEY MEANT ME": Ibid., p. 9.

216   "LOOKING FOR A POKER GAME": Ibid., p. 196.

217   "GET US TOO FAR DOWN": Peter Matthiessen and Ben Bradlee quoted in Shnayerson, *Irwin Shaw*, p. 213.

217   "AROUND FOR THAT REASON": Patsy Southgate quoted ibid., p. 206.

217   "POWERFUL IMPRINT ON ME": William Styron quoted ibid., p. 211.

218   "AND DARRYL ZANUCK!": Ibid.

218   "TURNED ON BY THAT": Southgate quoted ibid., pp. 212–13.

219   "MANUSCRIPT INTO THE FIRE": Thomas Guinzburg quoted ibid., p. 218–19.

219   PAGES OF THAT BOOK: Ibid., p. 219.

220   "GOODFELLOWSHIP AND FRIENDLINESS": Styron quoted ibid., p. 211.

221   "OUT OF PARIS ALTOGETHER": Buchwald and Buchwald, *Seems Like Yesterday*, pp. 112–13.

223   "THE GYPSY GUITARIST": James Jones quoted in "James Jones," in *Writers at Work: The Paris Review Interviews*, 3rd ser. (New York: Viking, 1967), p. 235.

223   "BUCKLE HIS SWASH": James Jones quoted in Arthur Goodfriend, "The Cognoscenti Abroad—James Jones's Paris," *Saturday Review*, Feb. 1, 1969, p. 37.

223   "DEAD NIGGER'S EAR": Ernest Hemingway to Charles Scribner, Sr., March 5, 1951, in Ernest Hemingway, *Selected Letters*, p. 721.

223   "PART OF THE WAY": Irwin Shaw quoted in Willie Morris, *James Jones: A Friendship* (Garden City, NY: Doubleday, 1978), p. 94.

224   "TOO MANY DISTRACTIONS": James Jones quoted in Michael S. Lasky, "James Jones Has Come Home to Whistle," *Writer's Digest*, Oct. 1976, p. 26.

224   "OF HUMAN CONFLICT": Budd Schulberg, "The Right-headed James Jones," *Los Angeles Times Book Review*, Jan. 19, 1977, p. 16.

225   "CLOSE AS BROTHERS": Morris, *James Jones*, p. 98.

225   "OR EXPECT TO SEE": James Jones to Jeff Jones, April 6, 1959, quoted in Frank MacShane, *Into Eternity: The Life of James Jones, American Writer* (Boston: Houghton Mifflin, 1985), p. 179.

225   "TODAY IN ANY FORM": Jones quoted in "James Jones," p. 235.

225   CAPACITY TO LOVE OTHERS: MacShane, *Into Eternity*, p. 183.

226   WRITE A CONVINCING BOOK: James R. Giles, *James Jones* (Boston: Twayne, 1981), p. 30.

226   "HUMAN REFERENCE ANY MORE": Jones quoted in "James Jones," p. 248.

227   "LOOKING AT THE SCENE": Jones quoted in Goodfriend, "The Cognoscenti Abroad—James Jones's Paris," p. 37.

227   "FIGHTING IN THE PACIFIC": George Whitman, conversation with author, July 17, 1990.

227   "I CAN HARDLY SEE": James Jones quoted in Bainbridge, *Another Way of Living*, p. 224.

227   "DARKEN THE MEMORY": Irwin Shaw quoted in Morris, *James Jones*, p. 102.

227   "ZEST AND FUN": William Styron quoted ibid., p. 110.

228   "BROKEN MARRIAGES ASSUAGED": Shaw quoted ibid., p. 115.

228   "WHERE THEY WERE": Morris, *James Jones*, p. 117.

228   "THROUGH HIS INTELLECT": Shaw quoted ibid., p. 104.

228 "EMASCULATED BY SCHOLASTICISM": James Jones to Burroughs Mitchell, November 19, 1959, quoted in MacShane, *Into Eternity*, pp. 180–81.

229 "THAT OF A FEW MEN": Ibid., p. 181.

229 "THE LITERARY ESTABLISHMENT": Jones quoted in Bainbridge, *Another Way of Living*, p. 221.

230 "WRITE A REAL NOVEL": MacShane, *Into Eternity*, p. 182.

230 " 'YOU DRUNKEN BUM' ": Styron quoted in Morris, *James Jones*, p. 129.

230 "*REDEYE*, YOU ASSHOLES": Jones quoted ibid., p. 135.

231 "AWKWARD, SPRAWLING PEOPLE": Jones quoted in "James Jones," p. 236.

231 "PERVADING EMOTIONAL CLIMATE": Ibid.

231 "OUTSIDE OF EVERYTHING": Jones quoted in Bainbridge, *Another Way of Living*, p. 220.

CHAPTER ELEVEN: *LOCUS SOLUS ET SOCII*: HARRY MATHEWS AND JOHN ASHBERY

234 "ANY PARTICULAR VEIN": Harry Mathews, conversation with author, July 21, 1990.

234 "IMPORTANT AT THAT TIME": Harry Mathews quoted in John Ashbery, "John Ashbery Interviewing Harry Mathews," *Review of Contemporary Fiction*, 7, no. 3 (Fall 1987), p. 46.

235 FINANCIAL EXIGENCIES: Mathews, conversation with author, July 21, 1990.

235 "I WAS THIRTEEN OR FOURTEEN": Ibid.

235 "IT WAS POWERFULLY SO": Ibid.

236 "THE FRENCH WERE DOING": Ibid.

236 "A WRITER WERE OVER": Ibid.

236 DESIRE TO WRITE: Harry Mathews, "Autobiography," in *The Way Home: Collected Longer Prose* (London: Atlas, 1989), p. 153.

236 "CERTAIN AMOUNT OF CONFUSION": Mathews, conversation with author, July 21, 1990.

237 "POETRY-MAKING DAYS AT SCHOOL": Mathews, "Autobiography," p. 154.

237 "I LOVED IT": Mathews, conversation with author, July 21, 1990.

237 "IN ITS PROPER PLACE": Mathews, "Autobiography," p. 156.

238 TOOK AN IMMEDIATE LIKING: Ibid., p. 134.

239 "SOMEONE NAMED JOHN ASHBERY": Ibid., pp. 135–36.
239 "YALE SERIES OF YOUNGER POETS": Ibid., p. 136.
240 "IN ORDER TO WORK MYSELF": John Ashbery, conversation with author, May 1, 1991.
241 "NEW YORK THAT FALL": Ashbery, conversation with author, Nov. 30, 1989.
241 "PRETEXT FOR GOING BACK": Ashbery, conversation with author, May 1, 1991.
242 "ON THOSE AROUND HIM": Mathews, "Autobiography," p. 136.
242 "YOU NEED TO READ IT": Mathews, conversation with author, July 21, 1990.
243 "INVENT WHAT I WROTE": Mathews, "Autobiography," pp. 136–37.
243 "ALL MY MATERIALS": Roussel, *How I Wrote Certain of My Books*, p. 3.
244 "IN THE REMOTEST FUTURE": Roussel's admirers quoted in John Ashbery, "In Darkest Language," in Raymond Roussel, *How I Wrote Certain of My Books*, trans. Trevor Winkfield (New York: Sun, 1977), p. 59.
244 "FELT BUT NOT COMMUNICATED": Ashbery, "In Darkest Language," p. 61.
244 "NEVER BE THE SAME": Ibid., p. 64.
244 "FASCINATED BY HIS WORK": Ashbery, conversation with author, Jan. 9, 1990.
245 "*LA GRANDE PERMISSION*": John Ashbery, "An Interview with Henri Michaux," in *Reported Sightings: Chronicles of the Art World, 1957–1987* (Cambridge, MA: Harvard University Press, 1989), p. 398.
245 "DO WITH LANGUAGE": Ashbery, conversation with author, May 1, 1991.
245 "PRODUCED ALMOST GRATUITOUSLY": Ashbery, "John Ashbery Interviewing Harry Mathews," p. 41.
245 "MY UNADMITTED SELF INTO VIEW": Mathews, "Autobiography," p. 155.
246 "LED ME TO ANOTHER": Ashbery, conversation with author, May 9, 1991.
246 "AS FRANÇOISE SAGAN!": Ibid.
247 "THE IDEA OF RETURNING": Ibid.
248 "VERY LITTLE EFFECT": Harold Bloom, "The Charity of the

Hard Moments," in *John Ashbery*, ed. Harold Bloom (New York: Chelsea House, 1985), p. 53.

248 "ITS LIMITATIONS": Ashbery, conversation with author, May 1, 1991.

250 "DESTINED FOR PUBLICATION": Ibid.

250 BEFORE WILBUR'S RETURN": Ashbery, conversation with author, April 27, 1991.

250 "THE ONLY FREAK IN PARIS": Ashbery, conversation with author, May 1, 1991.

251 "STARTED *THE CONVERSIONS*": Mathews, conversation with author, July 21, 1990.

252 "MOVINGLY NEUTRAL VOICE": Mathews, "Autobiography," p. 156.

253 "WE CALL FICTION": Georges Perec, "Avez-Vous Lu Harry Mathews?," *Review of Contemporary Fiction*, 7, no. 3 (Fall 1987), p. 83.

253 "HOW AMERICANS SOUNDED": Ashbery, conversation with author, May 1, 1991.

254 "LIVING AT HOME": Mathews, conversation with author, July 21, 1990.

254 "SELF-CONSCIOUS ABOUT IT": Ibid.

254 "THE WAY I WRITE": Ibid.

255 "OR TWO ON THAT": Ashbery, conversation with author, May 1, 1991.

255 "TO LIVE IN PARIS": Ibid.

256 "DISCUSSED, NOT EXPLAINED": John Ashbery, "Leland Bell," in *Reported Sightings*, p. 197.

256 "BEHIND PHYSICAL APPEARANCES": John Ashbery, "Parmigianino," in *Reported Sightings*, p. 31.

256 "IT WAS HELPFUL": John Ashbery quoted in "John Ashbery," in *The Craft of Poetry: Interviews from the New York Quarterly*, ed. William Packard (Garden City, NY: Doubleday, 1974), p. 129.

257 "CLOTHING FOR THE PICTURE": John Ashbery, "Niki de Saint Phalle," in *Reported Sightings*, p. 146.

257 "WELL OVER A DECADE": Mathews, "Autobiography," p. 144.

257 "DENIS ROCHE AND MARCELIN PLEYNET": Mathews, conversation with author, July 21, 1990.

258 "INSUFFICIENT PUBLISHING OUTFITS": Ibid.

258 "SUPPORTIVE EVER SINCE": Ibid.

259 "WRITING AND PERSONAL FRIENDSHIP": Ibid.

259 "RANDOM HOUSE [AND EPSTEIN] TOOK IT": Ibid.

259 "INDEPENDENT OF FASHION": John Ashbery, "American Sanctuary in Paris," in *Reported Sightings*, pp. 90–91.

260 "HAS BEEN REMOVED": Ibid., p. 97.

CHAPTER TWELVE: AT THE BEAT HOTEL

261 GIVING THEM A ROOM: Allen Ginsberg, conversation with author, July 15, 1989.

262 "AND THAT WAS THAT": William S. Burroughs, foreword to Harold Norse, *The Beat Hotel* (San Diego: Atticus, 1983), n.p.

263 "BEWILDERING BEAUTY OF PARIS": Ginsberg, conversation with author, July 15, 1989.

264 "MODERNISM IN FRANCE": Ibid.

264 "SPOOKY AND THRILLING": Ibid.

264 "DOESN'T SEEM A BURDEN": Ibid.

264 "CARS RACE THRU STREETS": Allen Ginsberg, "Europe! Europe!" in *Collected Poems: 1947–1980* (New York: Harper & Row, 1984), p. 173.

265 "POEM WAS LARGELY MISSED": Ginsberg, conversation with author, July 15, 1989.

265 "WITH YOUR EYES": Allen Ginsberg to Jack Kerouac, Nov. 13, 1957, Ginsberg Deposit, Columbia University.

266 "A RHYTHM UP TO CRY": Ibid.

266 "WERE SURE TO MAKE": Joan Dillon quoted in "The *Paris Review* Sketchbook," p. 369.

266 "A TOTAL FABRICATION": Ginsberg, conversation with author, May 4, 1992.

267 "NABOKOV, GENET, BECKETT": Ginsberg, conversation with author, July 15, 1989.

267 "MARGINAL ADDITIONS, ET CETERA": Ibid.

267 "FRAGMENT STRUNG TOGETHER": Ibid.

267 "CUMULATIVE ACCRETIONS": Ibid.

268 "*NAKED LUNCH* TO BE": Ibid.

268 *NAKED LUNCH* FOR PUBLICATION: Burroughs, conversation with author, July 22, 1989.

268 "DIDN'T IMPROVE THINGS A BIT": Ginsberg, conversation with author, July 15, 1989.

269 "DETECT [THEM] IN SECONDS": Ibid.

269 "RADIANT, CHILDLIKE CHARM": William S. Burroughs, foreword to Gregory Corso, *Mindfield* (New York: Thunder's Mouth, 1989), p. xvii.

270 "SERIOUSLY ANY LONGER": Ginsberg, conversation with author, July 15, 1989.

270 " 'BUT I'M ONLY HUMAN' ": Burroughs, conversation with author, July 22, 1989.

270 DUCHAMP COMPLIED: Ibid.; Morgan, *Literary Outlaw*, pp. 290–91.

271 "ALWAYS TO ENTHUSIASM": George Whitman, conversation with author, July 12, 1990.

271 "REMARKABLE, QUITE DIFFERENT": Ibid.

271 EVENT HAD BEEN: Ginsberg, conversation with author, July 15, 1989.

271 TEA AT HER CLUB: Ibid.

272 "A FEW STORIES": Burroughs, conversation with author, July 22, 1989.

273 " 'IN THE UNIVERSE!' ": Ginsberg, conversation with author, July 15, 1989.

273 NEVER RETURNED TO THE HOTEL: Ibid.; Burroughs, conversation with author, July 22, 1989.

273 "FRENCHMEN OF HIS CLASS": Burroughs, conversation with author, July 22, 1989.

273 "DETECT SUCH AN ACTION": Gregory Corso to Allen Ginsberg, November 28, 1958, quoted in Miles, *Ginsberg*, p. 247.

274 "WHAT ARE YOU, THE CIA?": Ginsberg, conversation with author, July 15, 1989.

274 "LOOK YOU IN THE EYES": Allen Ginsberg, "Message," in *Collected Poems*, p. 183.

275 "AS SIMPLE ALLEN ANYMORE": Allen Ginsberg to William S. Burroughs, Feb. 1959, quoted in Morgan, *Literary Outlaw*, p. 310.

275 "LIFE HE'D SET UP": Burroughs, conversation with author, April 28, 1987.

275 "REALLY SCORED WITH HIM": Brion Gysin, "Cut-ups: A Project for Disastrous Success," in William S. Burroughs and Brion Gysin, *The Third Mind* (New York: Viking/Seaver, 1978), p. 49.

276   GYSIN LOST THE RESTAURANT: Ibid., p. 48.

277   "OUTSIDE ROOM 15": Ibid., p. 42.

277   "UNDER ITS SPONSORSHIP": Jack Mabley quoted in Morgan, *Literary Outlaw*, p. 296.

278   " 'BREAKTHROUGH IN GREY ROOM' ": Gysin, "Cut-ups: A Project for Disastrous Success," p. 43.

278   "AT RANDOM—TO THE PRINTER": William S. Burroughs quoted in Gysin, "Cut-ups: A Project for Disastrous Success," pp. 42–43.

278   "THOSE FABULOUS SCENES": Ginsberg, conversation with author, July 15, 1989.

279   A FINE OF $80: Morgan, *Literary Outlaw*, pp. 311–17.

280   "MORPHINE AT THE TIME": William S. Burroughs, *The Job: Interviews with William Burroughs by Daniel Odier* (New York: Grove, 1974), p. 159.

281   UNDER *HIS* SPELL: Ginsberg, conversation with author, July 15, 1989.

281   "TO TAKE YOUR EYES AWAY": Morgan, *Literary Outlaw*, p. 305.

281   "A TRACE OF PRETENSION": William S. Burroughs, introduction to Brion Gysin, *The Last Museum* (New York: Grove, 1986), p. 8.

281   "PEOPLE AS AGENTS": Ginsberg, conversation with author, July 15, 1989.

281   "HEAVY PSYCHIC THINGS": Gregory Corso, conversation with author, July 27, 1988.

281   DIFFERENT INCARNATIONS: Morgan, *Literary Outlaw*, p. 306.

281   "HAVE PSYCHIC EXPERIENCES?": Burroughs, conversation with author, April 28, 1987.

281   "EXPLORER OF PSYCHIC AREAS": William S. Burroughs, "Fold-ins," in Burroughs and Gysin, *The Third Mind*, p. 95.

282   "THOROUGHLY SURVEYED": Ibid., p. 95.

282   "FUNNY AND HYSTERICALLY MEANINGFUL": Gysin, "Cut-ups: A Project for Disastrous Success," p. 44.

282   "PAINTERS FOR FIFTY YEARS": William S. Burroughs, "The Cut-up Method of Brion Gysin," in Burroughs and Gysin, *The Third Mind*, p. 29.

282   "NO DIFFERENCE AT ALL": Lewis Carroll, *Complete Works* (New York: Random House, 1939), p. 790.

282   "FUNCTION OF MEDIA": Brion Gysin quoted (in French) in Marc Dachy, *Journal du Mouvement Dada* (Geneva: Skira, 1989), p. 79.

283 " 'DERANGEMENT OF THE SENSES' ": Burroughs, "The Cut-up Method of Brion Gysin," p. 32.

283 "METHOD HE WAS USING": Burroughs quoted in Gysin, "Cut-ups: A Project for Disastrous Success," pp. 42–43.

283 "ONLY MINUTES TO GO": Morgan, *Literary Outlaw*, p. 324.

283 "SHACKLES OF WESTERN CIVILIZATION": Burroughs quoted in Conrad Knickerbocker, "Interview with William S. Burroughs," in Burroughs and Gysin, *The Third Mind*, pp. 5–6.

285 "WHIRLING OUT THROUGH SPACE": Brion Gysin, "Dream-achine," in *Brion Gysin Let the Mice In* (West Glover, VT: Something Else, 1973), p. 28.

285 "POUNDING TO GET IN": Ian Sommerville quoted ibid.

285 "TWENTY-FIVE FLASHES PER SECOND": Burroughs, *The Job*, p. 131.

286 "JUNK RAN OUT": William S. Burroughs, introduction to *Naked Lunch* (New York: Grove, 1966), p. xli.

287 "PAINTING, TALKING, AND PLANNING": Burroughs, foreword to Norse, *The Beat Hotel*, n.p.

287 "FEW MEN EVEN DREAM COULD EXIST": Norse, *The Beat Hotel*, pp. 59–60.

287 "ENERGY DAY AND NIGHT": Ginsberg, conversation with author, July 15, 1989.

THE CONTINUAL PILGRIMAGE

289 "APPREHEND THE MOTION": John Ashbery, "The New Spirit," in *Three Poems* (New York: Viking, 1972), p. 5.

290 "IT IS REALLY THERE": Stein, *Paris France*, p. 2.

290 "HAVING THOSE PRIVILEGES": Ibid., p. 21.

Selected Bibliography of Secondary Sources

Anderson, Elliot, and Mary Kinzie, eds. *The Little Magazine in America: A Modern Documentary History*. Yonkers, NY: Pushcart, 1978.

Applefield, David, et al., eds. *Fire Readings*. Paris: Frank Books, 1991.

Ashbery, John. *Reported Sightings: Chronicles of the Art World, 1957–1987*. Cambridge, MA: Harvard University Press, 1989.

Bainbridge, John. *Another Way of Living: A Gallery of Americans Who Choose to Live in Europe*. New York: Holt, Rinehart & Winston, 1968.

Bair, Deirdre. *Samuel Beckett*. New York: Harcourt Brace Jovanovich, 1978.

Baker, Carlos. *Ernest Hemingway: A Life Story*. New York: Charles Scribner's Sons, 1969.

Baldwin, James. *The Price of the Ticket: Collected Non-Fiction 1948–1985*. New York: St. Martin's/Marek, 1985.

Beach, Sylvia. *Shakespeare and Company*. New York: Harcourt, Brace, 1959.

de Beauvoir, Simone. *Force of Circumstance*, vol. 1: *After the War*, trans. Richard Howard. New York: G. P. Putnam's Sons, 1965; repr. Harper & Row, 1977.

Brian, Denis. *The True Gen*. New York: Grove, 1988.

Buchwald, Ann, and Art Buchwald. *Seems Like Yesterday*. New York: G. P. Putnam's Sons, 1980.

Burroughs, William S. *The Job: Interviews with William Burroughs by Daniel Odier*. New York: Grove, 1974.

Burroughs, William S., and Brion Gysin. *The Third Mind*. New York: Viking/Seaver, 1978.

Campbell, James. *Talking at the Gates: A Life of James Baldwin*. New York: Viking, 1991.

Cherkovski, Neeli. *Ferlinghetti: A Biography*. Garden City, NY: Doubleday, 1979.

Duras, Marguerite. *The War: A Memoir*, trans. Barbara Bray. New York: Pantheon, 1986.

Eckman, Fern Marja. *The Furious Passage of James Baldwin*. Philadelphia: M. Evans/Lippincott, 1966.

Fabre, Michel. *La Rive Noire: De Harlem à la Seine*. Paris: Lieu Commun, 1985.

———. *The Unfinished Quest of Richard Wright*, trans. Isabel Barzun. New York: William Morrow, 1973.

———. *The World of Richard Wright*. Jackson: University Press of Mississippi, 1985.

Flanner, Janet. *Janet Flanner's World: Uncollected Writings 1932–1975*. New York: Harcourt Brace Jovanovich, 1979.

———. *Paris Journal: 1944–1965*. New York: Atheneum, 1965.

———. *Pétain: The Old Man of France*. New York: Simon & Schuster, 1944.

Gallup, Donald, ed. *The Flowers of Friendship: Letters Written to Gertrude Stein*. New York: Alfred A. Knopf, 1953.

Gayle, Addison, Jr. *Richard Wright: Ordeal of a Native Son*. Garden City, NY: Doubleday, 1980.

Girodias, Maurice, ed. *The Olympia Reader*. New York: Grove, 1965.

Gysin, Brion. *Brion Gysin Let the Mice In*. West Glover, VT: Something Else, 1973.

Hemingway, Ernest. *By-Line Ernest Hemingway*, ed. William White. New York: Charles Scribner's Sons, 1967.

———. *Selected Letters: 1917–1961*, ed. Carlos Baker. New York: Charles Scribner's Sons, 1969.

Hemingway, Leicester. *My Brother, Ernest Hemingway*. Cleveland and New York: World, 1962.

Hemingway, Mary Welsh. *How It Was*. New York: Alfred A. Knopf, 1976.

Himes, Chester. *The Quality of Hurt: The Autobiography of Chester Himes* (vol. 1). Garden City, NY: Doubleday, 1972.

———. *My Life of Absurdity: The Autobiography of Chester Himes* (vol. 2). Garden City, NY: Doubleday, 1976.

Kert, Bernice. *The Hemingway Women*. New York: W. W. Norton, 1983.

Lee, Lawrence, and Barry Gifford. *Saroyan: A Biography*. New York: Harper & Row, 1984.

Lord, James. *Où Étaient les Tableaux . . .: Mémoire sur Gertrude Stein et Alice Toklas*, trans. Pierre Leyris. Paris: Mazarine, 1982.

Lottman, Herbert. *The Left Bank*. Boston: Houghton Mifflin, 1982.

MacShane, Frank. *Into Eternity: The Life of James Jones, American Writer*. Boston: Houghton Mifflin, 1985.

Mathews, Harry. *The Way Home: Collected Longer Prose*. London: Atlas, 1989.

Mellow, James. *Charmed Circle: Gertrude Stein and Company*. New York: Praeger, 1974.

Meyers, Jeffrey. *Hemingway: A Biography*. New York: Harper & Row, 1985.

Miles, Barry. *Ginsberg: A Biography*. New York: Simon & Schuster, 1989.

Morgan, Ted. *Literary Outlaw: The Life and Times of William Burroughs*. New York: Henry Holt, 1987.

Morris, Willie. *James Jones: A Friendship*. Garden City, NY: Doubleday, 1978.

Norse, Harold. *The Beat Hotel*. San Diego: Atticus, 1983.

————. *Memoirs of a Bastard Angel*. New York: William Morrow, 1990.

Plimpton, George, ed. "The *Paris Review* Sketchbook," *The Paris Review*, no. 79 (1981).

Review of Contemporary Fiction (Harry Mathews number), 7, no. 3 (Fall 1987).

Rogers, W. G. *When This You See Remember Me: Gertrude Stein in Person*. New York: Rinehart, 1948.

Roussel, Raymond. *How I Wrote Certain of My Books*, trans. Trevor Winkfield. New York: Sun, 1977.

Sevareid, Eric. *Not So Wild a Dream*. New York: Alfred A. Knopf, 1969.

Shaw, Irwin. *Paris! Paris!* New York: Harcourt Brace Jovanovich, 1977.

Shnayerson, Michael. *Irwin Shaw: A Biography*. New York: G. P. Putnam's Sons, 1989.

Silesky, Barry. *Ferlinghetti: The Artist in His Time*. New York: Warner, 1990.

Stein, Gertrude. *The Selected Writings of Gertrude Stein*, ed. Carl Van Vechten. New York: Random House, 1962.

Styron, William. *This Quiet Dust and Other Writings*. New York: Random House, 1982.

Sutherland, Donald. *Gertrude Stein: A Biography of Her Work*. New Haven: Yale University Press, 1951.

Thomson, Virgil. *Virgil Thomson*. New York: Alfred A. Knopf, 1966.

———. *A Virgil Thomson Reader*. New York: E. P. Dutton, 1984.

Toklas, Alice B. *What Is Remembered*. New York: Holt, Rinehart & Winston, 1963; repr. San Francisco: North Point, 1985.

Weatherby, William J. *James Baldwin: Artist on Fire: A Portrait*. New York: Donald I. Fine, 1989.

Webb, Constance. *Richard Wright*. New York: G. P. Putnam's Sons, 1968.

Whelan, Robert. *Robert Capa: A Biography*. New York: Harper & Row, 1985.

Williams, John, and Charles F. Harris, eds. *Amistad 1*. New York: Vintage, 1970.

Wineapple, Brenda. *Genêt: A Biography of Janet Flanner*. New York: Ticknor & Fields, 1989.

Index

S

Vian, Boris, 76
Vidal, Gore, 8
Viertel, Peter, 216, 228
View, 263
Villon, Jacques, 32, 158
Vogue, 58
"Voyage Out, Voyage Home" (Shaw),
221
VVV, 263

W

Wainhouse, Austryn, 129, 130, 134,
136, 138–39, 154
Waiting for Godot (Beckett), 131, 136–
37
Walter, Eugene, 5, 129–30, 150, 154,
155
Walter, William Grey, 285
Walton, William, 27
Wand & Quadrant (Logue), 136
War, The (Duras), 44
Warner, Jack, 213
Wars I Have Seen (Stein), 48, 49, 51,
52, 53, 55, 56
Waste Land, The (Eliot), 172, 180
Watt (Beckett), 131–32, 134, 135–36
Way of Dispossession, The
(Ferlinghetti), 167, 169
Webster, Daniel, 62
Weininger, Otto, 54
Welles, Orson, 81
Welsh, Mary, 15–16, 17, 18, 20, 22,
25–27, 28, 29
Welty, Eudora, 8
Wertenbaker, Charles, 15, 35
Weybright, Victor, 198
White, Theodore, 214
White, Walter, 201

White Goddess, The (Graves), 238
White Man, Listen (Wright), 93
Whitman, George, 8, 129, 130, 168–
69, 173, 180, 227, 270–71, 283
Whitman, Mary, 168
Whitman, Walt, 172, 174, 248, 263
Wilbur, Richard, 157, 250
Wilder, Thornton, 228
Williams, William Carlos, 128, 263
Wilson, Colin, 153
Winner Take Nothing (Hemingway),
18
Wolfe, Thomas, 164, 167, 175
Wouk, Herman, 182
Wright, Ellen, 67, 74, 96, 98
Wright, Julia, 67, 74, 98
Wright, Rachel, 81, 98
Wright, Richard, 4, 7–8, 9, 67–98,
99–102, 103, 109, 117, 123, 128,
151, 182, 183, 184, 185–86, 187–
88, 189, 190, 191, 192, 203

Y

"Year to Learn the Language, A"
(Shaw), 221
Yes Is for a Very Young Man (Stein), 48,
50–52
Young, Lester, 225
Young Adam (Trocchi), 139
Young Lions, The (Shaw), 16, 214

Z

Zanuck, Darryl, 218, 270
Zero, 5, 85, 100, 101, 103, 108, 127–
28, 177
Zone (Apollinaire), 265

345

About the Author

Christopher Sawyer-Lauçanno is the author of *An Invisible Spectator: A Biography of Paul Bowles* (Weidenfeld & Nicolson, 1989). His book-length translations include *The Destruction of the Jaguar: Poems from the Books of Chilam Balam*, and a volume of early surrealist prose poems and plays by Federico García Lorca, *Barbarous Nights: Legends and Plays from The Little Theater*. He teaches in the Program in Writing and Humanistic Studies at MIT.